W9-COZ-424

HUMOR AND AGING

HUMOR AND AGING

Edited by

Lucille Nahemow
Gerontology Center
West Virginia University
Morgantown, West Virginia

Kathleen A. McCluskey-Fawcett
Department of Psychology
West Virginia University
Morgantown, West Virginia

Paul E. McGhee
Department of Human Development and Family Studies
Texas Tech University
Lubbock, Texas

1986

ACADEMIC PRESS, INC.
Harcourt Brace Jovanovich, Publishers
Orlando   San Diego   New York   Austin
London   Montreal   Sydney   Tokyo   Toronto

COPYRIGHT © 1986 BY ACADEMIC PRESS, INC.
ALL RIGHTS RESERVED.
NO PART OF THIS PUBLICATION MAY BE REPRODUCED OR
TRANSMITTED IN ANY FORM OR BY ANY MEANS, ELECTRONIC
OR MECHANICAL, INCLUDING PHOTOCOPY, RECORDING, OR
ANY INFORMATION STORAGE AND RETRIEVAL SYSTEM, WITHOUT
PERMISSION IN WRITING FROM THE PUBLISHER.

ACADEMIC PRESS, INC.
Orlando, Florida 32887

United Kingdom Edition published by
ACADEMIC PRESS INC. (LONDON) LTD.
24-28 Oval Road, London NW1 7DX

LIBRARY OF CONGRESS CATALOGING-IN-PUBLICATION DATA

Main entry under title:

Humor and aging.

   Includes index.
   1. Aged—Psychology.   2. Aging—Psychological
aspects.   3. Wit and humor—Psychological aspects.
4. Old age—Anecdotes, facetiae, satire, etc.
5. Aging—Anecdotes, facetiae, satire, etc.
6. Death—Anecdotes, facetiae, satire, etc.
I. Nahemow, Lucille.   II. McCluskey-Fawcett, Kathleen A.
III. McGhee, Paul E.
BF724.85.H86H86   1985   155.67   85-7456
ISBN 0-12-513790-7 (alk. paper)
ISBN 0-12-513791-5 (paperback)

PRINTED IN THE UNITED STATES OF AMERICA

86 87 88 89   9 8 7 6 5 4 3 2 1

155.67
H883

MARTIN B. LOEB (1913–1983)

This book is dedicated to Martin Loeb, past president of the Gerontological Society of America, who first suggested that a comprehensive study of humor and aging be undertaken. His life, which was rapidly coming to a close (he died on 26 April 1983), served as an outstanding demonstration of the importance of humor in facing life and coping with aging. The following illustrations provided by his friends and colleagues exemplify the dynamic and multifaceted relationship among humor, growth, and aging.

Edgar F. Borgatta wrote:

> Martin Loeb was good humored and appreciated the foibles in life. If Murphy's Law had never been passed, if the Peter Principle had never been discovered, and if the book on Parkinson's Law had never appeared, Martin's appreciation of how things operate wouldn't have been different. His analyses of how bureaucracies operate, how the people in them behave, and what the consequences are were sardonic and humorous. No one would ever accuse Martin of being a statistician, but he understood the appropriate statistical model, and so his analyses and expectations were usually correct. If it can be done badly, it will be, and he almost universally predicted the bad outcome. He was usually correct, and his descriptions of how the events came about were always entertaining. And, he would note, you might as well think they are funny. What's the alternative?

Robert Havighurst provided an article from the *University of Wisconsin News* for 8 August 1973, which Martin Loeb had sent to him.

Director Named for Institute on Aging

Dr. Martin B. Loeb, Director of the School of Social Work at the University of Wisconsin–Madison, has been appointed Director of the new Faye McBeath Institute on Aging and Adult Life on the Madison campus.

v

257665

In his own handwriting, Martin wrote: "Bob: You started me on this—
They gave the Institute to me for my 60th Birthday."

Sandra Howell said:

> I remember Martin on an occasion of playful joy, in Grand Cayman Island,
> where he often drew varied friends to snorkel with him among the colorful fish.
> He kept there an assortment of well-worn tapes of his favorite music. On this
> evening, following a salubrious meal, Martin proceeded to conduct the
> Beethoven Ninth enthusiastically, in his shorts, from a folding chair in an
> otherwise bare room.

Millie Seltzer felt that

> to try to capture the essence of Martin Loeb in "fifty words or less" is the
> equivalent of pinning down light, laughter, love, and life itself. He could be
> extraordinarily outrageous, impossibly difficult, inordinately intelligent, and
> downright irascible. He was outgoing and lonely, creative and lazy. When he
> wanted to be, he could be a brilliant, incisive, and disciplined thinker. On the
> other occasions he could be insensitive and thoughtless. He added romance
> and drama to dull situations and excitement by just being around. He was, in
> other words, a fully human being whom many of us loved and will always miss.

Vivian Wood completed Martin's contribution to this volume when
he was unable to do so. She said:

> As one who appreciates humor in others, it will be Martin's sense of fun and
> humor that I will remember most affectionately from my years of colleagueship
> with him. As his friends know, Martin lived life fully. I doubt that there were
> many things he wanted to do that he never got around to doing. If there were
> any regrets about things undone, missing the publication of this book might be
> one. A zesty sense of humor and great conviviality were Loeb trademarks, and
> it is especially appropriate that a book on humor and aging be dedicated to him.

Contents

Contributors

Numbers in parentheses indicate the pages on which the authors' contributions begin.

Edward F. Ansello (233), Center on Aging, Division of Human and Community Resources, University of Maryland, College Park, Maryland 20742

Nancy J. Bell (253), Department of Home and Family Life, Texas Tech University, Lubbock, Texas 79409

Nancy Datan (161), Department of Human Development, University of Wisconsin, Green Bay, Wisconsin 54301-7001

James Duchon (139), Department of Psychology, Illinois Institute of Technology, Chicago, Illinois 60616

Nelda S. Duffey (253), Personal Growth Services, 401 Louisiana Street Southeast, Suite J, Albuquerque, New Mexico 87108

William F. Fry, Jr. (81), Department of Psychiatry, School of Medicine, Stanford University, Stanford, California 94305

Margaret Hellie Huyck (139), Department of Psychology, Illinois Institute of Technology, Chicago, Illinois 60616

Martin Loeb[1] (279), School of Social Work, University of Wisconsin–Madison, Madison, Wisconsin 53706

Carol Ann Lorenz (199), Department of Fine Arts, Colgate University, Hamilton, New York 13346

Kathleen A. McCluskey-Fawcett[2] (53), Department of Psychology, West Virginia University, Morgantown, West Virginia 26505

---

[1] Deceased.

[2] Present address: Department of Psychology, University of Kansas, Lawrence, Kansas 66045.

Paul E. McGhee (27, 253), Department of Human Development and Family Studies, Texas Tech University, Lubbock, Texas 79409

Lucille Nahemow (3, 265), Gerontology Center, West Virginia University, Morgantown, West Virginia 26506

Erdman B. Palmore (101), Duke University Medical Center, Durham, North Carolina 27710

Dennis R. Papini (53), Department of Psychology, Southeast Missouri State University, Cape Girardeau, Missouri 63701

Allen Raymon (265), 317 West 87th Street, Apartment 3B, New York, New York 10024

Edwin Rosenberg[3] (175), Department of Sociology, University of Pittsburgh at Bradford, Bradford, Pennsylvania 16701

Mildred M. Seltzer (121), Scripps Foundation Gerontology Center and Department of Sociology and Anthropology, Miami University, Oxford, Ohio 45056

C. J. R. Simons (53), Department of Psychology, Pennsylvania State University, Fayetteville, Pennsylvania 17222

Kathleen Fox Tennant (245), School of Nursing, West Virginia University, Morgantown, West Virginia 26506-6304

Christopher Vecsey (199), Department of Philosophy and Religion, Colgate University, Hamilton, New York 13346

Deborah G. Ventis (223), Department of Psychology, College of William and Mary, Williamsburg, Virginia 23185

Vivian Wood (279), School of Social Work, University of Wisconsin–Madison, Madison, Wisconsin 53706

[3] Present address: Department of Sociology, La Roche College, Pittsburgh, Pennsylvania 15237.

Preface

Humor has great potential for the study of aging, although it is hard to classify, difficult to categorize, and impossible to pin down. We can, nevertheless, study the humor of and about the old and thus explore a quality that is commonly assumed to be important for well-being across the life span. We can search for agreement concerning what is funny. We can document the fact that it changes over time, that it differs by gender, by cohort, and by ethnic subgroup, as well as by age. We can look at humor of the old and about the old and humor that amuses the old.

Much of the literature in gerontology has been devoted either to detailing the myriad problems of aging or to giving assurances that aging can be fun. The former dominates professional journals, the latter is mostly in the popular media. A popular psychological theory known as *object relations* states that when an issue is too hot to handle, people tend to exaggerate both the good and the bad elements, splitting them off from one another (Guntrip, 1971). The exaggeration represents an attempt to divide the issue into component parts that can be dealt with. If we both love and hate a person, what are we to do? There is no forthright action that can be taken. Americans are action oriented; they want to *do* something. The exaggeration of both the badness and the goodness is a kind of solution. However, because the problem is solved by altering the perception of reality, the facts keep intruding. Complexities of aging and of life keep reemerging. Thus one is often more disconcerted than reassured by posters stating brightly that "life begins at 40." Such an unbalanced position may trigger cognitive dissonance. Humor is a mechanism that can relieve the cognitive strain. Thus the poster stating, "Life may not begin at 40, but it does not end there either," is much more satisfying. Because humorous messages leave one free to get the point or not to get the point, to comprehend at one level while denying at another, or even to develop one's own delaying structure so that one misses the point now but gets it later, humor serves many functions. Aging is an issue that creates conflict in most of us. The popular humor of our time shows some brutal confrontations with both the realities of aging and the fact of denial. A case in point is the greeting card that reads, "Happy 29th Birthday! Welcome to fantasy land!"

Gerontologists spend endless hours discussing alternate definitions of aging only to conclude that it is relative. How much easier it is to quote the proverb: "An old maid who gets married becomes a young wife." How much more pleasant to tell about old Mr. Trabish:

Old Mr. Trabish, sitting near the pool in a Catskill resort, could not help noticing the white-haired man at the next table. There he sat with two beautiful sexy women as he had every day during the week, drinking and laughing and eating. Every day he went off the high diving board and swam seven lusty laps without stopping. And every night he was in the nightclub, dancing with different women until the wee hours.

After two weeks of observing this strenuous schedule, Mr. Trabish leaned over and said, "Mister, it's amazing the condition you're in, the way you live!"

"Thank you," said the white-haired man.

"Excuse me for asking, but how old are you?"

The white-haired man shrugged. "Twenty-seven." (Rosten, 1972)

Similarly, to express critical issues in geriatrics one can do no better than the story of the doctor who examined the 83-year-old woman and said, "Some things not even modern medicine can cure. . . . I can't make you any younger, you know, my dear." "Who asked you to make me younger?" replied the woman. "I want you to make me *older*."

Aging is a process that begins at birth and progresses throughout one's life. This book deals with humor throughout the life span, although primary attention is given to humor about and by the elderly. The book contains theoretical and review material from infancy to old age and includes empirical studies of death and dying in both our own and other societies.

The book is divided into four parts. In Part I theoretical models of humor development across the life span are considered, and physiological, psychological, and sociological processes are discussed. Part II deals with ways of considering humor and aging from different vantage points. They include (1) humor *about* people of different ages, (2) humor *for* people of different ages, and (3) humor *by* people of different ages. Part III deals with the grim subject of death and dying and how it lends itself to humorous treatment in our own and other societies. Part IV contains brief empirical reports. Since scientific research in humor and aging is only beginning, it seems important to discuss pilot work in hopes that others will follow. Finally, an epilogue by Loeb and Wood presents a compelling theoretical approach.

LUCILLE NAHEMOW

REFERENCES

Guntrip, H. (1971). *Psychoanalytic theory, therapy, and the self.* New York: Basic.
Rosten, L. (1972). *Treasury of Jewish quotations.* New York: McGraw-Hill.

Acknowledgments

Many individuals made important contributions to the conception of this volume, which grew out of the West Virginia University Gerontology Center Conference on Humor and Aging at the Coolfront Conference Center in Berkeley Springs, West Virginia. All who attended the sessions were collaborators in the book, and we are grateful to them all.

We thank the following members of the West Virginia University community for their participation: Betty Maxwell and Rita Rendina of the Gerontology Center; Donna Barre, Linda Holt, and Rosellen Rosich of the Department of Psychology; Beverly Hummel of the College of Agriculture and Forestry; Robert Waldman of the School of Medicine; Joseph Gluck of Student Affairs; and William Collins, Vice President for Academic Affairs. Their work and support were crucial to the success of this endeavor.

Several other individuals who participated in the conference were instrumental in generating ideas reflected in this volume. We particularly thank Donna Polisar, David Guttman, Harvey Sterns, Rubin Gur, Elias Cohen, Leonard Gottesman, Polly McConney, Maxine Ewers, Dorothy J. Lyons, and Virginia Powers for their creativity and insight. We thank Barbara Knight and Nancy Merrifield for editorial assistance.

PART I

THEORY

This part contains four chapters. In Chapter 1, Nahemow discusses potential uses of humor research to increase our knowledge of the aging process and the position of the aged in society. Major theories of aging are presented. In Chapter 2, McGhee considers the development of humor across the life span and addresses the very important issue of individual differences. Chapter 3, by Simons, McCluskey-Fawcett, and Papini, is concerned with theories and data regarding the origins and development of humor in infancy, childhood, and adolescence. Finally, Fry presents a comprehensive treatment of the physiology of humor and laughter in Chapter 4.

Copyright © 1986 by Academic Press, Inc.
All rights of reproduction in any form reserved.

Humor as a Data Base for the Study of Aging

LUCILLE NAHEMOW

INTRODUCTION

Aging is a natural and universal phenomenon common to all living things. The process starts at the moment of fertilization and continues throughout the life cycle. It involves rapid early growth, maturation, continual change and development during the major part of life, and, finally, a period of senescence, terminating in death. A disproportionate amount of attention has been focused on the first half of life and only recently has theory and research been directed toward the older adult (see Poon, 1981). *Humor* is a key element in the human repertoire—so much so that many consider it a defining human attribute. In this chapter, we examine the interrelationship of aging and humor. This focus, which seems obvious and logical to us, is quite new. Heretofore, humor has been examined from a developmental perspective but only concentrating on the earlier part of life. Similarly, aging theorists have rarely addressed the issue of humor production or appreciation. In general, we can look at the subject from two points of view: Changes with aging can be studied to increase our knowledge about humor, or humor can be studied to shed light on the process of aging. The latter is the approach taken in this chapter.

Copyright © 1986 by Academic Press, Inc.
All rights of reproduction in any form reserved.

EXAMINING HUMOR AND AGING

The Complexity of Humor

In order to study humor, we must first recognize its enormous complexity. Distinctions must be made among the following:

1. humor about age,
2. humor created by young, middle-aged, or old joketellers, and
3. humor intended for a particular age group.

We must also remain cognizant of the distinction between humorous products and feelings of playfulness, both of which deserve study. What one person finds hilarious, another finds offensive, dull, or incomprehensible. Implicit in the study of humor and aging is the expectation that there are differences in the perception of humor by young and old. However, we know that irrespective of age, an individual reacts differently to a humorous stimulus at different times. A sense of humor is simultaneously irrepressible and ephemeral. It is dependent upon such diverse contextual factors as whether people consider themselves to be among friends or strangers, whether they feel that laughing is the right thing to do—as when the boss tells the joke—and whether they are relaxed or tense at the time. To the extent to which these factors are shared with others present, social facilitation takes place. Finally, we should not forget to distinguish between the comprehension and the appreciation of humor and the relation between them and the phenomenon of laughter.

The Diversity of the Aged

As people age, the differences between them become greater. This is a little recognized implication of the generally accepted formula $B = F (I \cdot E)$, which states that behaviour (B) is a function (F) of the individual (I) and the environment (E) (Lewin, 1951). One is born with all one's genes. With aging, the environment makes its mark on the individual. Although babies are obviously quite different from one another, they are not *as* different as they will one day be. As we begin to develop norms for our aging population across a wide range of physiological and psychological areas, we find that the standard deviations for the older samples often tend to be greater (see Rossman, 1979). The effect of the environment in continaul interaction with the individual's inherited and developed propensities continually loops back on itself, creating unique older people. It has been said many times in many ways that as people age, they become more like themselves (Neugarten, 1977); that is, "At age 40 a man has the face he deserves," "Old people don't become crotchety, crotchety people become old," and so on, emphasizing the continuity of life and the variability of the aged.

Studying Humor and Aging Scientifically

It is in the nature of scientific inquiry to simplify. Research begins by finding and applying the lowest common denominator. When we look at the lowest common denominators of human functioning, the aged perform far worse than when we look at the highest levels of human functioning. For example, by age 40, reaction time, both simple and complex, has slowed down. The perceptual systems are not only slower, but less responsive and less efficient: vision is less acute, night vision less adaptive, loss of muscle tone creates the need for reading glasses. By age 80, acuity is further reduced. Glare becomes blinding, colors lose their saturation, and so on. (Storant, 1979).

The incredible strength of the old and the near old is not in those characteristics that they have in common but rather in those that are uncommon. Qualities of the elderly have been developed and nurtured over the years, thereby emphasizing individual differences. Clearly, some abstraction must take place to make it possible to engage in a scientific study. But by the same token, we simply cannot study aging without recognizing that which gives it meaning—time and the passage of time, memory, recollection, the integration of percepts and memories, and a sense of humor.

RESEARCH AND THEORY ON HUMOR AND AGING

In 1972, the American Psychological Association published the first book (Eisdorfer & Lawton, 1972) in which the society pulled together the available knowledge on aging and human development. To those acquainted with the traditional concerns of psychology, it was not surprising to find extensive treatment of physiology, perception, reaction time, and cognition. In his provocative "Epilogue," Kastenbaum concluded:

> Sleeping, dreaming, imaging, fantasizing, meditating, creating, loving, grieving, dying. These activities have something in common: lack of coverage by the American Psychological Association's Task Force on Aging. It is hard to

work up a grumble about omissions when so much material has been explored
with so much scholarship and skill. However, it would also be remiss to conclude this volume without at least a brief discussion of some of the questions
that remain in search of a task force. (p. 699)

It would be in the spirit of Kastenbaum's observation to add *humor* to
the to-be-studied list.

In this chapter we will examine the following classes of theories:
cognitive theories, psychoanalytic theories, drive-reduction theories,
disposition theory, and environmental theory. First, the theories are
described. For the first three, which are reviewed elsewhere in this
book, the initial description is very brief. Disposition and environmental theories are examined in more detail. In each case, implications for aging are discussed. Second, special difficulties that should
be anticipated in data collection are pointed out. This includes areas
in which it is suspected that already existing problems of measurement are magnified when an older population is studied. Finally,
insights that may be obtained by studying older individuals or
through using a greater age range are emphasized. We discuss ways in
which studying humor can enhance our knowledge of aging through
the life span.

Cognitive Theories

There is always an element of understanding in responding to humorous material. Getting the joke is an intellectual process whereas
enjoying it is an affective or emotional experience. Much of the scientific study of humor development follows a cognitive model. In *Humor: Its Origin and Development,* McGhee (1979) discusses the importance of intellectual challenge and the pleasure obtained through
cognitive mastery. He cites evidence that even 1-year-old infants derive pleasure from successful efforts to understand their world. Most
research and theory concerning the development of humor production
and appreciation focuses upon childhood. Simons, McCluskey-Fawcett, & Papini review this material in Chapter 3 of this book. We do
not repeat it here except where necessary to discuss some of the implications for aging.

STRUCTURE OF HUMOR

The structure of humor is characterized by incongruity. The discrepancy between the expected and that which transpires accounts for
the humorous experience. However, inconguity alone appears insuffi-
cient. There must also be resolution for the joke to make sense. Shultz

(1976) finds that about one-half of the verbal jokes that he analyzed obtain such resolution on the basis of linguistic ambiguity. Using Chomsky's (1965) linguistic theory, he differentiates levels of ambiguity as follows:

Surface structure ambiguity–"Can you tell me how long cows should be milked?" The farmer answers, "They should be milked the same as short ones, of course".

Deep structure ambiguity–"Did you know that the natives like potatoes even more than missionaries?" "Yes, but the missionaries are more nutritious" (p. 13).

Shultz states,

> "Any truly comprehensive theory of the structure of humor must take account of cognitive development. Although it seems obvious that the structure of humor for infants and young children is quite different from that for older children and adults, there have been very few theoretical attempts to account for these differences" (p. 17).

No cognitive theory of humor extends to the complete life span. Let us examine Shultz's examples with the older adult in mind. Both require knowledge of cultural as well as linguistic factors in order to comprehend the humorous elements. Comprehension of the one utilizing deep structure ambiguity depends upon a long chain of association that involves cultural awareness and diverse memories. A young person might not get the joke—not because he or she does not have the cognitive structure, but because a particular memory is lacking. In studying humor, we must consider not only cognitive development but also cognitive style, which sometimes differs markedly for old and young adults.

THE MEANING OF HUMOR

Differences in cognitive style typically distinguish old from young adults. Since the meaning of a communication depends upon one's past experiences and knowledge, the missionary joke that Schultz uses as an example of deep structure ambiguity makes no sense to a young person who knows about Third World people but not about "natives" as the word is used in the joke. Older people come from a different time. Howell (1972) found that older people were unable to learn to identify unfamiliar, standard material as rapidly as the young. However, when the material came from the 1908 Sears catalogue, they performed the same task as well as the young. It is easier to relate to those who have backgrounds and experience similar to our own. Seltzer (1983) refers to older people as "temporal immigrants" who are left out of the common culture. We should not be surprised, therefore, if there are times when they do not get the joke.

ISSUES OF UNDERSTANDING

The problems that confront people at different points along the life span are a function of both internal development and external imposition. Older people may devote more attention to humor that relates to problems of intelligence and comprehension because of the widespread, although misplaced, fear of senility. If issues of understanding are found to be a major theme in the humor of the aged, a domain of research would be uncovered. The following questions come to mind: At what age does interest in these areas increase? Is it comparable for men and women? Is it comparable for those of different educational levels? Does it appear to be related to the degree that society denegrates older people?

Many of today's elderly have had little formal education. In the main, their lives have been hard. They experienced economic reversal during the Depression; many are again experiencing economic strain. They appear to have developed humor as a coping strategy to deal with a difficult and sometimes painful life. However, in the absence of schooling, which tends to inculcate an analytic orientation, they have not necessarily developed an associated hypothetical attitude. Brought up in an age that preceded educational toys, the older generation was not *taught* to play. Schooling in the beginning of the twentieth century was usually brief and to the point, with no fooling around. I submit that the hypothetical–analytic attitude develops at the interface of play and education and that old people who lack formal education lack this hypothetical attitude, a requirement for some types of humor appreciation.

The recognition that something is funny contains both emotional and cognitive elements. One can laugh spontaneously and only later analyzes why. In a review of the physiological literature on humor and laughter, McGhee and Duffy (1983) suggests that the right cerebral hemisphere plays a more important role than the left in spontaneous comprehension of a joke or cartoon, while the left hemisphere is more involved than the right in analyzing why it is funny. Humor appreciation requires an attitude of playfulness that is impeded by anxiety. Jokes are more amusing in congenial surroundings, in the company of appreciative people. In addition to these factors, we expect that one's attitude toward one's self affects the level of amusement. If one is anxious about one's intellectual effectiveness, a joke that makes intellectual demands may increase anxiety, thus decreasing enjoyment. It is possible that a critical attitude readies the left hemisphere and damps the spontaneity of the right hemisphere of the brain.

We know that normal aging does not bring marked cognitive decline (see Baltes & Labouve-Vief, 1972). However, this information is not communicated adequately to older people themselves. Despite the weight of evidence, there remains a belief that old people become "senile." We have said that responsiveness to linguistic ambiguity varies with intellectual prowess and with a backlog of relevant information. We also expect it to vary with one's perception of one's own intellectual prowess. If a person fears he or she is losing mental ability, failing to understand a joke can result in distress.

Clayton (1982) required both old and young adults to list adjectives with which they associate the quality of *wisdom*. A complex data analysis revealed that having a sense of humor was closely associated with being a wise person. This association was stronger for older subjects than for young ones. We conclude therefore that humor is valued particularly highly by the old. It is always disconcerting to feel that one has missed the point of a joke, even more so for the older people who consider a sense of humor close to the quality of wisdom.

FEAR OF SENILITY

The fear of senility creates a self-fulfilling prophecy. Despite compelling evidence to the contrary, most old people are terrified of losing their minds. Unless one suffers a debilitating disease, such as senile dementia of the Alzheimer's type, one can expect to retain one's cognitive faculties throughout life. Forgetfulness that would be ignored in the young is seen in an old person as signaling progressive senility. Contemporary humor on aging often emphasizes this fear. A book of *Laughs and Limericks on Aging in Large Print* by Reggie the Retiree (1982) bears the instruction on the cover: "Gift Wrap for an Oldie." It is particularly distressing in this context to uncover such gems (in large print) as:

My bifocals are the best you can find
My teeth fit and don't bind
My ear plug's o.k.

and so's my toupee
but I sure do miss my mind. (p. 16)

and

Three things age does to you
First you forget who's who
That's not so bad
What makes me sad
I can't recall the next two. (p. 19)

Such negative expectations make older people fearful of their own forgetfulness. Thus, lack of comprehension in an older person may create enormous anxiety. Since anxiety inhibits humor appreciation, a serial effect is expected. If one joke falls flat because the person is not sure he or she got the point, increased tension might create proactive inhibition that impedes memory tasks that follow. The next joke or humorous situation would not be experienced as funny.

For older people, it is necessary to consider first, whether the person "gets" the joke in the sense that it is intended, and second, whether the person "gets" the joke to his or her own satisfaction. I hypothesize that the latter is far more important for an older than a younger adult because that subjective level determines whether or not anxiety is produced. This variable is particularly difficult to measure. A technique that could be applied involves the use of a confederate. Since, for many older people, there is considerable ego involvement in comprehension of humorous material, the issue has to be defused before it is possible for them to admit confusion. An elderly confederate, playing the role of a fellow subject could say, "Did you get that?" in a tone of voice that expresses doubt. The confederate could also request an explanation of the point of the joke without having it appear to be an examination, but rather a request for help. In this way we find out what the older individual considers humorous. Before such a design is undertaken, however, ethical issues have to be addressed. This is always the case when an experimental design requires deception, but it is even more problematic with older people, who are often more vulnerable and frequently less accepting of deception in the name of science.

Psychoanalytic Theories

As in so many other areas of human behavior, Freud was one of the first to posit a developmental theory of humor production and appreciation. Erikson's (1950) thoery was the first major extension of analytic developmental concepts into old age. Erikson detailed the stages of middle age and adulthood and reviewed some of the conflict areas that are resolved during the later stages of life. If laughter is seen as a result of areas of conflict, we predict that older people would laugh at different things than younger people. Erikson postulated that the major task during early childhood is to develop basic trust and in late life to develop ego integrity and confront the inevitability of death. Thus we predict that youngsters laugh more than old people at jokes that challenge and then reaffirm the trustworthiness of others. Old people seek out and are more amused than younger people by humor that reaffirms the integrity of the self despite myriad imperfections and challenges; for example, we expect more joking about illness and death in this group. Humor directed to conflict areas may backfire, for these are fearful subjects for us all. The delivery must not fully expose the underside of tragedy. An unobtrusive measure that could be applied involves examining the material with audiences of different ages (see Nahemow & Raymon, Chapter 15). Since the whole society is aging rapidly, we could predict alterations in popular comedy in years to come.

According to psychoanalytic theory, people's sense of humor should reflect their personal hangups. Areas of obsessional thinking and repetitive working through should be reflected in their perceptions of what is funny. We have hypothesized that older people are particularly responsive to issues that challenge personal integrity. However, we must bear in mind that older people may be stuck at an earlier level of development. When an older person is fascinated by scatological humor, it does not necessarily mean that we have uncovered a particular challenge of age; it may mean that this person, or even group of people, remains fixated at an earlier stage of development. With aging, people tend to become more individualistic. We hardly expect all older people to be amused by the same joke. Nevertheless, given a large enough sample, we expect age differences in humor appreciation to emerge.

It comes as no surprise that psychoanalytic theory is a difficult area in which to conduct controlled research. In order to differentiate between amusement elicited as a function of stage of life or as a result of individual fixations at earlier stages of development, we need to develop norms for different subgroups of young and old. We predict a greater range of humor appreciation for the old than for the young since they have experienced more potential stages in which fixations could occur.

Drive Reduction Theories

Drive reduction theories of learning have been a mainstay of American psychology (see Hall & Lindsay, 1970). These theories postulate that learning takes place when a particular behavior reduces an uncomfortable drive. An animal that is deprived of food will readily learn to turn left in a maze or to press a bar to obtain food, which is an unconditioned reinforcer. Drive reduction theory postulates that there are also conditioned reinforcers, which are stimuli that are associated with an unconditioned reinforcer. After a left turn in a particular maze is repeatedly associated with food, the behavior itself acquires drive properties. Until extinction of the drive occurs, gratification is derived from the behavior itself. The behavior becomes its own reward; other behaviors can be learned by association with that behavior. More complex behaviors may be learned as new stimuli are associated with the stimuli that reduce drives. Drive reduction theories explain all learning from a simple left turn to a complex musical composition, in this way.

These reductionistic theories have been extremely useful in developing a scientific psychology. The theories have generated an enormous body of research data. Because this research attempted to control as many factors as possible, it has usually been conducted in a laboratory. The development of a high specific drive state such as hunger makes data interpretation easier. Within limits, the longer the period of deprivation the stronger the drive. Therefore, animals would be deprived of food or water for specified intervals. Whenever possible, diffuse drive states were avoided. One did not work with an animal who was a little bit hungry, a little bit thirsty, and somewhat sexually aroused. One can readily see how difficult it would be to compare that animal to another with a different pattern of arousal.

When human subjects were used, they were almost always college students who were presented with simplified learning tasks, such as memorizing lists of nonsense syllables. Old people were never used as subjects; thus, anyone interested in the drive reduction theories of learning can make new discoveries simply by studying older people.

The drive state of the human being is typically much more diffuse than the powerful, highly focused drive of the starved mouse. Even when a person is quite hungry, the hunger drive has a complex of social overtones. For example, one refrains from eating while Grace is said because the need to appear socially acceptable is temporarily greater than the need for food. In general, old people appear to have more diffuse drive states than young people. Most young people who attempt to ignore hunger pangs while dieting are decidedly aware of those pangs. In contrast, old people sometimes suffer serious malnutrition because, without someone to cook for or to eat with, they forget to eat. In a similar vein, lack of sleep is often reported by the old. However, unlike the young who often try to stay awake, older people report problems in falling and staying asleep.

The assumption is often made that aging tends to blunt the libido. Certainly, many jokes relating to aging reflect that supposition. Despite the explosion of "sex over 60" books, no research deals with the issue directly. I believe it was Simone de Beauvior who stated, "In youth, sex is a drive, in old age, it is a pleasure." This statement has the play on the word *sex*, which is an integral part of humor. While there is no doubt that diffuse drive states are more difficult to define and to measure, they are so characteristic of human motivation that they demand study. Traditional research with drive reduction theory avoided ambiguous material, and, therefore, humor was not a subject of study.

The frustration–aggression hypothesis, which comes from drive reduction theory (Dollard, Doob, Miller, Mowrer & Sears, 1939), postulates that frustration always leads to aggression, although the behavior is sometimes blocked. In other words, one becomes angry but may be unable to act out the anger. The research generated by this interesting theory tends to be limited to a very brief unit of time, thereby making experimental control possible. However, the focus upon aging leads to the questions: What happens over time? Are there cumulative effects? Does frustration not expressed as aggression accumulate? Does it lose some sharp edges, perhaps develop greater depth? Folk wisdom suggests that humor serves as an outlet for pent up frustrations (see Datan, Chapter 8). Clearly, aggression may be disguised as humor (*Smile when you say that, pardner!*). Because our society lacks respect for age, old people experience considerable frustration. They are exposed to many losses and myriad insensitivities. The frustration–aggression hypothesis would predict that with advancing years put-down humor would seem funnier. The more powerless the elder, the funnier it would seem.

Disposition Theory

SUPERIORITY THEORY

Superiority theories of humor have a long history. The Greek philosophers first attempted to systematize the conditions under which exposing weakness or deformity leads to mirth (Zillmann, 1983). Plato and Aristotle both found that laughter could be punishing. Humor that belittles and humiliates derives its enjoyment from the fleeting sense of superiority experienced in comparison to the belittled other. The sudden sense of triumph triggers laughter. Humorous material that derives its zest from putting down individuals or groups is also referred to as disparagement humor (Zillmann, 1983). When a group is elevated in status or wisdom in the joke, it is always at the expense of another. Hostility and aggression are necessarily central to the point of the joke.

However, when a joke is at another's expense, it usually makes a difference who that person is. Wolff, Smith, and Murray (1934) contrast Jews to non-Jews in the appreciation of anti-Jewish jokes. As the superiority theory predicts, these jokes are considered funnier by non-Jews. When one's own group is disparaged, the joke generally is not funny. A distinction is made between those people and objects with whom we identify and those with whom we do not. Martineau (1972) notes that the fleeting sense of superiority that produces mirth is obtained only in the disparagement of objects with which we do not identify. Initial studies assumed that when one is a member of a particular group, such as Germans or blacks, one fails to be amused when one's own group is denigrated. Generally, this is found to be true (Zillmann & Bryant, 1974); however, there are people who do not identify with their own groups.

REFERENCE GROUP THEORY

Hyman (1942), who coined the term *reference group* to identify the group from which individuals derive their values, found that aspiring working class youth sometimes used the middle class as a reference group. He notes that anti-Semitic Jews derive their values from the Christian society. We are all members of many groups, but we do not subscribe to their values equally. LaFave (1961) demonstrated that the concept of reference group could be an effective predictor of humor reactions. Contrasting four experimental groups: Catholics, Jehovah's Witnesses, Southern Baptists, and agnostics, he found that "jokes tend to be judged as funny by [subjects] whose reference group is esteemed, and whose outgroup is disparaged, and to be judged unfunny by Ss whose reference group is disparaged and whose outgroup is esteemed" (p. 67). Refining the technique further, LaFave, McCarthy, and Haddad (1970) found that the effect was enhanced by measuring the degree of identification with the group. They found that avidly pro-Americans laugh more heartily at humor directed at non-Americans, and, similarly, pro-Canadians did not find anti-Canadian humor particularly funny. The humorous impact of disparagement increases in proportion to hostility felt toward the receiver group.

The disposition theory of humor is articulated by Zillman (1983) as follows:

> Prediction of the enjoyment of witnessing disparagement is based on affective dispositions toward the parties involved, that is, toward the disparaging and the disparaged entities. These dispositions may be positive (e.g., affection, admiration, love) or negative (e.g., resentment, condemnation, hate), and they are expected to vary in intensity. Both the hedonic quality and the intensity of affect are empirically ascertained, and the likelihood and magnitude of mirth resulting from witnessed disparagement is projected from this ascertainment. Obviously, the affective dispositions under consideration may correspond with group affiliations (e.g., a Jew may feel sympathy toward other Jews and antipathy toward KKK members), and if so, disposition theory can accommodate reference group theory. But such correspondence need not exist (e.g., a professor might hold a negative disposition toward other professors and be more sympathetic toward students than peers), and if this is the case, any conceptualization in terms of groups and classes is considered pointless, immaterial, and potentially misleading. (p. 90–91)

> In formal terms, the disposition theory of humor and mirth is based on the premise that persons respond affectively to a multitude of stimulus conditions, that the affective reaction is discernable as hedonically positive or negative, and that it varies in intensity. (p. 91)

DISPOSITIONAL CONFUSION

Middleton (1959) compares the appeal of racial jokes to matched groups of black and white students from southern universities in the 1950s. He found that blacks reacted more favorably than whites to antiwhite jokes. So far, we are following the expected pattern, but then we find that black students are surprisingly appreciative of anti-black jokes. In fact, they found them to be as funny as did white students. In the same vein, McGhee & Duffey (1983) found that girls from lower income families considered disparagement of girls to be funnier than disparagement of boys. Zillmann (1983) calls this *dispositional confusion*.

Certain transitory emotional states permit close friends and lovers to develop resentment-based mirth against one another. In addition, one can use disparagement humor against oneself. Zillmann argues that it is not contradictory to expect persons with high self-esteem to become temporarily annoyed with themselves and create jokes at their own expense (Zillmann & Cantor, 1977). However, we should question the self-evaluation of persons who constantly disparage themselves in jest.

LaFave (1972) said that most people, when asked who possesses a sense of humor, will claim that they do, and their friends do, but their adversaries do not. With much qualification, he defines sense of humor as the capacity to laugh at one's own expense. He points out that the definition contains a contradiction since the constructs *at one's own expense* and *amusement* refer to unhappy and happy states respectively.

McGhee and Duffey (1983) found that among 3- to 6-year old children, only whites found it funnier to see a child of another ethnic group disparaged than one of their own. Black and Mexican-American children do not exhibit such preferences. This is reminiscent of the findings of Clark and Clark (1947) that southern black children preferred white to black dolls. This became instrumental in the "separate is unequal" Supreme Court decision (Clark, 1950, in Brown v. Board of Education, 1953). Admittedly, the evidence is very limited, but there seems to be a relationship between appreciation of self-disparaging humor and societal status as a despised minority. The relationship betweeen the two constitutes a critical area of need for research in humor and aging. What is the function of self-debasing humor? To what extent does it dissipate negative dispositions, and to what extent does it exaggerate them? Under what circumstances might we expect one or the other to take place?

DISPOSITIONS TOWARD AGING

Agism, or negative societal stereotypes leading to discrimination against old people, is not the exclusive province of the young. In a review of the literature on attitudes toward aging and the aged, Bennett and Eckman (1973) found that most elderly have some negative attitudes toward old people. Fry (1976) examined sexual humor relating to aging. He found old age as depicted in jokes and cartoons to be a dreadful time in which problems confronting the old are exaggerated to the point of becoming grotesque. The following joke is offered as an example of how guilt plays a part in our humor about aging.

Two old veterans of "the war to end all wars" are chatting about their days "over there." "Do you remember that salt-peter they used to put in our coffee to try to keep us from chasing the women all the time?" "Yeah, it didn't have any effect at all." "Well, I wouldn't be too sure. I think it's starting to work on me now." (p. 146)

Fry feels that in our grandiosity we exaggerate the importance of our sins. We expect punishment to be forthcoming and see the aging process itself, terminating as it does in death, as fitting punishment. Palmore (1971) found that jokes about old people, and particularly older women, are often disparaging. Huyck (Chapter 7) finds that jokes about older people found in greeting cards are frequently quite nasty.

Humor is a many-edged sword. Complex and multifaceted, it can be used for coping with losses, but it can also be used to diminish the self as well as others. It can be light-hearted nonsense, but it can also be vicious. Laughter can be a giggle or a snicker. Thus, while humor is an effective tool for education (Robinson, 1977) and for therapy, it can also be destructive of self-esteem.

In order to appreciate most humorous interchanges, one must be able to perceive two or more facets of a situation. It is certainly possible for individuals to experience anger and, at the same time, understand that others might experience mirth. Furthermore, because human beings are so complicated and because humor taps into that complexity, it is possible for the same people to observe their own reactions and question the lack of mirth. They may think, "Is the joke despicable, or am I becoming a stodgy old fool?" Interpreting Freud's theory of humor, Zillmann (1983) states elegantly, "Humor permits us to be malicious with dignity" (p. 98). But, alas, when that maliciousness is directed full upon us, it is difficult to feel dignified. For that reason humor is a very effective weapon. It usually leaves the recipient in a state of confusion. At the time of the joketelling one is speechless; later on, one runs through a whole series of "I should have said's" in one's mind. This occurs when an individual is attacked "humorously" by another. How much more difficult it is when one is also the attacker! For a divided self, humor can be a strong poison. An attack through humor denies us the release of any active response. Thus, the answer to the question, Is it funny when the joke is on you? should be, No. When the old feel that they *should* laugh, they are in a serious bind. What a set up for generating self-hatred and guaranteeing failure! To repeat that oft-quoted line from Walt Kelly's *Pogo*, "We have met the enemy and he is us!"

Environmental Theory

The ecological theory of aging is an environmental theory which examines the complex interactions between person and environment (Lawton & Nahemow, 1972). A derivative of Lewin's topological field theory (1935), it explores the effect of the physical and the social environment on behavior. The ecological theory is concerned with the special vulnerability of the aged to the environment. With aging, there is a constriction of social space. Typically, as people age they do not get around as much as they once did. Consequently, problems created by the environment cannot readily be overcome by simply going elsewhere for a while. When this happens, problems seem to mount up. To make matters worse, sensory decrements and motoric impairments make it harder to cope with marginal environments. Minor nuisances become major obstructions. For example, in a poorly designed supermarket it is the older person who tends to trip, is unable to see what he or she is buying, and so on. Because old people are highly vulnerable to the environment and because they are very different from one another, the question of person–environment fit is critical (Kahana, Liang, & Felton, 1980).

The ecological theory is a homeostatic theory that is based upon the concept of level of adaptation of the person to the environment. Three major variables form the base of the theory: individual competence, environmental press, and adaptation level. We briefly describe each variable.

INDIVIDUAL COMPETENCE

Individual competence is conceived of as a summated variable that consists of the individual's strengths as they are used on a day-to-day basis in interaction with the environment. Individual competence fluctuates with mood, and different facets of the individual's potential surfaces in response to different demand properties of the environment. Competence is not a unitary variable. A highly competent football player may be an incompetent scholar. Nevertheless, there are general factors which seem to be useful across a wide variety of situations. These include general intelligence, the ability to keep one's head when all others are losing theirs, and a sense of humor that permits one to alter the perceived field. Individual competence is the utilization of those enduring abilities enabling the individual to function.

ENVIRONMENTAL PRESS

Environmental press refers to aspects of the environment that act in concert with a personal need to evoke behavior. The concept was first proposed by Murray (1938) who differentiated between alpha press (the sum total of motivators, perceived or not) and beta press (the aspects perceived as important). Our definition of environmental press includes *all* behavioral motivators, thus encompassing the demand properties of the environment. It is related to the complexity of the environment but is far from synonymous. Generally speaking, when one first enters an environment, the environmental press is greater than it is after acclimation takes place. One is much more alert to the demands of an unfamiliar than a familiar environment.

ADAPTATION LEVEL

Helson (1964) developed the concept of adaptation level. He points out that human beings are homeostatic systems in which a steady state is one of accustomed balance of inputs. White noise, which consists of a random pattern of noise of many frequencies, blocks out disturbing auditory signals. We adapt to the white noise so completely that we do not hear it. The individual adapts to environmental press so that, with time, most environmental stimul are perceived as neutral. In a neutral setting, one which we experience as neither hot nor cold, dark nor light, pleasant nor unpleasant, we are able to screen out most environmental stimuli and concentrate on focal tasks.

THE ECOLOGICAL THEORY OF AGING

The ecological theory posits that the adaptation level that develops is dependent upon individual's competence, environmental press, and accustomed activities. The adaptation level balances these factors over time and maximum comfort is experienced with a narrow range of the adaptation level achieved. When the environmental press is too far from this level, maladaptive behavior occurs, particularly for those of limited competence. In general, the closer one is to one's adaptation level, the more comfort is experienced. Variation in the direction of greater or lesser environmental press is irrelevant where feelings are concerned because the model is symmetrical. However, regarding the behavior that affects individual competence, the theory is asymmetric. Keeping the individual at or below the level of environmental press to which he or she has adapted produces lethargy and ultimately lowers the individual's competence. In contrast, environmental press that is above the accustomed level results in heightened activity, leading to improved competence. Thus, maximum performance is obtained by slight increases in environmental press. If the increase is maintained over time, the adaptation level becomes elevated, and the individual functions at a higher level.

Let us consider a hypothetical case as an example: A woman enters a domiciliary home after a fire destroys her home, to which she clung for many years after her children moved far away and her husband died. It was a drafty house that she could neither heat nor repair. Cardboard boxes filled every room because the woman, who was always a saver, was afraid to throw anything away for fear of being unable to replace it. The house had been a fire hazard for a long time. Entering the domiciliary home, the woman had many fears; at first, the environmental press was almost too much for her to bear. This new environment seemed extremely complex, with potential threat lurking in every nook and cranny. When her fears were allayed she began to blossom in the new environment. However, a year and a half later she was morose and withdrawn. Why? Analysis of the change in her mood and behavior reveals that at first the new environment was terrifying, then stimulating and enriching, then comfortable though dull, and finally excruciatingly boring. As her capabilities expanded and developed in what seemed to be stimulating new surroundings and as the anticipated threat consistently failed to materialize, she relaxed and grew. The environment was not able to grow with her; for environments, like people, can have growth potential. Unfortunately, some of the environments to which the old are relegated lack this quality. They remain static, day after day, year after year: the arts and crafts are always at the same level, the foreign language class is always for beginners. One characteristic of such environments is that they are not amusing. Humor is consistently lacking.

ENVIRONMENTAL ENRICHMENT

How can such a situation be alleviated? There are many ways in which the environment can be enriched. New elements can be introduced into the physical environment, which stimulate the senses; the social environment can be changed, for example, by giving certificates of achievement in classes, and by offering other courses. Many ways to alleviate the inherent boredom of the limited institutional environment have been discussed by those involved in research and practice in aging (Poon, 1981). Since the ecological theory was posited, an array of therapeutic interventions directed at increasing the environmental press have been recommended. However, all of them intercede through increasing environmental complexity.

A major problem with the ecological theory is that many intervening variables defy direct measurement. While we can measure environmental complexity, we cannot directly measure environmental press.

Similarly, we can measure competence in a particular area with some reliability, but a summated construct consisting of enduring intraindividual characteristics lacks even estimated reliabilities. Efforts to test the theory have relied upon objectively different environments with high or low environmental press (Lawton, 1976). However, when individuals demonstrate maladaptive behavior, it is difficult to tell whether that behavior is a function of too much environmental press or too little. The subjective nature of the construct mitigates against its use in attempts to apply the theory. The juxtaposition of a theory of humor introduces new possibilities into this research domain.

The theory of psychological reversals posited by Smith and Apter (1977) is a form of incongruity theory. In contrast to drive reduction theory, it argues that arousal can be pleasurable and that one can be motivated to seek varied experiences. The theory discriminates between telic (goal orientated) and paratelic (fun-seeking) behavior. Fun seeking increases arousal level. An intriguing implication of the psychological reversal theory is that if humor and fun could be introduced into nursing home environments, they would increase arousal and, by extension, increase effective environmental complexity. This would be accomplished by the elderly person rather than by a therapeutic change agent. In this way, the press is not only appropriate for the individual, but if sustained long enough, increases the level of adaptation.

We tend to think of a sense of humor as being an individual attribute despite the weight of evidence to the contrary. Research data show marked effects of social facilitation (see McGhee & Goldstein, 1983). This scientific evidence is flanked by our subjective sense of feeling grim in certain places. Fun seeking, or paratelic behavior in Smith and Apter's terms, declines when one is anxious or angry. Anger is a strong element in boredom. How else could we explain our ability to spend hours on the beach doing absolutely nothing in contrast to feeling bored in 3 minutes by a lecturer we did not choose to hear?

Simultaneous consideration of the ecological theory and the theory of psychological reversals permits us to reexamine the important question of how to sustain an individual in a home for the aged. Fun seeking permits the individual to see two sides of a situation simultaneously. An environment that is perceived as containing a flip side is both more complex and less intimidating. The author experienced the following unforgettable encounter in a nursing home many years ago. An old woman, looking grim, was hemming a square of cloth. I sat down to talk with her and made the mistake of admiring her stitches. She looked at me with an unexpected clarity and said, "I am a tailor.

For 60 years I am a tailor." We both looked down at the pathetic cloth with new understanding. I was appalled and my expression must have reflected my feelings. She looked at me kindly and turned tragedy into humor by laughing suddenly and saying, "She don't know. I let her teach me. She's a nice lady. I make her happy." I started to giggle, then to laugh, and finally we both roared.

If we can develop experimental paradigms in this difficult area, we will accomplish two things: (1) We improve function through the introduction of humor into environments hitherto bereft of fun, and (2) we establish new parameters for the prediction of improvement.

SUMMARY AND CONCLUSIONS

We have briefly described theories that can be extended to encompass both humor and aging. These range from the broad-based classes of theories that are central to academic psychology (drive reduction and cognitive theories) to more limited midrange theories. Disposition theory is primarily a theory of humor that derives from a social psychological base, and the ecological theory is primarily an aging theory with roots in Lewinian psychology. Each theoretical area develops its own insights and can generate considerable additional research by examining both humor and aging simultaneously.

Drive reduction theory has focused upon specific drives and has tended to beg the questions, What happens when drives are muted and drive states become a composite of different needs? Do multiple, interlocking drives enhance or diminish one another? Are specific motivators responsible for the powerful learning impetus that we study in our laboratories, or are they created by the conditions of the laboratory? As evidence accumulates demonstrating that learning is not the exclusive province of the young, modifications will be required in this classical theory. The study of humor using an aging sample will point out where modifications must be made.

Cognitive theories lend themselves more readily to the study of the aged than does drive theory. The exclusion of the elderly as subjects simply reflects more global societal values; the old are excluded from many areas of concern. Once we introduce individuals in the second half of their lives as subjects worthy of study, we learn a great deal about being a mature human being. Work in this area needs to avoid pitfalls that we have thrown in our own way such as drawing too many conclusions about aging from institutionalized populations of the aged. Research that was not representative of the entire age range has provided little information concerning the aged. The vacuum thus created was filled with the myths and misconceptions about the old that permeated the larger society. Thus, by extending our samples to include human beings of all ages and by focusing upon humor rather than eye-blink reaction, we will rapidly increase our knowledge base.

Psychoanalytic theory has a different set of problems when applied to the issues of humor and aging. The ideas, particularly those of Erik Erikson, lend themselves to analysis of this complex area. However, the theory itself is and always has been difficult to translate into hypotheses amenable to controlled study. Consequently, much of the richness of the theory has been better utilized by clinicians and by those in fields where scholarly research and systematic speculation are preferred to empirical research.

Disposition theory offers great promise for research on humor and aging. Since it deals with issues of affiliation and power, it can provide many insights into the role of older people as a class and the position of their different subgroups. It can also be used to track changes that occur in these domains. Humor research can serve as a very effective form of unobtrusive analysis. Disposition theory is amenable to small research projects. I predict that many doctoral dissertations and masters' theses will be generated from it.

Finally, the ecological theory of aging can serve as a useful base for research on humor and aging. The person–environment focus of the theory can explain feedback phenomenon. Whether something strikes one as funny or not need not be explained in terms of one's sense of humor alone. For one thing, there is a strong buildup effect in comedy. In a stand-up routine, the tenth joke usually seems funnier than the first. That is why there is so often a warm-up act before a star performance. There are environmental conditions that engage one's sense of humor. The ecological theory could most fruitfully be used to study the interaction effect. It has also been suggested that when considered jointly with the theory of Smith and Apter, the ecological theory could be used to study ways in which humor is used by individuals to alter their perceived environment.

In conclusion, we can learn a great deal about an individual by examining what strikes him or her as funny. We can also learn about ourselves by considering what does *not* strike us as funny. For example, we compliment one another with the absurdity, "You are growing younger every year," without as much as a smile to show that we have registered the silliness of the statement. Our jokes about old people have limited themes and may be stilted. Our heroes are cowboys and comic strip characters lacking a past (Berger, 1973). Berger (1973) states flatly, "In theory, a society which creates grotesques must, in some way, be grotesque itself" (p. 30). Humor, and particularly popular humor, is used as an index of popular concerns. Exposure to popular forms of humor consumes vast amounts of time in the lives of most Americans. It is argued that scientific studies of aging that focus upon the lowest common denominator of human functioning make aging look particularly unappealing and therefore have contributed to the distaste that we have for the old, and to our own fear of aging. In addition to adding an important dimension to our knowledge of human functioning, a comprehensive examination of humor and aging will contribute a body of data that will serve to celebrate the aging process.

REFERENCES

Baltes, P. B., & Labouve-Vief, G. (1972). Aging and human development. In C. Eisdorfer & M. P. Lawton *The psychology of adult development and aging*, pp. 157–219. Washington, DC: American Psychological Association.

Bennett, R., & Eckman, J. (1973). Attitudes toward aging: A critical examination of recent literature and implications for future research. In C. Eisdorfer & M. P. Lawton (Eds.), *The psychology of adult development and aging* (pp. 575–597). Washington, DC: American Psychological Association.

Berger, A. A. (1973). *The comic stripped American.* New York: Walker.

Brown v. Board of Education, 347 U.S. 483 (1953).

Chomsky, N. A. (1965). *Aspects of the theory of syntax.* Cambridge, MA: MIT Press.

Clark, K. B. (1950). *Effect of prejudice and discrimination on personality development.* Mid Century White House Conference on Children and Youth, Washington, DC.

Clark, K. B., & Clark, M. P. (1947). Racial identification and preference in Negro children. In T. M. Newcomb & E. L. Hartley (Eds.), *Readings in social psychology.* New York: Holt, Rinehart & Winston.

Clayton, V. (1982). Wisdom and intelligence: The nature and function of knowledge in the later years. In S. Brent (Ed.), *Aging and wisdom: Individual development and social functions.* New York: Springer Press.

de Beauvoir, S. (1972). *The coming of age.* New York: G. P. Putnam's Sons.

Dollard, J., Doob, L. W., Miller, N. E., Mowrer, O. H., & Sears, R. R. (1939). *Frustration and aggression.* New Haven, CT: Yale University Press.

Eisdorfer, C., & Lawton, M. P. (Eds.). (1972). *The psychology of adult development and aging.* Washington, DC: American Psychological Association.

Erickson, E. H. (1950). *Childhood and society.* New York: Norton.

Fry, W. F. (1976). Psychodynamics of sexual humor: Sex and the elderly. *Medical Aspects of Human Sexuality, 10,* 140–148.

Hall, C. S., & Lindsay, G. (1957/1970). *Theories of personality.* New York: Wiley.

Helson, H. (1964). *Adaptation level theory.* New York: Harper & Row.

Howell, S. C. (1972). Familiarity and complexity in perceptual recognition. *Journal of Gerontology, 27,* 364–371.

Hyman, H. (1942). The psychology of status. *Archives of Psychology*, No. 269.

Kahana, E., Liang, J., & Felton, B. (1980). Alternative models of person–environment fit: Prediction of morale in three homes for the aged. *Journal of Gerontology, 35,* 584–595.

Kastenbaum, R. (1972). Epilogue. In C. Eisdorfer & M. P. Lawton (Eds.), *The psychology of adult development and aging* (pp. 699–708). Washington, DC: American Psychological Association.

LaFave, L. (1961). *Humor judgments as a function of reference groups: An experimental study.* Unpublished doctoral dissertation, University of Oklahoma.

LaFave, L. (1972). Humor judgments as a function of reference groups and identification classes. In J. H. Goldstein & P. E. McGhee (Eds.), *The psychology of humor: Theoretical perspectives and empirical issues* (pp. 195–210). New York: Academic Press.

LaFave, L., McCarthy, L., & Haddad, J. (1970, May). *Humor judgments as a function of identification classes: The student sit-in issue.* Paper presented at the meeting of the Canadian Psychological Association, Winnipeg. (Abstract, Canadian Psychologist, 1970, *11*, 187–188.

Lawton, M. P. (1976). The relative impact of congregate and traditional housing on elderly tenants. *The Gerontologist, 16,* 237–242.

Lawton, M. P., & Nahemow, L. (1972). An ecological theory of aging. In C. Eisdorfer & M. P. Lawton (Eds.), *The Psychology of adult development and aging* (pp. 619–674). Washington, DC: American Psychological Association.

Lewin, K. (1951). *Field theory in social science.* New York: Harper & Row.

Lewin, K. (1935). *Dynamic theory of personality.* New York: McGraw-Hill.

Martineau, W. H. (1972). A model of the social functions of humor. In J. H. Goldstein & P. E. McGhee (Eds.), *The psychology of humor: Theoretical perspectives and empirical issues* (pp. 101–125). New York: Academic Press.

McGhee, P. E. (1979). *Humor: Its origin and development.* San Francisco: Freeman.

McGhee, P. E. (1979). Sex differences in children's humor. *Journal of Communication, 26,* 176–189.

McGhee, P. E., & Duffey, N. S. (1983). The role of identity of the victim in the development of disparagement humor. *Journal of General Psychology, 108,* 257–270.

McGhee, P. E., & Goldstein, J. H. (Eds.). (1983). *Handbook of humor research: Vol. 1. Basic Issues.* New York: Springer-Verlag.

Middleton, R. (1959). Negro and white reactions to racial humor. *Sociometry, 22,* 175–182.

Murray, H. A. (1938). *Explorations in personality.* New York: Oxford University Press.

Nesselroade, J. R., Schaie, K. W., & Baltes, P. B. (1972). Ontogenetic and generational components of structural and quantitative change in adult cognitive behavior. *Journal of Gerontology, 27,* 222–228.

Neugarten, B. (1977). Personality and aging. In J. E. Birren & K. W. Schaie (Eds.), *Psychology of aging* (pp. 626–649). Van Nostrand Reinhold.

Palmore, E. (1971). Attitudes toward aging as shown by humor. *The Gerontologist, 2* (3, Pt. 1), 181–186.

Poon, L. N. (1981). *Aging in the 80's: Psychological issues.* Washington, DC: American Psychological Association.

Reggie the Retiree. (1982). *Laughs and limericks on aging in large print.* Wells, ME: Reggie the Retiree Co.

Robinson, V. M. (1977). *Humor and the health profession.* Thorophare, NJ: Slack.

Rossman, I. (1979). *Clinical geriatrics.* Philadelphia: Lippincott.

Seltzer, M. (1983). Unstarted projects, unused paragraphs and unfinished business. *The Gerontologist, 23,* 120–122.

Schulz, T. R. (1976). A cognitive–developmental analysis of humor. In A. J. Chapman & H. C. Foote (Eds.), *Humor and laughter: Theory, research and applications* (pp. 11–36) New York: Wiley.

Smith, K. C. P., & Apter, M. J. (1977). Humor and the theory of psychological reversals. In A. J. Chapman & H. C. Foote (Eds.), *It's a funny thing, humor.* Oxford: Pergamon Press.

Storant, M. (1979). Psychological aspects of aging. In I. Rossman (Ed.), *Clinical geriatrics* (pp. 551–567). Philadelphia: Lippincott.

Wolff, H. A., Smith, C. E., & Murray, H. A. (1934). The psychology of humor: A study of responses to race-disparagement jokes. *Journal of Abnormal and Social Psychology, 28,* 341–365.

Zillmann, D. (1983). Disparagement humor. In P. E. McGhee & J. H. Goldstein (Eds.), *Handbook of humor research: Vol. 1. Basic Issues* (pp. 86–107). New York: Springer-Verlag.

Zillmann, D. & Bryant, J. (1974). Retaliatory equity as a factor in humor appreciation. *Journal of Experimental Social Psychology, 10,* 480–488.

Zillmann, D., & Cantor, J. R. (1976). A disposition theory of humor and mirth. In A. J. Chapman & H. C. Foote (Eds.), *Humor and laughter: Theory research and applications.* London: Wiley.

Zillman, D., & Cantor, J. R. (1977). Affective responses to the emotions of a protagonist. *Journal of Experimental Social Psychology 13* 155–165.

Humor across the Life Span: Sources of Developmental Change and Individual Differences

PAUL E. MCGHEE

INTRODUCTION

Philosophical speculations about humor have a long history, but serious empirical studies of humor were not undertaken until the present century. A few studies of children were completed between 1930 and 1960, but it was not until the 1970s that the development of humor in children began to be studied in earnest. We have learned a great deal about children's humor since then, but we continue to have virtually no information on developmental changes in humor beyond adolescence. The present chapter is designed to draw attention to the void in our understanding of life-span humor development and to stimulate research along these lines by examining various influences that might be expected to lead to both general developmental changes for all individuals and individual differences in patterns of humor development. This should help direct future investigators into research domains that will be most fruitful within a life-span approach.

     27   Copyright © 1986 by Academic Press, Inc.
All rights of reproduction in any form reserved.

SOURCES OF GENERAL DEVELOPMENTAL CHANGE

Maturation

Most general age-related changes in humor, appear to have a strong maturational link. I argue elsewhere (McGhee, 1979) that general developmental changes in children's humor reflect underlying cognitive developmental changes. That is, as new levels of cognitive skill are achieved, they lead to new forms of humor comprehension and appreciation (and presumably, production). Thus, humor begins once events can be stored and recalled in terms of simple images. As language is increasingly used to represent objects and ideas, it begins to be used in humor as well as in more serious interchanges. As the child's thinking becomes conceptual in nature, humor also becomes conceptually based. The acquisition of concrete operational thinking enables the child to keep two ideas in mind at the same time, and this leads to the onset of enjoyment of riddles and other jokes based on double meanings. The impact of formal operational thinking on humor is only beginning to be studied (see Couturier, Mansfield, & Gallagher, 1981), but the new capacities for abstract thinking and formal logic undoubtedly lead to new forms of humor (e.g., satire or irony).

A maturational framework, then, points to a general developmental function for the kinds of humor children can enjoy and produce. This pattern of change mainly reflects a continuum of complexity or abstractness of humor and has no implications for thematic content or the extent to which an individual seeks out or produces humor. A maturational explanation should also have no usefulness beyond adolescence. No attempt has been made to demonstrate age-related changes in humor beyond adolescence, but if such changes are eventually shown, investigators will need to consider other explanations. It is unlikely that anything approaching the universality of age trends found for childhood will be obtained for adulthood and old age, but strong age trends may be found for selected groups of individuals who are similar in important respects (e.g., common life experiences).

Alternative Explanations

The theoretical frameworks advanced by Goldstein, Suls, and Anthony (1972), Zillmann (1983; Zillmann & Cantor, 1976) and LaFave (1972; LaFave, Haddad, & Maesen, 1976) offer a means of explaining age trends through the adult years without relying on the notion of maturation. Portions of Freud's (1905/1960) theory may also be used in the same way.

EMOTIONAL AND COGNITIVE SALIENCE

Freud (1905/1960) argues that jokes provide a vicarious means of gratifying repressed sexual and aggressive impulses. Grotjahn (1957), Levine (1977), Mindess (1971), and Wolfenstein (1954) stress the general value of humor in coping with sources of anxiety and distress. They argue that the fear or anger associated with a person or event can be mastered by joking about it. Wolfenstein, for example, notes that children often use joking as a means of overcoming anxiety and distress that inevitably accompany being a child. If different points of the life cycle can be characterized by different sources of anxiety, then, this view provides a basis for predicting developmental change in the content of preferred humor. Thus, if the elderly are more concerned than younger persons with death, lack of money, or being alone, jokes that tap these themes should be funnier for them. Loeb and Wood's (see *Epilogue*) attempt to use Erickson's stage theory as a basis for predicting changes in humor appreciation across the life span is consistent with this general approach to studying humor development. In addition to providing a basis for predicting particular developmental changes in humor and particular preferences of groups of individuals at a given time, this approach enables one to predict varying preferences for different individuals either at the same time or at different age levels.

Predictions about the relative funniness of different themes within Freudian theory are based on differences in the emotional salience of content areas. Goldstein et al. (1972) argue that mere cognitive salience is sufficient to increase appreciation of a joke or cartoon; that is, simply making a person more cognizant of even such neutral themes as automobiles or music is enough to make humor including these themes funnier. No attempt has been made to further test this view, but if cognitive salience does contribute to humor, investigators may be able to predict age differences in enjoyment of different themes simply by determining content areas that are more relevant to people's lives at particular ages. Future research along these lines would profit most by including humor material previously found to vary along a continuum of salience that is anchored by nonsalient material on one end and by emotionally salient material on the other, with cognitively salient (emotionally neutral) humor in the middle.

DISPARAGEMENT THEORY

Two theoretical positions have been advanced to explain disparagement or "put-down" humor. LaFave (1972; LaFave et al., 1976) proposes that the extent to which one identifies positively or negatively with an individual or group is pivotal in determining the extent of appreciation of humor that disparages that individual or group. Positive identification with the disparaged group interferes with humor, while negative identification facilitates humor. In short, humor should be greatest when the "good guy" disparages the "bad guy". Zillmann and Cantor's (1976) closely related disposition theory proposes that "humour appreciation varies inversely with the favourableness of the disposition toward the agent or entity being disparaged, and varies directly with the favourableness of the disposition toward the agent or entity disparaging it (p. 100–101). Considerable support has been obtained for these views in connection with such areas as racial, ethnic, and political humor, but no attempt has been made to use them as a basis for predicting life span developmental changes in humor preferences.

If it is assumed that individuals identify more strongly with or are more favorably disposed toward their own age group than other age groups, there is a clear basis for predicting general developmental changes in enjoyment of put down humor. Children should find jokes victimizing adults funnier than jokes victimizing a child, while older adults should find jokes victimizing other age groups funnier than jokes victimizing the aged. Parents should find jokes victimizing children funnier than jokes victimizing parents. Consistent with these predictions, McGhee and Duffey (1983a, 1983b) and McGhee and Lloyd (1981) found that even preschoolers from varying socioeconomic and racial–ethnic backgrounds found drawings depicting a minor mishap experienced by a mother or father funnier than drawings showing the same event happening to a child. Data from adult samples in response to comparable sets of cartoons or jokes have not yet been obtained.

Disposition and identification theories may similarly be used to predict age differences in enjoyment of humor putting down other types of individuals. Any group or person toward whom large numbers of a given age group are negatively disposed may become a favorite target of put down humor for that age group. For example, if the President of the United States were to suddenly remove all Social Security benefits from the elderly, older persons would be expected to suddenly experience greater enjoyment of jokes putting down the President; and this effect should be progressively weaker with younger individuals since they are less directly affected by the action. In short, if different age groups show different affective dispositions toward any particular persons or groups, they should show corresponding differences in appreciation of humor victimizing those persons or groups.

SOURCES OF INDIVIDUAL DIFFERENCES

Genetic Factors

There is little doubt that genetic factors account for species differences in the capacity to experience humor. All normal humans are capable of experiencing humor, although it is not clear just when humor begins in infancy (see McGhee, 1979; Pien & Rothbart, 1980, for opposing views). McGhee (1983) argues that apes have also demonstrated their capacity for humor. The most interesting question to be raised in connection with genetic influences on humor in humans, of course, concerns impact of these influences on individual differences.

Nias and Wilson (1977) and Wilson, Rust, and Kasriel (1977) compared identical and fraternal twins and found no significant differences in the correlations between identicals and fraternals for appreciation of nonsense, sexual, aggressive, or satirical humor. Their basis for expecting significant heritability of differences in the kind of humor enjoyed is the finding that strong genetic influences operate in producing differences in extroversion–introversion (Scarr, 1969), which has been found to be significantly related to preference for either sexual and aggressive humor or nonsense and incongruity humor (Eysenck & Wilson, 1976). The limited evidence, then, suggests that environmental factors may be more important than genetic factors in accounting for the content of humor preferences. No attempt has been made to determine the role of genetic factors in degree of humor initiation or responsiveness.

Temperament and Personality

Eysenck (1982) states, "Genetic factors contribute something like two-thirds of the variance in major personality dimensions. This estimate applies to the 'true' variance in each case, purified of errors of measurement" (p. 28). If genetic factors contribute to humor development, then they may do so through their impact on personality development. Surprisingly few attempts have been made to link humor with different personality types or traits. A number of studies, however, have shown significant relationships between humor appreciation and such dimensions as conservatism (see Ruch, 1984; Ruch & Hehl, 1983; Wilson, 1973, for a review), dogmatism, (see Smith & Levenson, 1976) and authoritarianism (see Granfield & Giles, 1975; Surlin & Tate, 1976). Numerous studies have also tested Freudian hypotheses by examining the relationship between sexual or hostile arousal or repression and appreciation of sexual and aggressive humor (see Wilson, 1979).

EXTROVERSON–INTROVERSION

The dimension of personality that holds the most promise for studies of humor development may be extroversion–introversion. Scarr (1969) concludes that "moderate-to-high genetic contributions to social introversion–extroversion were found in all of the studies" (p. 286). Bronson (1966) similarly concludes that "if there are any personality traits that show a strong genetic influence, the dimension of extroversion–introversion heads the list" (p. 165). It is also important to note that individual differences in extroversion–introversion appear early in childhood and remain highly stable through adulthood (Eysenck, 1982; Morris, 1979; Schaie & Parham, 1976). This suggests that differences in extroversion–introversion may have a biological basis and may reflect a basic underlying difference in temperament.

As noted earlier, extroverts tend to prefer sexual and aggressive humor, while introverts tend to prefer nonsense or incongruity humor (Eysenck, 1942; Eysenck & Wilson, 1976; Verinis, 1970). Extroverts also give higher ratings than introverts to jokes in general (Eysenck & Wilson, 1976). Given the pervasiveness of the impact of extroversion–introversion on a broad range of behaviors (see Eysenck, 1981, 1982; Morris, 1979), it is surprising that attempts to link this aspect of personality to humor have been so limited. A number of characteristics of extroversion appear to predispose extroverts toward greater interest in, production of, and responsiveness to humor in comparison with introverts.

Extroverts are generally social, lively, impulsive, emotionally expressive, and seekers of novelty and change, while introverts are generally quiet, introspective, emotionally unexpressive, well-ordered and prefer small groups of friends (Morris, 1979). According to Eysenck (1982), there is a clear biological basis for the differences between extroverts and introverts.

Extroversion–introversion is related to the amount of arousal in the cortex when in the resting state, and this cortical arousal itself is mediated by the *reticular formation*. The theory states that people in whom the arousal level is relatively low in the resting state will tend to behave in an extroverted fashion, whereas people in whom arousal level in the resting state is relatively high will behave in an introverted manner. (p. 13)

Eysenck notes that the reason for this unexpected pattern is that

the main activity of the cortex is the *inhibition* of lower centers, so that the more aroused the cortex is the stronger the inhibiting function it plays. Alcohol . . . is a depressent drug—it lowers the arousal level of the cortex; in this way it liberates the lower centers from inhibition, and leads to extroverted behavior. (p. 14)

Because of these characteristics, Eysenck argues that extroverts are typically below their optimal level of arousal, while introverts are generally above theirs. This leads us to expect various forms of stimulation-seeking in extroverts. Consistent with this prediction, Zuckerman, Bone, Neary, Mongelsdorff, and Brustman (1972) found a significant positive relationship between extroversion scores on the Eysenck Personality Inventory and all of the subscales of a sensation-seeking measure except the one for boredom susceptibility. Mere increased social contact would contribute to the desired increased arousal, as would other forms of outgoing behavior. But humor, experienced either alone or in a social context, is also ideally suited to fill this need. Sexual and aggressive themes within humor are typically highly arousing, and this may account for extroverts' preference for these forms of humor. Berlyne (1972) notes, however, that characteristic arousal fluctuations accompany any kind of humor. Thus, extroverts should seek out and initiate all kinds of humor more often than introverts.

I argue elsewhere (McGhee, 1979) that most children are attracted to make-believe and humor in the early preschool years because these experiences provide an easy means of maintaining an optimal level of stimulation. Given the early appearance and stability of extroversion–introversion and the generally heightened need of extroverts for stimulation, it follows that extroverts should become more interested than introverts in humor during childhood and should maintain that interest throughout their lives. The greater emotional expressiveness of extroverts should also lead them to be generally more responsive (i.e., to show more laughter) to humor. Converseley, the tendency toward behavioral control and inhibition among introverts should lead them to show reduced responsiveness to humor as well as less frequent humor initiation.

Finally, extroversion has also been shown to be associated with assertiveness and dominance (Averett & McManis, 1977; Dana & Cocking, 1969; Vestewig & Mass, 1976). Research has shown that both of these qualities are associated with frequent humor initiation across the life span (see discussion that follows); this provides an additional basis for predicting greater humor initiation among extroverts. In combination, these qualities suggest that their influence on humor should contribute to stability of both humor initiation and humor responsiveness across the life span.

COGNITIVE STYLE

One other personality dimension has consistently been found to be related to the responsive aspects of sense of humor. Cognitive syle refers to the way in which an individual processes information. Degree of reflection–impulsivity (Kagan, Rosman, Day, Albert, & Phillips, 1964), or conceptual tempo, is one aspect of cognitive style that is closely related to measures of humor comprehension and appreciation (Brodzinsky, 1975, 1977; Brodzinsky, Feuer, & Owens, 1977; Brodzinsky & Rightmyer, 1980; Brodzinsky, Tew, & Palkovitz, 1979). These studies have all shown that impulsive children (fast inaccurates on the Matching Familiar Figures Test) laugh more than reflectives (slow accurates) at cartoons and jokes, but reflectives show better comprehension than impulsives. Thus, impulsive children show more laughter at humor even though they do not understand "the point" as well as reflectives. Impulsive individuals' laughter is generally at an elevated level, while reflectives tend to show varying degrees of laughter depending on such factors as complexity of the joke and degree of comprehension (Brodzinsky, 1977).

To this point, the relationship between reflection–impulsivity and humor has only been shown for children. However, the fact that this dimension has been found to be stable over periods of several years (Bronson, 1966, 1967; Sigel & Brodzinsky, 1977) suggests that its relationship to humor responsiveness may also be relatively stable. It is not clear how cognitive style dimensions relate to frequency or quality of initiated humor, but degree of reflection–impulsivity should contribute to within-person stability of the responsive aspects of sense of humor across the life span. Both extroversion–introversion and reflection–impulsivity, then, should have a major impact on the early appearance of individual differences in humor and these differences should be retained into the aging years.

Behavioral Precursors and Correlates

In addition to these specific personality dimensions, several other correlates of heightened humor development have been identified. In some cases, they consist of early childhood characteristics that are predictive of current sense of humor; in other cases, they include links with current behaviors. Consideration is restricted here to frequency of humor initiation; attention is not given to humor responsiveness or the kind of humor initiated. One finding stands out from studies using a broad range of subjects and experimental procedures. Individuals who initiate more humor have consistently been shown to be both more aggressive and more socially assertive. This has been found for elementary school children (Damico & Purkey, 1978; McGhee, 1976, 1980), college students and an elderly group of women (Bell, McGhee, & Duffey, in press), and both amateur (Fisher & Fisher, 1981) and professional (Janus, 1975, 1981) comedians. Both McGhee (1980) and Janus (1981) argue that humor in social interaction can be viewed as a vehicle for exercising social power and as a means of rechanneling aggressive tendencies into more socially acceptable directions. McGhee (1979, 1980) concludes that it is during the early elementary school years that children who already have a history of dominance and assertiveness begin to convert these behavior patterns into making more frequent attempts at being funny than their peers do. This link between humor and assertiveness appears to hold across the life span, both for people generally and for professionals who earn their living by being funny. This breadth of prediction indicates that assertiveness and aggressiveness are key behavioral prerequisites for development that includes frequent production of humor in social interaction.

Other behavioral correlates of frequent humor production do not share the above consistency across subject samples and data gathering procedures. McGhee (1980) found that, for both boys and girls, early attempts to seek attention, recognition, affection, emotional support, and help on tasks were all positively related to frequency of initiation of some form of humor. Thus, in spite of their dominating and generally assertive style of interaction with peers, young humorists had a history of being especially sensitive to adult reactions and appeared to gear much of their behavior toward getting positive reactions from adults. Among boys, this pattern was accompanied by a tendency to be highly conforming to adult demands. This conformity is surprising in view of their strong assertiveness with peers and underscores the importance to them of positive forms of adult attention. In a final finding, young humorists of both sexes were especially persistent in their efforts to master gross motor skills but were lacking in such persistence at mastering fine motor skills. This difference may simply reflect the fact that gross motor activities are generally more socially involving than fine motor activities.

Fisher and Fisher (1981) review the literature on amateur comics and conclude that the following attributes (along with aggressiveness) are characteristic of them: spontaneity, unconventionality, leadership, favorable self-image, above-average intelligence, verbal fluency, and creativity. Salameh (1980) found a similar list of attributes (along with dominance and aggressiveness) to be characteristic of stand-up comedians: social ambition, impulsivity, self-confidence, outspokenness, self-centeredness, and verbal fluency. Fisher and Fisher (1981, 1983), using projective tests, found that professional comics show high concern about issues of good and evil (presumably reflecting persistant concerns about their own worth), a preoccupation with size and smallness (presumably reflecting their own feelings of inferiority and failure), a concern with things not always being what they seem, and a conviction that life is full of contradictions.

Finally, Bell, McGhee and Duffy (in press) argue that high scores on the Snyder (1974) Self-Monitoring scale could be used as an index of higher levels of interpersonal competence. Given this assumption, both college students and elderly women who rated themselves as being frequent initiators of humor also scored higher in interpersonal competence. Turner (1980) obtained similar data, showing that, in comparison with low self-monitors, high self-monitors rated themselves as more witty, wrote cartoon captions judged to be more humorous, and initiated more humorous remarks in two different tasks. Levine and Zigler (1976), using the Phillips–Zigler Social Competence Index, found that high-social-competence individuals showed higher comprehension of a group of cartoons than did low-social-competence persons; the high-social-competence individuals also laughed more and rated the cartoons as funnier. These studies suggest that in spite of (or perhaps because of) assertive and dominating tendencies, humor initiators have excellent social skills, are viewed positively by others and are sought out for social interaction.

Environmental Influences

All of the behavioral characteristics described as predictors of humor in the previous section are undoubtedly heavily influenced by experience. Several investigators have attempted to determine the relationship between early experiences and subsequent humor development, although the number of such studies remains limited. Since most of these studies focus on early relationships with parents, we continue to know very little about whether effective humor skills can be developed at other points in the life span.

PARENT INFLUENCES

Since widespread individual differences in both the productive and responsive aspects of sense of humor are easily detectable by the preschool years (and especially by age 6 or 7), if a child's environment does have a significant impact on humor development, a strong part of this impact is likely to result from interactions with parents. Bariaud (1983) argues that early parental laughter actually leads the child to first discover the experience of humor. This new source of pleasure in social interaction should strengthen those behaviors that produce laughter in others. Most of the data pertaining to this influence consists of recall by adults of early experiences and attitudes toward parents. While recall data should always be treated with caution, at least certain aspects of these data are consistent with findings of McGhee's (1980) longitudinal study, which included actual observation of both early parent behavior and current humor behavior.

Several interesting investigations of the early backgrounds and experiences of comedians or comedy writers have been published (e.g., Fry & Allen, 1975; Janus, 1975; Wilde, 1968). These sources of information are given only minimal attention here since they failed to obtain comparable information on control groups. Thus, they may be used as sources of hypotheses about influences on humor development, but it is difficult to draw even tentative conclusions from the data they present. Fisher and Fisher (1981, 1983) studied comedians, clowns, and "schlemiel" children and included appropriate control groups for comparisons of background information so primary attention is given here to their data. They note:

> Comics had, from an early age, been expected by their parents to take an unusual amount of responsibility. As children, comics had typically been called upon to be adult beyond their years; to begin earning money very early; to act as caretakers for siblings; and even to provide partial support for their parents. They were given the basic message that they were to grow up fast and that they did not have the right to experience the normal dependency and privileges that go with the status of being a child. (Fisher & Fisher, 1983, p. 46)

Consistent with this pattern, mothers of schlemiel children "tended to endorse the view that children should be urged to take responsibility for themselves as early as possible" (Fisher & Fisher, 1983, p. 49). These same mothers also showed evidence of a lack of kindness, sympathy, and unselfishness toward their children. Three studies of nonprofessional adult comics (Bales, 1970; Block, 1971; Fisher & Fisher, 1981) also indicated that the mothers of male comics tended to be nonnurturant and generally nonmaternal.

McGhee's (1980) longitudinal study of children from birth to the early elementary school years produced data comparable to those obtained for preselected groups of comics. Children who were more frequent initiators of humor between 6 and 11 years of age tended to have mothers who babied them very little (both genders) and were unprotective of them (girls only) during the preschool years. For boys, this relationship was primarily associated with increased hostility of subsequent humor. For girls, however, it was associated with increased verbal and behavioral humor without any evidence of accompanying increased hostility in humor. In both school-aged children and adults functioning as comics, then, a lack of maternal nurturance and maternal exposure of the child to challenging and potentially hazardous situations with which the child may not be ready to cope appear to contribute in some way to increased interest in humor and increased development of humor skills.

Fisher and Fisher (1981, 1983) note that, with this pattern of interaction with their mothers, it is not surprising that individuals who eventually become comics seem to have such doubts about their selfworth. This history would also account for McGhee's (1980) finding that children who initiated more humor were more focused on obtaining various positive reactions from adults. These children may all have learned very early that doing or saying funny things got them the warmth and positive attention they lacked. This early maternal pattern may also (to some extent) account for the early aggression and assertiveness that has consistently been found to be a precursor of enhanced humor development. McGhee (1980) found dominance and verbal and physical aggressiveness to be predictive of subsequent humor initiation as early as the preschool years. Amount of physical and verbal aggressiveness even predicted frequency of behavioral attempts at humor (this among a different group of 3–5½-year-olds). Additional research is needed to isolate the possible causes of the increased aggressiveness among humor initiators, but an early environment that placed heavy demands on them to earn nurtrance and positive attention may have hardened these children into assertive, dominating, and aggressive individuals. It should be noted in this regard that Salameh (1980) found that although stand up comedians obtained significantly higher Minnesota Multiphasic Personality Inventory (MMPI) Depression scores than the general population, they also obtained higher MMPI Ego Strength scores. Thus, both children and adults who become comics give every indication of having developed real personal and social strength as a result of early difficult demands on them rather than succumbing to these demands and developing signs of poor adjustment. Fisher and Fisher also acknowledged the "difficulties that comics have with their mothers, but were more impressed with their psychological resilience than their weakness" (1983, p. 56).

Maternal behavior appears to have an entirely different impact on humor displayed by children before and after entry into elementary school. For the 3–5½-year-old group studied by McGhee (1980), the amount of maternal babying and protectiveness from birth up to their present age was positively predictive of a combined measure of sense of humor (all correlations were .63 or higher). Mothers of humor initiators in this age group also were generally approving and uncritical of their children. For preschool children, then, it is a very positive and supportive maternal environment that seems to promote humor development. The one sign of the reversal in predictions that is about to come as children move into elementary school is the −.48 correlation between these children's attempts at humor and maternal affection during the period between age 3 and their current age. Since the humor measures for the preschool and elementary school groups were obtained on different samples of children, it is impossible to assess the continuity of the children's attempts at humor across this age period. It seems likely, however, that the children who initiate more humor as preschoolers are not the same children who do so 5 years later. That is, the maternal pattern of nurturance, babying, and protectivenss is not likley to suddenly change at school age. On the other hand, such a reversal could occur among mothers who feel that very young children should be protected and nurtured up to a point; and that point may come at age 5 or 6, when mothers feel the child is old enough to begin taking more responsibilities. Future, similar longitudinal studies are required to resolve this issue.

The available evidence regarding fathers' influence on children's humor development does not show the coherent pattern present in the data for mothers. Salameh (1980) found that stand-up comedians reported more conflict with their fathers than did a comparison group of actors and musicians. Prasinos and Titler (1981) found that humor-oriented adolescents showed greater distance from fathers than did other adolescents on a Figure Placement Test. Fisher and Fisher

(1981, 1983), however, found that comics held more positive attitudes toward their fathers (and more negative attitudes toward their mothers) than did a group of actors. To complicate matters further, Janus (1975) found that comedians of both genders viewed their same-gender parent more negatively than their opposite-gender parent. In McGhee's (1980) study, data were unavailable for fathers. Given the available evidence, no conclusions can be drawn at present regarding these aspects of fathers' influence on children's humor development.

THE ROLE OF EARLY GENERAL STRESS AND CONFLICT

Psychoanalytic writers such as Freud (1905/1960), Kris (1938), and Wolfenstein (1954) have long emphasized the role that humor is capable of playing in coping with stress and anxiety. Wolfenstein argues that all children enounter numerous sources of distress and conflict in growing up and that laughter and humor can help master a stressful situation. The key question for this chapter is whether an especially stressful childhood increases the probability of heightened humor development. To my knowledge, no investigator has attempted to predict interest in or use of humor in a general population using specific measures of early stress or conflict during childhood. In the closest approximation to this approach, McGhee (1980) found that elementary school girls whose homes were judged to be poorly adjusted in their first 3 years of life initiated more verbal humor and showed more hostility in their humor. No comparable relationship was obtained for boys.

The most typical approach to examining the role of early stress and conflict in humor development consists of taking a group of comedians, comedy writers, or other individuals who have demonstrated special talent in using humor and determining whether they had very stressful childhoods. It was noted earlier in this chapter that these studies typically have not had any form of nonhumor comparison group, although a few studies have included such groups. Clearly, such control groups are needed to determine whether individuals who become more skilled at humor or who simply become more frequent initiators of humor have higher levels of stress in their childhood than the average child—or at least higher levels than the noninitiator of humor. Fisher and Fisher (1981, 1983) did not specifically measure amount of early stress in their subjects, but the pattern of general interaction with mothers suggests that their humorists did have more stressful childhoods than did the comparison group of actors. Wilhelm and Sjoberg (1958) also used a control group of actors and showpeople and found that comedians were more likely to have grown up in broken homes.

Several studies without control groups have produced results supportive of the suggestion that early stress plays an important role in producing the comic personality. Fry and Allen (1975) and Janus (1975) found that comedians and comedy writers tend to come from homes judged to be in conflict or in stress. Janus found that the early lives of 55 nationally known comedians were characterized by high amounts of suffering, isolation, and feelings of depression. Prasinos and Titler (1981) similarly found that the homes of a group of humor-oriented adolescents were characterized as low in cohesion and high in conflict on a Family Environment Scale. Numerous articles in the popular press have also drawn attention to the stressful early lives of specific comic performers. For example, Meryman (1978) notes that Carol Burnett's parents were both alcoholics who often fought with each other. Burnett indicated in that interview that she had to somehow get stronger in this situation or else "buckle under." Her solution was to use humor as a means of gaining the necessary strength to cope.

The sketchy available data suggest that humor does help many individuals deal effectively with stress. However, not all comedians and comic writers have this kind of background, and many individuals who do have such a background do not adopt humor as a coping mechanism, since early stress is merely one contributing factor to heightened humor development and there are other routes to becoming a clown or joker that do not involve the need for such coping. Future research should attempt to determine behavior patterns that differentiate those in high stress groups who do and do not show increased humor development. If children have already acquired the patterns of dominance and assertiveness described earlier by the time they encounter serious life stresses and conflict, this acquisition may be the key to determining which children have the strength to rise above their troubles through the use of humor.

Future research should also give attention to the age at which continued stresses are encountered. If such experiences do promote heightened humor development (in some individuals), do they have the same power to spur on humor development in early, middle, or late adulthood that they have in childhood? This seems unlikely since the disposition to show frequent or few attempts at being funny seems to be relatively firmly entrenched by late adolescence. It may be that individual patterns of coping with stress are already established by this age, so that, if this incentive has not motivated extra interest in humor by early adulthood, it is not likely to do so later.

MODELING AND REINFORCEMENT EFFECTS

One of the most obvious explanations for individual differences in degree or quality of both responsiveness to and initiation of humor is specific modeling and reinforcement effects that operate in connection with both parents and friends. Thus, parents who do a lot of joking and clowning around and who also laugh a lot should be more likely to have children who do the same. Parents who provide frequent models of humor should provide their children with specific ideas for the kinds of humor the children might attempt and should also be more responsive to their children when they do make their own primitive attempts at humor. Friends who are heavily into humor should have similar effects.

All of the available data on parent modeling of humor are based on recall of prior parent behavior. In all but one case, this recall has been provided by individuals whose own sense of humor is the main focus of interest. No attempt has yet been made to observe parental joking in the presence of children or parental responses to children's humor and to study the effects these behaviors have on the children's own humor development. Fisher and Fisher (1981, 1983), Fry and Allen (1975), Janus (1975), and Wilde (1968) found that professional humorists tend to have models of joking or clowning in one or both parents (or other close relative, such as a grandmother) during childhood. These individuals also occasionally referred to the impact of radio or television models on their own development as humorists (Schwartz, 1978).

Since professional humorists are a very select group, it might be argued that these individuals are already predisposed toward heightened humor development for reasons discussed earlier in this chapter. It may be that frequent modeling and reinforcement of humor leads to extreme degrees of humor development only when predispositions are already present. A more convincing case for the importance of modeling and reinforcement could be made if they could be shown to have a strong impact on humor initiation and responsiveness for a general cross-section of persons of different ages. The available data along these lines provide a coherent picture of modeling influences among adult subjects, although the picture for child subjects remains unclear. In McGhee's (1980) longitudinal study, a home visitor observed a broad range of parent and child behaviors (humor was not a focus of these observations) in the home twice a year through the first 6 years of life of the child. When the children's humor and laughter were subsequently observed in a spontaneous play context (children ranged from 6 to 11 years of age), the home visitor provided a rating of the amount of maternal joking or other attempts at humor that had been observed during visits in the home throughout the 6 year period. The children's current humor initiation and responsiveness were not significantly related to the amount of early humor shown by mothers. No data were obtained for fathers, since fathers were generally not home during the home visits. The problem with these data is that the home visitor was not interested in humor and laughter at the time observations in the home were being made. Since it is impossible to determine how reliable these humor data are, the conclusion that maternal humor has no impact on children's humor should be viewed as a very tentative one.

Two recent studies of adults asked subjects to recall how much early joking and playful teasing their parents did during the subjects' childhood years. These data are discussed in detail in Chapter 14 of this volume, so they are given only brief attention here. McGhee, Bell, and Duffey (see Chapter 14) asked groups of college students and elderly women to rate themselves on a number of dimensions of humor initiation as well as several pertinent background characteristics regarding their early childhood. Both the female college students and the elderly women who rated themselves as currently being frequent initiators of humor also tended to rate their mothers as having done frequent joking, clowning, and playful teasing when they were growing up. No significant relationships were obtained in either study for fathers' humor. For male college students, the reverse pattern was obtained. Males who rated themselves higher in their own initiation of humor tended to recall their fathers as having done frequent joking, clowning and playful teasing, but no significant relationship was obtained between early maternal humor and males' own present humor initiation. These data suggest, then, that early modeling influences on humor development are strongest for the same gender parent. The fact that this relationship holds even for elderly women suggests that once the impact of such early modeling has occurred in childhood and adolescence, its effect remains relatively stable across the life span.

Modeling effects on the responsive aspects of humor have been better studied than modeling effects on humor initiation. Several studies show that laughter is increased in the presence of others who are laughing (Chapman, 1973a; Chapman & Wright, 1976; Fuller & Sheehy-Skeffington, 1974; Smyth & Fuller, 1972). This effect also holds for individuals watching a comedy film with a laugh track (Chapman, 1973b; Cupchik & Leventhal, 1974; Leventhal & Cupchik,

1975; Leventhal & Mace, 1970). The influence of others' laughter on one's own laughter is clear, but its influence on the actual level of appreciation experienced remains uncertain. That is, these may be social facilitation effects that hold for overt laughter but not for true enjoyment of the humorous event. The three studies by Leventhal and associates indicate that only females show a corresponding increase in funniness ratings for a film or comedy sequence. Males do not elevate their funniness ratings when their laughter is increased as a result of others' laughter. Does this mean that exposure to laughing models actually increases females' enjoyment of humor, but not that of males? This issue remains unresolved.

Brown and his associates (Brown, Brown, & Ramos, 1981; Brown, Wheeler, & Cash, 1980) obtained data for both children and adults that separates out genuine imitation learning effects from social facilitation effects on laughter. They conclude that imitation learning does contribute significantly to the amount of laughter shown to humorous material. While these data were obtained in a laboratory context, they suggest that children raised by parents who show frequent laughter should themselves be more overtly responsive to humor than they would otherwise be. Since parents who show a lot of laughter in response to humor are likely to also initiate more humor, heightened responsiveness to humor by parents should also be associated with greater attempts at humor by their children. Alford (1983) completed an anthropological study that indicates that joking relationships are very typical of American parents and their children. She found that 70% of a large sample of college students reported having a joking relationship with their mothers; 65% reported the same with their fathers. The extent of the joking relationship with parents was positively correlated with the degree of intimacy students felt with their parents. Unfortunately, Alford made no attempt to link the amount of joking or extent of a joking relationship exhibited by parents with the frequency or quality of their children's humor and laughter. The sheer prominence of humor within family interaction suggested by this study, however, underscores the assumption held here that parent modeling and support of children's attempts at humor has a major impact on humor development.

No investigator has yet examined the effect of either parent or peer reinforcement of efforts at humor upon any aspect of subsequent humor development. The positive forms of attention and affection that result from successful humor should be highly reinforcing at any age but should have their greatest impact during childhood. That is, most children show some early interest in humor—especially at around age

6 or 7, when the ability to understand riddles and other jokes based on double meanings appears. A child who receives considerable support for these early attempts at humor from either parents or other children should, as a result, spend more time trying to be funny. This should sustain joking and clowning, so that the child who has an early start at initiating more frequent humor than his or her peers should continue to do so with increasing age. But the fact that the successful production of humor in a social context reflects both cognitive and social skills suggests that it should be possible to strengthen one's humor competency at any age. Goodman (1983) found that with specialized training adults can improve their humor skills. Many children get this training on their own, simply as a result of their interest in humor. The only disadvantage adults should have over children in expanding skills at gaining humorous insights and successfully expressing them should be a lifetime of habits that do not include humorous or other playful interactions. Children may be allowed to demonstrate less competency in their insights or delivery because parents realize their general lack of sophistication and because other child recipients of their humor are not yet very good themselves at discriminating good and well-delivered humor from bad or poorly delivered humor. Adults are not generally allowed these luxuries, so consistent poor reception of one's atempts at humor should make one cautious about trying to be funny in the future.

CONCLUSIONS

This chapter is designed to draw attention to the kinds of influences that produce both general similarities and areas of uniqueness in humor development. The strongest case for universals in humor development can be made for childhood, where basic trends in humor reflect underlying cognitive changes. While developmental changes in adolescents' humor have not yet been linked to cognitive development, future studies should demonstrate such a link—especially in connection with the acquisition of formal operational thought. Disparagement theory and theories focusing on cognitive and emotional salience offer a means of predicting general developmental changes in humor across the life span, but it is not likely that future research will demonstrate any form of developmental changes that bear the close age relationships found for children. The greatest promise for predicting life span developmental changes in humor lies in identifying similarities in life circumstances and making predictions separately for individuals with different life patterns.

While all normally developing children should show basic similarities in the kinds of humor they understand, appreciate, and produce up to adolescence, numerous factors contribute to the development of a unique sense of humor within these stagelike similarities. Genetic factors have not been shown to directly contribute to any aspect of humor; they may operate in a more indirect fashion, however, by increasing the probability of development of certain personality characteristics or behaviors which predispose the individual toward heightened humor development. Degree of extroversion–introversion should have a significant impact on both the amount and the kind of humor one initiates in social interaction. Cognitive style also influences humor development by predisposing a child toward greater or lesser responsiveness to humor. Future investigators should be able to improve our understanding of humor development immensely by sorting out the nature of the interaction between general maturational influences and specific personality dimensions.

The role of social assertiveness in humor development should also be given special attention in future life span humor studies. The limited available data point toward a close connection between assertiveness and humor across the life span. Since humor is a cognitive event commonly assumed to be associated with creative thinking, social assertiveness alone should not be sufficient to produce effective humor skills—regardless of the age at which the assertiveness is acquired. Thus, future investigators should study the differences between assertive individuals who do and who do not show high levels of skills or interest in humor. It may be that only those assertive individuals who already have a high need for intellectual stimulation and show other forms of creativity are drawn to humor.

Finally, while some environmental influences on humor development have been identified, we remain ignorant of the role of experience in humor development. There is some evidence that same-gender modeling of humor may be important for heightened development of humor skills, but virtually nothing is known of the effect of parent reactions to their children's efforts at humor upon subsequent humor development in the child. Tentative support can be claimed for the view that early conflict and stress foster humor development, but this issue is far from settled. Investigators need to identify large groups of individuals who grew up with comparable levels of stress and search for factors that discriminate those who did and did not subsequently show enhanced humor development. The finding that humor initiators tend to have mothers who made premature demands for responsible behavior suggests that this form of early stress somehow draws children into an interest in humor as a means of coping with the demands of growing up.

Perhaps the most important question for any life span investigation of humor concerns whether or not the basic characteristics of our sense of humor are set during childhood or adolescence. There is every reason to expect high levels of stability for most aspects of humor, but this does not mean that these characteristics are impossible to change at any point of the life span. It remains to be seen just which characteristics of (and to what extent) our sense of humor can be changed at different ages. Efforts to enhance our sense of humor should help all of us as we strive to age successfully and happily.

REFERENCES

Alford, K. F. (1983). Privileged play: Joking relationships between parents and children. In F. Manning (Ed.), *The world of play*. West Point, NY: Leisure Press.

Averett, M., & McManis, D. L. (1977). Relationship between extraversion and assertiveness and related personality characteristics. *Psychological Reports 41*, 1187–1193.

Bales, R. F. (1970). *Personality and interpersonal behavior*. New York: Holt, Rinehart & Winston,

Bariaud, F. (1983). *La genèse de l'humour chez l'enfant* [The development of children's humor]. Paris: Presses Universitaires de France.

Bell, N. J., McGhee, P. E., & Duffey, N. S. (in press). Interpersonal competence, social assertiveness and humor. *British Journal of Developmental Psychology*.

Berlyne, D. E. (1972). Humor and its kin. In J. H. Goldstein & P. E. McGhee (Eds.), *The psychology of humor* (pp. 43–60). New York: Academic Press.

Block, J. (1971). *Lives through time*. Berkeley, CA: Bancroft Books.

Brodzinsky, D. M. (1975). The role of conceptual tempo and stimulus characteristics in children's humor development. *Developmental Psychology, 11*, 843–850.

Brodzinsky, D. M. (1977). Children's comprehension and appreciation of verbal jokes in relation to conceptual tempo. *Child Development, 48*, 960–967.

Brodzinsky, D. M., Feuer, V., & Owens, J. (1977). Detection of linguistic ambiguity by reflective, impulsive, fast–accurate and slow–inaccurate children. *Journal of Educational Psychology, 69*, 237–243.

Brodzinsky, D. M., & Rightmyer, J. (1980). Individual differences in children's humour development. In P. E. McGhee & A. J. Chapman (Eds.), *Children's humour* (pp. 181–212). Chichester, England: Wiley.

Brodzinsky, D. M., Tew, J. D., & Palkovitz, R. (1979). Control of humorous affect in relation to children's conceptual tempo. *Developmental Psychology, 5*, 275–279.

Bronson, W. C. (1966). Central orientations: A study of behavior organization from childhood to adolescence. *Child Development, 37*, 793–810.

Bronson, W. C. (1967). Adult derivatives of emotional expressiveness and reactivity-control: Developmental discontinuities from childhood to adulthood. *Child Development, 38*, 801–817.

Brown, G. E., Brown, D., & Ramos, J. (1981). Effects of a laughing versus a nonlaughing model on humor in college students. *Psychological Reports, 48,* 35–40.

Brown, G. E., Wheeler, K. J., & Cash, M. (1980). The effects of a laughing versus a nonlaughing model on humor responses in preschool children. *Journal of Experimental Child Psychology, 29,* 334–339.

Chapman, A. J. (1973a). Funniness of jokes, canned laughter and recall performance. *Sociometry, 36,* 569–578.

Chapman, A. J. (1973b). Social facilitation of laughter in children. *Journal of Experimental Social Psychology, 9,* 528–541.

Chapman, A. J., & Wright, D. S. (1976). Social enhancement of laughter: An experimental analysis of some companion variables. *Journal of Experimental Child Psychology, 21,* 201–218.

Couturier, L. C., Mansfield, R. S., & Gallagher, J. M. (1981). Relationship between humor, formal operational ability, and creativity in eighth graders. *Journal of Genetic Psychology, 139,* 221–226.

Cupchik, G. C., & Leventhal, H. (1974). Consistency between expressive behavior and the evaluation of humorous stimuli: The role of sex and self-observation. *Journal of Personality and Social Psychology, 30,* 429–442.

Damico, S. B., & Purkey, W. W. (1978). Class clowns: A study of middle school students. *American Educational Research Journal, 15,* 391–398.

Dana, R. H., & Cocking, R. R. (1969). Repression-sensitization and Maudsley Personality Inventory scores: Response sets and stress effects. *British Journal of Social and Clinical Psychology, 8,* 263–269.

Eysenck, H. J. (1942). The appreciation of humor: An experimental and theoretical study. *British Journal of Psychology, 32,* 295–309.

Eysenck, H. J. (Ed.). (1981). *A model for personality.* New York: Springer-Verlag.

Eysenck, H. J. (Ed.). (1982). *Personality genetics and behavior: Selected papers.* New York: Praeger.

Eysenck, H. J., & Wilson, G. (1976). *Know your own personality.* Baltimore, MD: Penguin.

Fisher, S., & Fisher, R. L. (1981). *Pretend the world is funny and forever: A psychological analysis of comedians, clowns and actors.* Hillsdale, NJ: Erlbaum,

Fisher, S., & Fisher, R. L. (1983). Personality and psychopathology in the comic. In P. E. McGhee & J. H. Goldstein (Eds.), *Handbook of humor research: Vol. 2. Applied studies.* New York: Springer-Verlag. pp. 41–59.

Frued, S. *Jokes and their relation to the unconscious.* (1960). New York: Norton, (Original work published in 1905)

Fry, W. F. Jr., & Allen, M. (1975). *Make 'em laugh.* Palo Alto, CA: Science and Behavior Books.

Fuller, R. G. C., & Sheehy-Skeffington, A. (1974). Effects of group laughter on response to humorous material: A replication and extension. *Psychological Reports, 35,* 531–534.

Goldstein, J. H., Suls, J. M., & Anthony, S. (1972). Enjoyment of particular types of humor content: Motivation or salience? In J. H. Goldstein & P. E. McGhee (Eds.), *The psychology of humor* (pp. 159–171). New York: Academic Press.

Goodman, J. (1983). How to get more smileage out of your life: Making sense of humor, then serving it. In P. E. McGhee & J. H. Goldstein (Eds.), *Handbook of humor research: Vol. 2. Applied studies* (pp. 1–21.) New York: Springer-Verlag.

Granfield, A. J., & Giles, H. (1975). Towards an analysis of humor through symbolism. *International Journal of Symbology, 6,* 17–23.

Grotjahn, M. (1957). *Beyond laughter.* New York: McGraw-Hill.

Janus, S. S. (1975). The great comedians: Personality and other factors. *The American Journal of Psychoanalysis, 35,* 169–174.

Janus, S. S. (1981). Humor, sex and power in American society. *American Journal of Psychoanalysis, 41,* 161–167.

Kagan, J., Rosman, B. L., Day, D., Albert, J., & Phillips, W. (1964). Information processing in the child: Significance of analytic and reflective attitudes. *Psychological Monographs, 78*(1, Whole No. 578).

Kris, E. (1938). Ego development and the comic. *International Journal of Psychoanalysis, 19,* 77–90.

LaFave, L. (1972). Humor judgments as a function of reference groups and identification classes. In J. H. Goldstein & P. E. McGhee (Eds.), *The psychology of humor* (pp. 195–210). New York: Academic Press.

LaFave, L., Haddad, J., & Maesen, W. A. (1976). Superiority, enhanced self-esteem, and perceived incongruity humour theory. In A. J. Chapman & H. C. Foot (Eds.), *Humour and laughter: Theory, research and applications* (pp. 63–91). London: Wiley.

Leventhal, H., & Cupchik, G. C. (1975). The informational and facilitative effects of an audience upon expression and evaluation of humorous stimuli. *Journal of Experimental Social Psychology, 11,* 363–380.

Leventhal, H., & Mace, W. (1970). The effect of laughter on evaluation of a slapstick movie. *Journal of Personality, 38,* 16–30.

Levine, J. (1977). Humour as a form of therapy: Introduction to symposium. In A. J. Chapman & H. C. Foot (Eds.), *It's a funny thing, humour.* Oxford, England: Pergamon.

Levine, J., & Zigler, E. (1976). Humor responses of high and low premorbid competence alcoholic and nonalcoholic patients. *Addictive Behaviors, 1,* 139–149.

McGhee, P. E. (1976). Sex differences in children's humor. *Journal of Communication, 26,* 176–189.

McGhee, P. E. (1979). *Humor: Its origin and development.* San Francisco: Freeman.

McGhee, P. E. (1980). Development of the sense of humour in childhood: A longitudinal study. In P. E. McGhee & A. J. Chapman (Eds.), *Children's humour* (pp. 213–236). Chichester, England: Wiley.

McGhee, P. E. (1983). The role of language in the onset of humor in animals and human infants. In D. L. F. Nilsen & A. P. Nilsen (Eds.), The language of humor and the humor of language. Tempe: Arizona State University Press.

McGhee, P. E., & Duffey, N. S. (1983a). Children's appreciation of humor victimizing different racial–ethnic groups: Racial–ethnic differences. *Journal of Cross-Cultural Psychology, 14,* 29–40.

McGhee, P. E., & Duffey, N. S. (1983b). The role of identity of the victim in the development of disparagement humor. *Journal of General Psychology, 108,* 257–270.

McGhee, P. E., & Kach, J. A. (1981). The development of humor in black, Mexican-American and white preschool children. *Journal of Research and Development in Education, 14,* 81–90.

McGhee, P. E., & Lloyd, S. A. (1981). A developmental test of the disposition theory of humor. *Child Development, 52,* 925–931.

Meryman, R. (1978, February). Carol Burnett's own story. *McCall's.*

Mindess, H. (1971). *Laughter and liberation.* Los Angeles: Nash.

Morris, L. W. (1979). *Extraversion and introversion: An interactional perspective.* New York: Hemisphere.

Nias, D. B. K., & Wilson, G. D. (1977). A genetic analysis of humour preferences. In A. J.

Chapman & H. C. Foot (Eds.), *It's a funny thing, humour* (pp. 371–373). Oxford, England: Pergamon.

Pien, D., & Rothbart, M. K. (1980). Incongruity humour, play, and self-regulation of arousal in young children. In P. E. McGhee & A. J. Chapman (Eds.), *Children's humour* (pp. 1–26). Chichester, England: Wiley.

Ruch, W. (1984). Konservativismus und witzbeurteilung: konvergenz gegenstandsbereichsinterner und -ubergreifender variabilitat? *Zeitschrift für Differentielle und Diagnostische Psychologie, 5,* 221–245.

Ruch, W., & Hehl, F. (1983). Intolerance of ambiguity as a factor in the appreciation of humour. *Personality and Individual Differences, 4,* 443–449.

Prasinos, S., & Titler, I. (1981). The family relationships of humor-oriented adolescents. *Journal of Personality, 49,* 295–305.

Salameh, W. A. (1980). *La personalité du comedien. Théorie de la conciliation tragicomique* [The personality of the comedian. Theory of the tragicomic reconciliation]. Unpublished doctoral dissertation, University of Montreal.

Scarr, S. (1969). Social introversion–extraversion as a heritable response. *Child Development, 40,* 823–832.

Schaie, K. W., & Parham, I. A. (1976). Stability of adult personality traits: Fact or fable? *Journal of Personality and Social Psychology, 34,* 146–158.

Schartz, T. (1978 April 3). Comedy's new face. *Newsweek,* pp. 60–71.

Sigel, I. E., & Bordzinsky, D. M. (1977). Individual differences: A perspective for understanding intellectual development. In H. L. Hom & P. L. Robinson (Eds.), *Psychological processes in early education.* New York: Academic Press.

Smith, D., & Levenson, H. (1976). Reactions to humor as a function of reference group and dogmatism. *Journal of Social Psychology, 99,* 57–61.

Smyth, M. M., & Fuller, R. G. C. (1972). Effects of group laughter on responses to humorous material. *Psychological Reports, 30,* 132–134.

Snyder, M. (1974). Self-monitoring of expressive behavior. *Journal of Personality and Social Psychology, 30,* 526–537.

Surlin, S. H., & Tate, E. D. (1976). "All in the Family": Is Archie funny? *Journal of Communication, 26,* 61–68.

Turner, R. G. (1980). Self-monitoring and humor production. *Journal of Personality, 48,* 163–172.

Verinis, J. S. (1970). Inhibition of humor enjoyment: Effects of sexual content and introversion–extraversion. *Psychological Reports, 26,* 161–170.

Vestewig, R. E., & Moss, M. K. (1976). The relationship between extraversion and neuroticism to two measures of assertive behavior. *Journal of Psychology, 93,* 141–146.

Wilde, L. (1968). *The great comedians.* Secaucus, NJ: Citadel,

Wilhelm, S., & Sjoberg, G. (1958). The social characteristics of entertainers. *Social Forces, 37,* 71–76.

Wilson, C. P. (1979). *Jokes: Form, content, use and function.* London: Academic Press.

Wilson, G. D. (1973). Conservatism and response to humour. In G. D. Wilson (Ed.), *The psychology of conservatism.* London: Academic Press.

Wilson, G. D., Rust, J., & Kasriel, J. (1977). Genetic and family origins of humor preferences: A twin study. *Psychological Reports, 41,* 659–660.

Wolfenstein, M. (1954). *Children's humor.* Glencoe, IL: Free Press. (reprinted by Indiana University Press, 1978).

Zillmann, D. (1983). Disparagement humor. In P. E. McGhee & J. H. Goldstein (Eds.), *Handbook of humor research: Vol 1. Basic issues* (pp. 85–107). Springer-Verlag.

Zillmann, D., & Cantor, J. R. (1976). A disposition theory of humour and mirth. In A. J.
    Chapman & H. C. Foot (Eds.), *Humour and laughter: Theory, research and appli-
    cations* (pp. 93–115). London: Wiley.
Zuckerman, M., Bone, R. N., Neary, R., Mongelsdorff, D., & Brustman, B. (1972). What
    is the sensation-seeker? Personality trait and experience correlates of the sensa-
    tion-seeking scales. *Journal of Consulting and Clinical Psychology, 39,* 308–321.

3

Theoretical and Functional Perspectives on the Development of Humor during Infancy, Childhood, and Adolescence

C. J. R. SIMONS
KATHLEEN A. MCCLUSKEY-FAWCETT
DENNIS R. PAPINI

INTRODUCTION

The general goal of this chapter is to underscore the interactive process that occurs between the changing child, the environment, and the development of humor. As an infant progresses through childhood and adolescence, the nature and functions of humor change through the interactions between the child and the environment. Since other chapters in this text are devoted to humor during adulthood and the aging years, the addition of this chapter will give the reader a more thorough understanding of humor in the context of a life-span perspective.

The portion of the life-span prior to adulthood is relatively short given the length of the normative life course. The first 20 years, however, are characterized by remarkable growth and development, during which the adult life course is shaped. The developmental and

Copyright © 1986 by Academic Press, Inc.
All rights of reproduction in any form reserved.

environmental tasks that challenge the infant, child, and adolescent are multitudinous in both number and diversity. Accordingly, the first section of this chapter is an examination of how humor and its functions develop and are the products of child–environment interactions during the early part of the life-span.

The second section is a consideration of three theories that have been applied to both humor and child development. The interpretation of humor from psychoanalytic, cognitive-developmental, and social-learning perspectives has resulted in each theory emphasizing either the child's or the environment's contribution to humor development: None has examined humor as the product of child–environment interactions. Consequently, we conclude the discussion of theory application to humor development by suggesting how an interactive approach could be more useful to our understanding of humor than the traditional psychoanalytic, cognitive-developmental, and social-learning theories.

THE FUNCTIONS OF HUMOR FOR HUMAN DEVELOPMENT

Social behaviors that appear and become more refined in the repertoire of the human organism do so because of their functional value for the survival of the individual and the social structure. Humor as a social behavior has survival value for the infant, enhances cognitive and linguistic development, deflects aggression, facilitates communication, and is important to the formation of peer group identity and affiliation. The value of humor throughout infancy, childhood, and adolescence has been empirically demonstrated, and the results of these research endeavors constitute the major portion of the following discussion.

One of the major difficulties in discussing humor is the fact that the "terminology situation in the area of humor remains perplexing" (Keith-Spiegel, 1972, p. 14). However, whether one observes behavior and then infers processes internal to the organism (see Anderson, 1980) or describes the relationship between stimulus and response, observed behavior is a common denominator for most research methodologies. Thus, we examine humor functions as they relate to such observable behaviors as smiling, laughing, or verbal reports that a stimulus has been perceived as being humorous.

A second assumption here is that humor is evident shortly after birth. This issue continues to be controversial, as some investigators argue that humor requires a level of cognitive sophistication which is attained about 2 years of age (McGhee, 1979). However, we base our position upon two premises: (1) Even if early laughing and smiling are not regarded as indices of cognitive humor, they may be represented as forerunners of laughing and smiling responses to cognitive humor, and (2) early smiling and laughing may serve as stimuli for humor responses from other persons in the environment. Both of these premises are consistent with the theoretical framework presented in the following section and are elaborated more fully in that discussion.

Infancy

One of the major developmental tasks of the first stage of the human life span is the formation of attachment relationships to caregivers and other significant persons (Bowlby, 1958, 1969). These attachment relationships, which are defined as exclusive and affectionate ties between adult and infant, are considered necessary for a range of critical developmental tasks. The initial survival of the infant is predicated upon a caregiver providing adequate physical care for the helpless infant. Additionally, it has been repeatedly and tragically demonstrated that lack of affection, of physical contact, and of experiential stimulation provided by a caregiver lead to failure to thrive, developmental delays, and anaclytic depression (Dennis, 1960; Skeels, 1966; Spitz, 1946). These early attachment relationships are also considered to be precursors of the relationships that develop across the human life span (Kagan & Moss, 1962). This process and its outcome, therefore, are of major developmental significance.

Attachment is a bidirectional process, and is characterized by reciprocal interchanges between the infant and caregiver. The infant exhibits many behaviors at birth that will elicit nurturant behavior from a normal caregiver. These reflexive behaviors include rooting, sucking, eye contact, cuddling, and hand-grasping. As the infant matures, these reflexive behaviors are replaced by more elaborate and organized social signals that continue to strengthen an infant's attachment to a caregiver. Bowlby (1958, 1969) has noted that smiling is one of five instinctual responses that bind the infant to the mother and the mother to the infant in a reciprocal dynamic. It is through this reciprocal dynamic that the infant's probability of survival is increased. If the infant survives and reproduces in adulthood, then the species survives.

Smiling and laughing are effective behaviors by which the infant can indicate both attention and interest in a caregiver (Cairns, 1979).

Just as importantly, these behaviors provide a means for transactional interchanges between the developing infant and a changing environment, such as the familial context. For example, infants may indiscriminately smile at books, lamps, and persons prior to approximately 2 months of age, while the social smile reliably appears around 2 months of age. Social smiling has been described as an indicator both of cortical maturation and of the infant's receptivity to social influences by the environment. But this social phenomenon is not a unidirectional process: Through the social smile the infant is capable of modifying the caregiver's behavior (see Rheingold, 1969). Thus, affective behaviors, such as smiling and laughing, become a communicative modality through which the infant and caregiver learn how, or how not, to coordinate their interactive exchanges.

As the infant continues to develop, the range of environmental stimulation also expands. A third general function of humor behaviors concerns the infant's relationships with this broader environmental context. For example, Hayes and Watson (1981) demonstrated that 14- and 20-week-old infants smiled more at upright than at sideways-presented faces, and longer at female than at male faces. In this same investigation, 14-week-old infants smiled more at their mothers than at a stranger, and they smiled more at upright, talking faces than at silent faces presented at a 90° angle. In comparison to less cognitively advanced infants, babies at 5 months have been reported to smile more at a female stranger than at their mothers (Roe, 1978). The reciprocating portion of this particular development is that mothers of 5-month-old infants demonstrate more cardiac acceleration to videotapes of their own smiling infants than to tapes of unfamiliar smiling infants (Wiesenfeld & Klorman, 1978). In an investigation of infants 9 months through 2 years or age, Brooks-Gunn and Lewis (1981) reported that the older infants more frequently smiled at pictures of familiar versus unfamiliar faces while the younger infants more frequently smiled at strange women than at strange men. However, these infants did not differentially smile at pictures of their own parents. Similar to the infants studied by Hayes and Watson (1981), these infants selectively responded to differing aspects of their social environment.

Again, the most prominent hallmark of humor development is its changing functions as the developing infant and the environment mutually influence one another. The infant's discriminating responsiveness to parents must surely enhance particular familial relationships and modify the behavior of unfamiliar persons. The infant's wary scrutiny of a stranger may reinforce the unfamiliar adult's attempt to elicit smiling or laughing from the infant, or it may serve as a potent stimulus that immediately stops any social bids on the stranger's part. An empirical demonstration of this infant–environment interaction and humor functions has been provided by Sroufe and Wunsch (1972). These investigators noted that tactile and auditory stimulation became less potent stimuli for laughter elicitation as infants progressed beyond 6 months of age, while the reverse was true for visual and some social stimuli. Thus, humor expression is a function of how the infant and environment continue to adapt to one another.

Toddlerhood

A child's ability to establish an autonomous identity that is separate from caregivers is as important to development as the formation of secure attachment relationships. The establishment of this identity is necessary for the individual's growth into a self-sufficient, self-reliant adult. This separation and evolving autonomy are viewed by many theorists as a necessary and desirable, yet a traumatic developmental task for the young child (Freud, 1933). Humorous or playful behaviors are one way the infant can cope with the conflictual need to maintain a bond with the caregiver while simultaneously breaking free from this bond. Frequently, the mother is also taking steps to redefine the attachment relationship by requiring more independent behaviors from the infant. This change in mothering patterns may also arouse feelings of anger in the infant, followed by subsequent anxiety over these feelings. Humor is one mechanism that is available to the infant for coping with and deflecting these unacceptable feelings.

An excellent example of the separation process and the infant's use of humor is the young child's behavior during the weaning process. When the mother begins to withdraw the breast from the infant at the onset of weaning, the infant will often begin to nip playfully at the mother's breast while smiling and laughing (Kaplan, 1978). In order to cope with the anxiety and anger aroused by this withdrawal, the infant resorts to a playful means of coping. Anger at the mother can be expressed through this type of "I'm only joking" behavior without risk of retaliation. It is an attempt to deal with the ambivalent feelings surrounding the weaning process by redefining aggressive acts as humorous ones. The biting serves an immediate function of providing an outlet for the infant's stress and anger. It also serves as a developmental function in providing an opportunity for the infant to turn passivity into activity, thereby assuming an active role in the desired separation from the mother. Somewhat paradoxically, smiling, laughter, and humorous episodes are as important to easing the process of separation as they are to the formation of the initial attachment.

Early Childhood

One of the most important outcomes of the young child's successful mastery of the developmental tasks of attachment and separation is the subsequent ability to expand the sphere of significant others to include peers. This is a dramatic step in the child's socialization process, as it is the first foray into the social world beyond the familial boundaries. The child's success or failure in initiating and maintaining these relationships is of particular importance as it is predictive of later ability to establish adult bonds (Kagan & Moss, 1962).

The broader environmental context beyond the familial situation is one that includes how the infant initiates and maintains relationships with age-mates. Vandell (1980) reports that 6- , 9- , and 12-month-old infants smiled equally frequently at their mothers and at a peer, and interprets this as a parallel in smiling development between mother–infant and infant–infant interaction. Consequently, the early function of humor as a facilitator of parent–infant relationships may serve as the basis for infant–peer exchanges. Sherman (1975) has extended this concept to older children (2–5 years of age) through his documentation of "group glee". Sherman characterized this phenomenon as laughing, joyful screaming, and intense physical actions that are spontaneous or contagious within groups of children. Both child variables and environmental factors determined the occurrence and topography of group glee.

According to McGhee (1979), the larger environmental context assumes a new importance around 2 years of age as the child begins to understand cognitive incongruities and attempts to share humor with other persons. While McGhee's research has emphasized the cognitive aspects of humor, he has implicated the role of the environment in humor expression. For example, McGhee and Grodzitsky (1973) suggest that boys with high levels of gender–role mastery were in a secure enough position to view inappropriate gender-role behavior as humorous; McGhee and Lloyd (1981) report that boys preferred humor that victimized persons dissimilar to themselves, and this may represent an earlier gender-role development or different environmental sanctions for boys than girls. In both of these investigations, humor appears to be associated with child–environment interactions.

Groch (1974) has elaborated further upon preschool humor by noting how it may be expressed in the forms of responsiveness, production, or hostility. Children 3–4 years of age in a nursery school setting displayed more productive humor in loosely structured situations, such as free play, and more responsive humor in situations that allowed for unexpected events, such as storytelling. Also, boys more frequently engaged in hostile and aggressive humor while girls demonstrated more instances of responsive humor.

The three functions of humor between infancy and the preschool period—infant and species survival, facilitation of parent–infant and infant–peer relationships, effective transactions with the environment beyond the familial context—may be considered within the broader process of socialization. The larger environmental context we have referred to, including peers, adults, and extrafamilial experiences, socializes the infant or child on a macroscopic level as to what the collective social structure supports in the form of humor expression. On the microscopic level, the infant or child socializes the environment as to what he or she personally finds humorous and what humorous behaviors he or she will express. Through the child–environment interaction, neither the macroscopic goal of the environment nor the microscopic goal of an individual infant or child is realized. What is realized is a mutant of the two goals, or an interactive expression of behavior that results from the mutual socialization between the individual and the environment. If this interactive concept of humor expression were not so, then the humor of today's infant or child would be the humor of tomorrow's offspring. As this is not the case, nor could it be due to individual and environmental change, humor is represented best as an interactive phenomenon.

Childhood

The functions of humor during infancy and early childhood are diverse, changeable, and interactive in nature and these same functional characteristics of humor continue across the childhood years. Generally summarized, the functions or humor are twofold during this period. The first function is that of a communication system with multiple facets. One of these facets is a relatively straightforward one in which the child relates to other persons on a social level through the use of humor. The second and third facets are somewhat less direct, as children utilize humor for personally satisfying demonstrations of their developmental level while at the same time indicating these abilities to other persons in the environment. Much like the multifaceted nature of this first function, developmental level incorporates dimensions of adjustment, cognitive mastery, and sociopersonal growth.

The second general function of humor is that of a mutual socialization process whereby the child socializes and is socialized by other persons. Humorous situations are contexts in which the child learns socially acceptable behaviors or demonstrates these behaviors to others through the expression of humor. Although the social facilitation of humorous laughter may be determined by sharing the social situation rather than by sharing humor (Chapman, 1975), it is through these humorous contexts that the child learns what is perceived as being humorous by the culture. Likewise, it is in these same contexts that the child produces variations of traditional cultural humor or new humorous themes (Wolfenstein, 1951). Thus, the process of humor expression is one in which the child socializes and is socialized by the environment.

McGhee (1979) has addressed the general communication function through his discussion of private and public humor. Very early humor, according to McGhee, is a private event that is personally gratifying to the child. Because the child does not have the cognitive prerequisites, humor is not shared with other persons. However, humor becomes a more social one as the child's developmental level becomes more mature and sophisticated.

One aspect of the child's changing developmental level is increased cognitive differentiation, and of all the humor correlates, the relationship between cognition and humor seems to be the most emphasized. Studies of this particular relationship have operationalized cognitive development through conceptual tempo, which is a measure of the child's latency and accuracy of response to uncertain humor stimuli (Brodzinsky, 1975). Reflective children tend to have a conceptual tempo that is cautious and accurate, while impulsive children demonstrate the opposing tempo polarities. In addition, two other conceptual tempo groups, fast–accurate and slow-inaccurate children, have been identified and described (Brodzinsky, 1975).

In comparison to impulsive subjects, reflective children demonstrate better spontaneous comprehension of humor material, more mirth to understood versus not understood humor (Brodzinsky, 1977), and seem to appreciate (measured by smiling and laughing) humor less (Brodzinsky, 1975). Although impulsive and slow–in accurate children demonstrated less spontaneous comprehension of humor than their counterparts, this difference was eliminated when the children's answers were probed by an examiner (Brodzinsky, 1977). Brodzinsky has argued that the spontaneous measure for impulsive children is an indicator of a production deficiency rather than a cognitive one. Thus, the incorrect responding of these children may be amenable to correction by teaching them to slow down and to scrutinize alternative solutions more closely in a systematic fashion (Brodzinsky, 1977).

Brodzinsky (1975) has also noted that 6- and 8-year-old reflective boys show greater comprehension of cartoon humor than their counterparts, but this difference between reflective and impulsive subjects is not evidenct in 10-year-old boys. This would seem to indicate a differential rate of cognitive development depending upon the child's individual style. Other age-related research has been interpreted to indicate increasing comprehension and decreasing enjoyment of joking riddles with increasing age (Prentice & Fathman, 1975), increasing discrimination of joking and nonjoking solutions to riddles with increasing age, increasing ability to create examples of joking relationships as the child grows older, but no proportional increase in the child's ability to verbalize the prerequisites for a joking relationship with increasing age (McGhee, 1974). Although the enjoyment of joking riddles appears to decrease as the child grows older, Brodzinsky (1975) has noted that the appreciation of visually determined cartoons decreases with age, while the appreciation of conceptually determined ones increases. Thus, the child's enjoyment or appreciation of humor does not decrease with advancing age; rather, the material that a child perceives as humorous qualitatively changes over time. As one might expect, humorous material that is moderately complex and stimulating for a child at a given developmental level tends to receive the most appreciation (Brodzinsky, 1975).

The primary social task to be mastered by school age children is the development of relationships with members of the same-sex group. While this task has its roots in early childhood, it becomes increasingly important in middle and later childhood, and the topography of these relationships changes. Children come to affiliate closely with a small group of peers who share similar qualities, such as appearance, physical skill level, cognitive achievement, social status, and gender. Humor is used frequently by children in this age group to define the parameters of who is in and who is out of their desired social sphere and to learn what is acceptable behavior (McGhee, 1979).

As illustrated by Datan (see Chapter 8, this volume), humor functions to define and to reinforce the value of ethnic and age groups and to regulate social boundaries. This same phenomenon is observable in the humor of school age children.

The preponderance of jokes about morons, the opposite sex, and other outgroups all illustrate the functional utility of humor for children in this age group. The moron jokes (i.e., Why did the moron throw the clock out the window? He wanted to see time fly.) serve to define and reinforce group identity by emphasizing the low regard in which the moron is held. The desirable, acceptable behavior is to be dissimilar to a moron (see Lorenz & Vecsey, Chapter 10, this volume, for a similar analysis of the Hopi Indians). Through these jokes that deride individual or group behavior, the child learns that specific types of activities are acceptable and that others are laughable and make one subject to derision.

While the relationship between cognitive development and humor seems to have received a major emphasis, the sociopersonal aspect of developmental level has not been neglected: "The normal child's response to humor obviously represents a complex interplay of affective and cognitive components, and efforts to identify more sharply the contribution of each are required" (Prentice & Fathman, 1975, p. 215). For example, of the four conceptual tempo groups described by Brodzinsky (1975), fast–accurate children were the least affectively responsive to cartoon humor. Other researchers have reported that reflective children are less distracted by the stimuli of visual humor than impulsive children (Brodzinsky, 1975), impulsives smile more than reflectives when their responses are incorrect (Brodzinsky & Rightmyer, 1976), and impulsives laugh more with audience laughter than do reflective children (Brodzinsky, Tew, & Palkovitz, 1979). Brodzinsky and his associates have suggested from these findings that impulsive children are more affectively labile and more affected by social cues from the environment than their counterparts and that reflectives' production of observable humor is dependent upon both humor stimuli in the environment and the children's evaluation of that information.

Perhaps one of the most interesting aspects of the relationship between sociopersonal growth and humor is that researchers have acknowledged the interplay between a child's characteristics and the nature of the environment. Impulsive children have demonstrated a heightened sensitivity to social cues from the environment when compared to reflective subjects (Brodzinsky, Tew, & Palkovitz, 1979); visually determined cartoons have been comprehended more than conceptually determined ones (Brodzinsky, 1975); children seemingly avoid cartoons with affective components that are strong and negative, and cartoons with low affective components are understood better than those with high affective content (Brodzinsky, 1975). Thus, observable humor is not determined by either the child's characteristics or the environmental context; rather, humor is the product of an interaction between the child's characteristics and the environmental situation.

The third dimension of developmental level that has been related to humor is adjustment. Adjustment, which is inseparable from cognitive mastery and sociopersonal development, has been investigated and operationalized through the content of jokes and riddles utilized by children. Consequently, the examination of this developmental dimension and humor has been the province of psychoanalysts (e.g., Wolfenstein, 1951, 1954). Wolfenstein has described the riddles and jokes of latency stage children, while noting how the content of humor displays are related to forbidden desires, haunting dangers, or emotional conflicts that were dominant during earlier psychosexual stages. Through the expression of the humorous material and its content, the child confronts the desire, danger, or conflict and is gratified through cognitive mastery over a previously troublesome issue. Yet the gratification of cognitive mastery is not totally egocentric: Especially through the telling of a riddle, children indicate that they are smarter than the riddle respondent. Thus, children are reassured of their adjustment through humor, while indicating this phenomenon to persons in the environment through the expression of humorous material.

> They (children) force themselves to face a danger situation (through humor) and demonstrate that they can take it. We thus have in relation to jokes a paradoxical situation. Children, who in real life presumably use denial more than adults do, use it less in jokes. We might conclude that while adults use jokes regressively, permitting themselves to employ an otherwise devalued mechanism in a playful way, children use jokes progressively in the service of their growing mastery of reality. (Wolfenstein, 1951, p. 349)

Wolfenstein's concept of humor as a paradox can also be utilized to describe the general function of humor as a communication system during childhood. The expression of humor during this period of development is both egocentric and socialized. On one hand, humor functions as a medium through which children find gratification in the exercise of their cognitive mastery, sociopersonal growth, and adjustment on a somewhat egocentric plane. However, on the other hand, children use these very same skills to engage other persons in social interaction. Consequently, it appears that this general function of communication, both to oneself and to others through humor, strengthens the child on a personal level and prepares both the environment and the child for the child's increasing participation in the culture's social structure.

The second general function of humor during childhood is a mutual socialization process whereby the child socializes and is socialized by other persons. In a series of carefully designed studies, Chapman (1973, 1974, 1975) has identified a number of factors that are associated with the social facilitation of laughter. (While laughter and humor may not be comparable concepts [Chapman, 1973], we find it difficult to separate the two, and we consider laughter as an index of humor, even though these two concepts may not be identical.) Chapman (1973) noted how 7-year-old children in coacting humorous situations with another child laughed and smiled more than children in audience or alone situations. Thus, "overt responsiveness to humorous situations [is] not simply a function of humor perception and comprehension. . . . Perhaps jokes seem funnier when shared with another" (Chapman, 1973, pp. 535, 539).

A succeeding study in 1974 yielded the finding that the level of a child confederate's mirth determined the subjects' amount of laughter and smiling: Increased mirth resulted in increased laughter and smiling (Chapman, 1974). In addition, the subjects' ratings of how funny the confederates had perceived the material was associated with the subjects' duration of time spent observing the confederates' faces. A further examination of 7- and 8-year-old children in monadic, dyadic, and triadic humorous situations yielded an inverse relationship between a subject's response to humor and the amount of interaction (face-to-face observation) that occurred between companion pairs (Chapman, 1975). Specifically, as the amount of face-to-face contact increased between two companions in a triadic situation, the amount of humor responsiveness for the third child decreased. This companion influence existed even when subjects were told that they were not listening to the same humorous material. Chapman has interpreted this finding as evidence that humorous laughter is facilitated more by sharing the social situation than by sharing humor.

In conjunction with the previous discussion of humor as a communication system, these findings indicate how humor functions as a mutual socialization process between the child and the environment. A child may control the amount of face-to-face contact with a partner during humorous exchanges, or the child may be controlled by the partner's amount of en face behavior. Similarly, the culture transmits forms of socially acceptable humor to successive generations, yet it is the active child who produces variations of traditional cultural humor or new humorous themes. Thus, the inseparability of cognitive mastery, sociopersonal growth, and adjustment is reflected also in the process of humor development as the child socializes and is socialized by the environment.

Adolescence

The functional implications of humor for adolescent development must be tempered by an understanding of the changing physical, social, and cognitive characteristics associated with this period of growth. Havighurst (1973) has noted that developmental tasks during adolescence are dependent upon the interaction between the physical changes induced by the onset of puberty and the expectations of society. Three of the more prominent developmental tasks include coming to terms with physical–sexual maturation, identity decisions, and vocational choices. The available studies on adolescence are primarily examinations of developmental tasks and of how the adolescent child attempts to master these tasks. Despite the limited availability of data, there is support for developmental changes in the adolescent's appreciation of the content of humor.

In her psychodynamic study of young female adolescents, Ransohoff (1975) found that:

> When humor was successful and giggling and laughter a pleasureful release, the material, spontaneous talk and jokes, resonated with current developmental tasks. Among them were those dealing with bodily changes, early relationships with boys, disguised masturbatory wishes, and ambivalent feelings towards mothers. . . . . Humor failed when content was too grownup: when the subject matter stimulated frightening fantasies of male penetration and damage and frightening images of the mature female body or fears of punishment. (p. 155)

Ransohoff's adolescents employed humor to relieve some of the anxiety or conflict generated by sexual topics. When the level of maturity exhibited by the sexual humor was greater than their personal level of genital maturity, the humor was no longer funny. Thus, humor during adolescence may be seen to have adaptive and developmental significance. While humor reflects an individual's psychosexual development, it also provides a process whereby physical–sexual changes that are anxiety producing can be dealt with according to the adolescent's own timetable. Additional research reported by Prerost (1980a) revealed that sexual humor was appreciated more by middle (16-year-old) adolescents than by early (13-year-old) or late (19-year-old) adolescents. This is not a particularly surprising finding given that 16-year-old adolescents are either in the midst or near the completion of the developmental task of accepting sexual maturity. Sexual humor resonates with the main developmental task of middle adolescence, while younger adolescents may be concerned with cognitive challenges, and older adolescents may be concerned with identity and vocational decisions.

Prerost (1980a, 1980b, 1982) has also been active in the investigation of the social factors that influence the adolescent's perception of humor. The general findings from these studies indicate that growing inhibits the adolescent's perception of joking humor, beginning in middle adolescence (16 years old) and extending into late adolescence (19 years old). Again, the self-consciousness engendered by the physical changes of puberty may influence the adolescent's appreciation of humor. Viewed as a whole, these findings highlight the notion that those events or processes that the adolescent sees as most humorous are related to the child's ongoing attempts to master current developmental tasks. In addition, these findings implicate a cognitive link between the adolescent's ability to master developmental tasks and the ability to produce and to consume humor.

The major cognitive development during adolescence is the emergence of formal operational thought (Piaget, 1952). The emergence of this novel cognitive ability enables the adolescent to think abstractly, but it simultaneously ensnares the adolescent in egocentric (and oftentimes humorous) forms of thought since it is idealistic (Elkind, 1967). Given that the leading activities of children between the ages of 11 and 15 consist of intimate personal and socially useful communication (El'konin, 1972), it should not be surprising that cognitive egocentrism during adolescence is exemplified during, and overcome through, social interaction (Looft, 1972). In research examining the relationship between operational thought and the child's appreciation and comprehension of humorous stimuli, McGhee (1972) found that the concept of egocentric thought (the child's inability to decenter) was useful in explaining humor responses. A similar analysis of the role of adolescent egocentric thought patterns for humor appreciation and comprehension has not been attempted.

Although the data are limited, there is an apparent developmental pattern that allows for the interpretation of humor based upon the tasks of adolescence. Young adolescent children are often engaged in the reality testing of new cognitive abilities, the results of which are grounds for the continued use of these strategies or grounds for change. The product, as many parents will attest to, is often humorous. Children of middle adolescence are faced with physical changes, sexual maturity, and how these developments are linked to general social and cognitive processes. Jokes and cartoons that match their developmental maturity are perceived as funny; jokes that are too advanced are threatening. Children of late adolescence are confronted with an identity search that incorporates vocational, educational, and companionship decisions. While there are few data on later adolescents' humor preferences, it may be the case that job-specific jokes are appreciated most.

Thus, humor is both an index of growth and a source of change during the adolescent years. Humor is a vehicle whereby the environmental context socializes and brings the child closer to the culture's expectations of adult functioning. Yet it is also the adolescent child who uses humor in the service of transforming the environment. Through this process of mutual socialization from infancy through adolescence, humor is described best as a developmental phenomenon that is conducive to successful interactions between the growing human organism and the culture's social context.

THEORETICAL PERSPECTIVES OF HUMOR

The empirical findings of the previously cited investigations appear to be useful in representing the functions of humor as interactive phenomena during the course of early development. If this representation of humor is the most useful description that is currently available, then it seems logical to infer that this interpretation has resulted from the application of interactive theories to the study of humor and its functions. On the contrary, theories that have been utilized to interpret humor development and humorous behaviors have not been based upon the premise that humor expression is a product of child–environment interactions. Accordingly, two issues are the foci of this discussion.

First, we describe how psychoanalytic, cognitive-developmental, and social-learning theories have been applied to humor development or humorous behaviors during the early part of the life-span. Within this process, we note whether a particular theory has been designed to emphasize the child's or the environment's contribution to humor while bypassing an interactive orientation toward the human organism and its environment. Our second goal is a consideration of (1) how an interactive framework can be used to interpret humor development, and (2) issues associated with an interactive orientation.

Psychoanalytic Theory

Psychoanalytic theorists have approached the concept of humor in primarily two ways. Humor is viewed functionally as one of the mechanisms individuals use to cope with anxiety, guilt, aggression, rage, lust, and other conflictual emotions. This defense mechanism is generally more socially acceptable and considered less pathological than some of the other defense mechanisms, such as reaction formation or denial. The second psychoanalytic interpretation of humor is that it can be a useful clinical tool which is analogous to dream interpretation. Specifically, the content of humor produced or responded to by an individual can be used as an index of the person's psychosexual development. While most of the research to date has been with adults, the current focus is upon the psychodynamic explanation of the development and functions of humor during childhood.

Freud (1933) proposed five invariantly ordered psychosexual stages of development—oral, anal, phallic, latent, and genital—with each stage having its own individual conflicts and processes. Psychoanalytic investigators of humor have consequently noted how humor is related to the child's psychosexual growth. For example, infants toward the end of the first year of life—when weaning begins—will often nip playfully at the mother's breast while smiling and laughing (Kaplan, 1978). This teasing of the mother by pretending to inflict pain illustrates two points. It is a demonstration of the predominant focus of the infant's activity—oral gratification—and it is an expression of the primary psychosexual conflict and tension of the oral stage—the gradual dissolution of the exclusive love relationship between mother and child.

Perhaps the most comprehensive interpretation of children's humor from a psychoanalytic perspective has been provided by the research of Wolfenstein (1951, 1954, 1955). While focusing her attention upon children's jokes and riddles, Wolfenstein (1954) has noted how

> jokes represent a certain way of overcoming emotional difficulties. They vary in content and in form depending on the phase of development whose characteristic impulses and defenses they express. The preference of children of a certain age for a certain kind of joke gives us a clue to its underlying significance, which may be further confirmed by the analysis of the joke itself. (p. 156)

Thus, Wolfenstein has viewed the analysis of children's jokes to be valuable for two reasons. First, the themes of the riddles and the jokes children produce parallel the stages of psychosexual development. Secondly, the function of joking serves an important developmental purpose in helping the child to cope with stress, anxiety, guilt, and other emotions that pervade childhood. For example, the content of jokes and riddles used by latency stage children has been reported to contain forbidden desires, haunting dangers, or emotional conflicts that were dominant during the preceding oral, anal, and phallic stages of psychosexual development (Wolfenstein, 1951). The confrontation of these conflicts through humor has been described as personally gratifying to a child on a cognitive level, while the content of the humorous material reveals the child's psychosexual development (Wolfenstein, 1951).

Thus, psychoanalytic theorists have noted how children use humor as a functional defense mechanism and how the content of jokes and riddles can be utilized as an index of the child's psychosexual development. This approach yields information about children and their characteristics, yet the social environment and the interaction between a child and the environment are virtually neglected (see Chodorow, 1978). The expression of humor is represented as a process that is internal to the developing child, while the influence of social factors upon humor is given minimal attention. This almost exlusive focus upon the child, the maturation of psychosexual stages, and the concept that these stages are controlled by mechanisms internal to the child (such as behavior being motivated by sexual and aggressive instincts) has precluded the examination of how the environment and child–environment interactions affect humor development. Thus, this noninteractive orientation of psychoanalysis poses major limitations for the researcher who chooses to represent humor as the product of child–environment interactions.

Cognitive-Developmental Theory

Similar to the stage concept of psychoanalysis, a stage orientation has been applied to the examination of the relationships between humor and cognitive development. Piaget (1952) has identified four invariant stages of cognitive development—sensorimotor, preoperational, concrete operational, and formal operational—, with each stage reflecting different cognitive accomplishments and a progression toward the abstract, and most mature, thought process of formal operations. Cognitive-developmental investigators have, in general, attempted to define relationships between Piaget's four stages of cognitive development and the child's expression of humor. For example, McGhee (1971a, 1974b) has pointed out how a child's cognitive ability is related to the comprehension, appreciation, and production of humor. Inquiries of this genre have yielded an overall finding of more sophisticated comprehension, appreciation, and production of humor as a child progresses from the sensorimotor through the formal operational stages of cognitive development (McGhee, 1971a, 1979).

One illustration of this research is an investigation that examined the relationship between conservation of matter, which is a cognitive accomplishment of concrete operations, and children's understanding of incongruity humor (McGhee & Johnson, 1975). McGhee and Johnson provided a set of concrete cues, through demonstrations of matter conservation, prior to the telling of jokes that relied upon incongruity as the source of humor. The conservation demonstrations were then followed by such jokes as the following.

> Mary is 6 years old and went to the bakery one day to get 5 one-pound loaves of bread for her mother's party. When she saw that the bread was cut into very thick slices, she said, "Oh, you'd better slice them thin! I could never carry them home sliced that thick." (McGhee & Johnson, 1975, p. 24)

The demonstrations of matter conservation inhibited the appreciation of incongruity, but they produced greater surprise reactions among conserving then nonconserving children. Perhaps more importantly, conserving children both interpreted and understood violations of the principle of matter conservation.

Researchers who have examined the relationships between cognitive development and humor have frequently focused their attention upon various operationalizations of incongruity humor (e.g., Suls, 1972). While there is no single definition of incongruity humor, this type of humor relies upon the child's ability to identify and to resolve a discrepancy between perceived and already-known information. In the above McGhee–Johnson joke, discrepancy identification may be defined as a child's ability to note that Mary's request seems silly or unusual. However, discrepancy resolution is a child's ability to note that Mary's behavior is funny since the thickness of the bread slices has nothing to do with the bread being carried home. Both types of discrepancy require a child to compare already-known information about the transportation and thickness of bread slices with the information provided by the joke. This comparison between already-known and perceived information results in a discrepancy that can then be identified and resolved by a child.

McGhee (1971a, 1971b, 1974b) has reported that discrepancy resolution is more sophisticated than discrepancy identification, that both types of discrepancy are related to a child's cognitive level, and that children's production of humor becomes more complex as their cognitive abilities mature. Discrepancy identification versus discrepancy resolution may be defined further as two levels of comprehension, with identification reflecting knowledge and resolution indicating understanding. Thus, children who could both identify and resolve the discrepant information in a joke, riddle, or cartoon, have been reported to demonstrate more advanced cognitive abilities than those children who could only identify discrepancies in humorous materials (McGhee, 1971a, 1971b).

This cognitive-developmental distinction between humor knowledge and humor understanding is an issue that reflects two primary characteristics of this theoretical orientation. First, theories of cognitive development, such as Piaget's, are based upon the premise that the child does not perceive the environment as it actually is, but cognitively acts upon individualized perceptions of the environment. During this process, the child constructs an environment that is organized, adaptive, and meaningful. The second characteristic logically follows from the first: Developmental theorists have appeared to focus their interest upon children and their expanding abilities while failing to describe environmental influences upon child development, as well as child–environment interactions. This process of reducing interactions into their component child and environment parts violates tenets of an organismic world view, upon which most cognitive-developmental theories are based (Overton & Reese, 1973; Reese & Overton, 1970).

According to an organismic world view, if the interaction between a child and the environment is sufficiently strong, then it is not feasible to dissect an interaction into its component child and environment parts. While most researchers would argue that child–environment interactions are strong, investigators using the organismic world view have repeatedly emphasized the child and his or her characteristics while dismissing child–environment interactions. This convenient fiction (Reese & Overton, 1970) indicates either a rejection of a strong interaction or a violation of the organismic world view, and the latter is more likely than the former possibility. While inquiry may be served by this form of reductionism, an accurate description of the human organism acting in multiple contexts may not be. For whatever reason this fiction exists, the investigation of humor development is served more usefully by an orientation that emphasizes the child–environment interaction, rather than either the child or the environment.

Social-Learning Theory

While psychoanalytic and cognitive-developmental theorists have focused their attention upon children and their emerging abilities, social-learning theorists have emphasized the exclusive influence of environmental factors upon childhood behaviors. Also, social-learning theorists have chosen to examine childhood behaviors, rather than child development (Baldwin, 1980). Accordingly, the topic of *humor development* in the previously outlined theories becomes an issue of *humorous behaviors* in this theoretical framework. Although a number of social-learning theories currently exist (Cairns, 1979), a strict operant analysis (e.g., Skinner, 1953) is perhaps the most representative application of this theoretical orientation to humorous behaviors.

From an operant perspective, the acquisition of humorous behaviors, such as laughing, joketelling, and riddletelling, occurs when a child is reinforced for attempting to produce these various responses. If a humorous behavior is totally new to a child, then shaping or physical guidance with reinforcement can be used to produce the final form of a given response (such as joketelling). Totally new responses, for which the child does not have the prerequisite behaviors, cannot be imitated and, subsequently, reinforced. However, "already-learned behaviors may be organized into novel combinations as a part of imitating a model. These reorganizations may appear to be new responses, but, in fact, they are only new combinations of familiar elements" (Baldwin, 1980, p. 448). Thus, the child learns a humorous response by reproducing a reinforced humorous behavior or through shaping or physical guidance of a humorous behavior followed by contingent reinforcement.

An acquired humorous response in an operant paradigm is maintained through either continous or partial reinforcement of a given behavior. Thus, the child who has acquired a behavior for joketelling will continue to exhibit this particular response as long as the environment provides contingent reinforcement for its production. However, most naturalistic settings provide partial-reinforcement schedules, and any behavior, including humorous ones, may become relatively resistant to extinction (Baldwin, 1980). A child may continue to repeat a relatively bland joke for an extended period of time, even though reinforcement is infrequent. In addition, environmental contingencies may be arranged so that certain humorous behaviors are differentially reinforced. For example, young children are reinforced frequently for acts of physical humor, such as clowning behavior, while older children are reinforced for verbal humor, such as joketelling.

Humorous behaviors in a social-learning perspective have been operationalized through such observable phenomena as smiling, laughing, and verbal reports that a stimulus has been perceived as being humorous. For example, Brackbill (1958) has demonstrated that infant smiling can be conditioned differentially according to the type of reinforcement that is instituted. This classic study of early conditioning has been followed by a number of investigations (e.g., Wahler, 1967) that have clarified further the learning parameters associated with infant smiling.

A more recent investigation (Brown, Wheeler, & Cash, 1980) manipulated a humorous situation as three groups of children individually listened to tape-recorded jokes and riddles. One group of children saw no model listening to the tape while the remaining two groups observed a laughing or nonlaughing model listening to the tape. Children who observed a laughing model laughed more when they listened to the tape than did the other two groups of children. However, children who observed no model and those who watched a laughing model smiled more than the group of children who observed a nonlaughing model. Brown et al. concluded that imitation is a primary method whereby children learn humorous responses, and social facilitation may appear to account for humorous behaviors, but imitation is a strong, rival explanation that may equally well describe this dimension of childhood behavior.

Social-learning theory accentuates the controlling nature of the environment while dispensing with the organism and such childhood characteristics as developmental level (Baldwin, 1980). In this process of neglecting the organism, these theories have not provided an explanation for the origin of aggressive, sexual, or affiliative behavior (Cairns, 1979). Thus, this theoretical orientation has represented the expression of humor as a passive response to active environmental stimulation.

While social-learning theory may be applied to humor expression at any point in the life-span, this seeming advantage loses its potency if the developmental level of the human organism is ignored. Change is a primary characteristic of human development, yet social-learning theory has been constructed as a framework that primarily emphasizes environmental influences and the impact of external forces upon behavior expression. It is precisely through this environmental focus that this theoretical framework provides a convincing explanation for anything and everything (Baldwin, 1980). If one is willing to entertain an interactive perspective between organism and environment, then this explanatory power becomes a hypothetical poltergeist, which can be understood as a reality only when we provide empirical demonstrations of the mutual influences between the changing organism and the changing environment. Bandura (1971, 1977), Mischel (1973), and other social-learning theorists (e.g., Cairns, 1979) have begun to address the complexity of an interactive network, and it is this theoretical position that appears to hold the potential for more adequately describing humor development and humorous behaviors than do psychoanalytic, cognitive-developmental, or social-learning approaches.

Humor Development from an Interactive Perspective

In a general sense, either the child or the environment is disregarded in the orientations provided by psychoanalytic, cognitive-developmental, and social-learning theories. The reduction of sophisticated child-environment interactions into their elemental parts may seem to facilitate our investigation of the component elements, but it tells us little about how the child and the environment mutually change one another. A child's expression of humor does not change in a vacuum; neither do cultural forms of humor survive and undergo modification in the child's absence.

The theoretical foci of the theories we have reviewed become even more perplexing if we reconsider the functions of humor between infancy and adolescence. We have illustrated the functions of humor as diverse, changeable, and interactive in nature across the early period of the human life-span. These three functional characteristics contain striking manifestations of how the developing child and the changing environment modify one another through reciprocal transactions. It is therefore paradoxical that the data for these humor functions have been generated by theories that are noninteractive; yet an interactive approach yields a more cogent explanation of these aggregated data than do any of the noninteractive orientations.

The position we have been proposing for humor development and humorous behaviors is an interactive perspective, which is derived from the world view of dialectic contextualism (Reese, 1977). According to Reese,

> The aim (of contextualism) is to identify the rules of change and to describe transitions and the contexts in which they occur. . . . In psychology, the contextualistic model is reflected by an active organism model, in which not only the organism but also the context actively transform reality as known, each at the same time influencing the nature of the transformation. (p. 207)

Change is given in this orientation: The interaction between the developing child and multiple, changing contexts is the expression of human development and behavior. Also, the environment and the child are reflections of a historical past, and this historical element is related directly to child-environment interactions. Very briefly summarized, an interactive perspective is based upon the premise that children and their environment are inseparable since they mutually change one another: Both change through their interactions, and it is not useful to examine the unitary contributions of either the child or the environment to these mutual transformations.

While an interactive perspective is an appealing theoretical framework, its recognition and utilization by investigators will occur only if it is more useful than other orientations in its explanation of humor development. Perhaps the most illustrative example of this framework's development and utilization has been the research of current social-learning theorists. When these researchers were unable to use the traditional principles of operant conditioning to explain the maintenance of childhood behaviors (Cairns, 1979), they began construction of an interactive framework to explain their empirical findings. Specifically, Bandura (1971, 1977) has suggested that the maintenance of a behavior depends upon four interactional factors: (1) attention the child has directed toward the model's behavior, (2) the child's memory, (3) the child's motivation, and (4) the child's prerequisite skills for reproducing the modeled behavior. Thus, any observable behavior can be described as a result of the interaction between child and environment.

The fascinating characteristic of Bandura's interactive framework is the ease with which it can be applied to humorous behaviors. For example, the maintenance of a child's joking behavior may depend upon the same factors outlined above: (1) attention the child has directed toward a model's joking behavior, (2) the child's memory of the joke's information, (3) the child's motivation for reproducing the joke, and (4) the child's prerequisite skills for reproducing the modeled behavior. Two promising characteristics are especially apparent in this application of an interactive orientation. First, an interactive framework capitalizes on the two strengths of traditional theories (focus upon the child or the environment) by merging the two in a conceptual framework of reciprocal influence. Second, an interactive model can be applied across the entire life-span, and this continuity seems to have more utlity than age-period theories (such as Piaget's) or the application of one approach (child-oriented) to child development and another (environment-oriented) to adult development (Reese, 1976).

While Bandura's interactive framework is easily applied to humorous behaviors, the challenges for current and future investigators are the refinement and successful utilization of an interactive approach for the description of humorous behaviors and humor development. Verbal acknowledgement that an interactive approach is warranted is no longer an adequate justification for this framework's existence. Responsible researchers must cogently define and then empirically demonstrate how an interactive orientation is useful for our understanding of humor and human development (see Cairns, 1979).

Accordingly, two issues need to be addressed before this utilization can occur.

The first issue is a clear delineation of what constitutes an interactive perspective. Reese (1977), Reese and Overton (1970), Overton and Reese (1973) have begun the task of defining the philosophical and theoretical aspects of this approach, while such investigators as Bandura (1971, 1977) and Mischel (1973) have utilized an interactive approach for their empirical findings. These efforts have been meritorious, but they are not enough. If the scientific community is willing to acknowledge the concept of interaction in a relatively loose and frequent fashion (Cairns, 1979), then it behooves us to provide definitions and empirical demonstrations of this construct.

Consequently, the empirical investigation of humor as an interactive phenomenon is in need of a lucid theoretical foundation. Methodologically, Bandura (1971, 1977) has provided an interactive framework for the interpretation of behavior maintenance, but it is not an orientation that can account for the origins of humor development or humorous behaviors. Thus, the theoretical premises of an interactive orientation (Reese, 1977) have not been completely recognized in methodologies, such as Bandura's. If we are to represent humor expression as the result of child–environment interactions, then a unitary focus upon behavior maintenance is inadequate. Rather, we need to examine the ramifications of how the changing child and the changing environment mutually influence humor and its expression.

The second issue is whether new methodologies need to be created for the collection of interactive humor data. Meacham (1984) has noted that this will not be necessary, but interpretations of data will need to change in order to be consistent with an interactive orientation. This is perhaps the crux of an interactive perspective and its utilization: Researchers will have to change their thinking of humor as the product of either child- or environment-dominated influences and to begin a reconceptualization of humor as an interactive phenomenon. Once the premises of traditional theories have been dispensed with, it will then be possible to initiate more comprehensive investigations and interpretations of humor from an interactive perspective.

CONCLUSION

The period of human development between infancy and adolescence can be described as diverse, changeable, and the product of mutual interactions between the child and his or her environment.

These very same characteristics can be applied to humor development from infancy through adolescence. The diversity of humor is represented by its functions as a facilitator of parent–infant and infant–peer relationships, of infant survival, of communication, of peer group affiliation and identification, and of the child's display of cognitive mastery over humorous materials. Throughout all of this diversity, the functions of humor constantly change as the child's developmental abilities continue to mature: The young infant may interact with a caregiver through laughter and smiles while an adolescent may approach sexual issues through jokes with peers. Lastly, the expression of humor and its function are the products of mutual interactions between children and their environments. Although the environment may teach a generations-old riddle to a child, it is the child who has the option to repeat the humorous material or to alter its content and form. Humor, on a general dimension, is a process of mutual adaptation between the child and the environment. Consequently, both the child and the environment change, and are changed, through their humorous transactions. A child, through these mutually adaptive exchanges, progressively exhibits more mature levels of functioning via humor and its expression.

The concept of humor as an interactive process between child and environment is a relatively contemporary issue, and its implications for future research are copious. For example, What child and environmental characteristics facilitate a child's expression of humor? Are there parent and child variables that stimulate or hamper humor? What is the origin for the class clown's propensity for humor? Previous research has been focused primarily upon the child's or the environment's contribution to expressions of humor. Neither of these approaches fully shows the richness of the child's humor in relation to the environment or environmental forms of humor as they affect the child. Consequently, further development of an interactive orientation holds a major potential for a more comprehensive analysis of humor and its relationships with child–environment interactions.

REFERENCES

Anderson, J. R. (1980). *Cognitive psychology and its implications*. San Francisco: Freeman.

Baldwin, A. (1980). *Theories of child development* (2nd ed.). New York: Wiley.

Bandura, A. (1971). *Psychological modeling: Conflicting theories*. Chicago: Aldine-Atherton.

Bandura, A. (1977). *Social learning theory*. Englewood Cliffs, NJ: Prentice-Hall.

Bowlby, J. (1969). *Attachment and loss* (Vol. 1). New York: Basic Books.

Bowlby, J. (1958). The nature of the child's tie to his mother. *International Journal of Psychoanalysis, 39,* 350–373.

Brackbill, Y. (1958). Extinction of the smiling response in infants as a function of reinforcement schedule. *Child Development, 29,* 114–124.

Brodzinsky, D. M. (1975). The role of conceptual tempo and stimulus characteristics in children's humor development. *Developmental Psychology, 11,* 843–850.

Brodzinsky, D. M. (1977). Children's comprehension and appreciation of verbal jokes in relation to conceptual tempo. *Child Development, 48,* 960–967.

Brodzinsky, D. M., & Rightmyer, J. (1976). Pleasure associated with cognitive mastery as related to children's conceptual tempo. *Child Development, 47,* 881–884.

Brodzinsky, D. M., Tew, J. D., & Palkovitz, R. (1979). Control of humorous affect in relation to children's conceptual tempo. *Developmental Psychology, 15,* 276–279.

Brooks-Gunn, J., & Lewis, M. (1981). Infant social perception: Responses to pictures of parents and strangers. *Developmental Psychology, 17,* 647–649.

Brown, G., Wheeler, K., & Cash, M. (1980). The effects of a laughing versus a nonlaughing model on humor responses in preschool children. *Journal of Experimental Child Psychology, 29,* 334–339.

Cairns, R. (1979). *Social development: The origins and plasticity of interchanges.* San Francisco: Freeman.

Chapman, A. J. (1974). An experimental study of socially facilitated humorous laughter. *Psychological Reports, 35,* 727–734.

Chapman, A. J. (1975). Humorous laughter in children. *Journal of Personality and Social Psychology, 31,* 42–49.

Chapman, A. (1973). Social facilitation of laughter in children. *Journal of Experimental Social Psychology, 9,* 528–541.

Chodorow, N. (1978). *The reproduction of mothering.* Berkeley and Los Angeles: University of California Press.

Dennis, W. (1960). Causes of retardation among institutional children: Iran. *Journal of Genetic Psychology, 96,* 47–59.

Elkind, D. (1967). Egocentrism in adolescence. *Child Development, 38,* 1025–1034.

El'konin, D. B. (1972). Toward the problem of stages in the mental development of the child (M. Vale, Trans.). *Soviet Psychology, 10,* 225–251. (Original work published in *Voprosy Psikhologii, 4,* 6–20)

Freud, S. (1933). *New introductory lectures on psychoanalysis.* New York: Norton.

Groch, A. (1974). Joking and appreciation of humor in nursery school children. *Child Development, 45,* 1098–1102.

Havighurst, R. J. (1973). History of developmental psychology: Socialization and personality development through the life-span. In P. B. Baltes & K. W. Schaie (Eds.), *Life-span developmental psychology: Personality and socialization.* New York: Academic Press.

Hayes, L., & Watson, J. (1981). Facial orientation of parents and elicited smiling by infants. *Infant Behavior and Development, 4,* 333–340.

Kagan, J., & Moss, H. A. (1962). *Birth to maturity.* New York: Wiley.

Kaplan, L. J. (1978). *Oneness and separateness: From infant to individual.* New York: Simon and Schuster.

Keith-Spiegel, P. (1972). Early conceptions of humor: Varieties and issues. In J. H. Goldstein & P. E. McGhee (Eds.), *The psychology of humor: Theoretical perspectives and empirical issues.* New York: Academic Press.

Looft, W. R. (1972). Egocentrism and social interaction across the life-span. *Psychological Bulletin, 78,* 73–92.

McGhee, P. H. (1979). *Humor: Its origin and development.* San Francisco: Freeman.

McGhee, P. H. (1977). A model of the origins and early development of incongruity-based humour. In A. Chapman and H. Foot (Eds.), *It's a funny thing, humour.* Oxford: Pergamon Press.

McGhee, P. H. (1974b). Development of children's ability to create the joking relationship. *Child Development, 45,* 552–556.

McGhee, P. H. (1974a). Cognitive mastery and children's humor. *Psychological Bulletin, 81,* 721–730.

McGhee, P. H. (1972b). On the cognitive origins of incongruity humor: Fantasy assimilation versus reality assimilation. In J. H. Goldstein & P. H. McGhee (Eds.), *The psychology of humor: Theoretical perspectives and empirical issues.* New York: Academic Press.

McGhee, P. H. (1971b). Development of the humor response: A review of the literature. *Psychological Bulletin, 76,* 328–348.

McGhee, P. H. (1971a). Cognitive development and children's comprehension and appreciation of humor. *Child Development, 42,* 123–138.

McGhee, P. H., & Grodzitsky, P. (1973). Sex-role identification and humor among preschool children. *Journal of Psychology, 84,* 189–193.

McGhee, P. H., & Johnson, S. F. (1975). The role of fantasy and reality cues in children's appreciation of incongruity humor. *Merrill-Palmer Quarterly, 21,* 19–30.

McGhee, P. H., & Lloyd, S. A. (1981). A developmental test of the disposition theory of humor. *Child Development, 52,* 925–931.

Meachman, J. A. (1984). The individual as consumer and producer of historical change. In K. A. McCluskey & H. W. Reese (Eds.), *Life-span developmental psychology: Historical and cohort effects.* New York: Academic Press.

Mischel, W. (1973). Toward a cognitive social learning reconceptualization of personality. *Psychological Review, 80,* 252–283.

Overton, W. F., & Reese, H. W. (1973). Models of development: Methodological implications. In J. R. Nesselroade & H. W. Reese (Eds.), *Life-span developmental psychology: Methodological issues.* New York: Academic Press.

Piaget, J. (1952). *The origins of intelligence in children.* New York: International Universities Press.

Prentice, N. M., & Fathman, R. E. (1975). Joking riddles: A developmental index of children's humor. *Developmental Psychology, 11,* 210–216.

Prerost, F. J. (1982). The development of the mood-inhibiting effects of crowding during adolescence. *The Journal of Psychology, 110,* 197–202.

Prerost, F. J. (1980b). The effects of high spatial density on humor appreciation: Age and sex differences. *Social Behavior and Personality, 8,* 239–244.

Prerost, F. J. (1980a). Developmental aspects of adolescent sexuality as reflected in reactions to sexually explicit humor. *Psychological Reports, 46,* 543–548.

Ransohoff, F. (1975). Some observations on humor and laughter in young adolescent girls. *Journal of Youth and Adolescence, 4,* 155–170.

Reese, H. W. (1977). Discriminative learning and transfer: Dialectical perspectives. In N. Datan & H. Reese (Eds.), *Life-span developmental psychology: Dialectical perspectives on experimental research.* New York: Academic Press.

Reese, H. W. (1976). Models of memory development. *Human Development, 19,* 291–303.

Reese, H. W., & Overton, W. F. (1970). Models of development and theories of development. In L. R. Goulet & P. B. Baltes (Eds.), *Life-span developmental psychology: Research and theory*. New York: Academic Press.

Rheingold, H. (1969). The social and socializing infant. In D. Goslin (Ed.), *Handbook of socialization theory and research*. Chicago: Rand McNally.

Roe, K. (1978). Mother-stranger discrimination in the three-month-old infants and subsequent Gesell performance. *The Journal of Genetic Psychology, 133*, 111–118.

Sherman, L. (1975). An ecological study of glee in small groups of preschool children. *Child Development, 46*, 53–61.

Skeels, H. M. (1966). Adult status of children with contrasting early life experiences. *Monographs of the Society for Research in Child Development, 31* (3, Serial No. 105).

Skinner, B. (1953). *Science and human behavior*. New York: Macmillan.

Spitz, R. A. (1946). Anaclitic depression. *Psychoanalytic study of the child* (Vol. 2). New York: International Universities Press.

Sroufe, L., & Wunsch, J. (1972). The development of laughter in the first year of life. *Child Development, 43*, 1326–1344.

Suls, J. M. (1972). A two-stage model for the appreciation of jokes and cartoons: An information-processing analysis. In J. H. Goldstein & P. H. McGhee (Eds.), *The psychology of humor: Theoretical perspectives and empirical issues*. New York: Academic Press.

Vandell, D. (1980). Sociability with peer and mother during the first year. *Developmental Psychology, 16*, 355–361.

Wahler, R. (1967). Infant social attachments: A reinforcement theory interpretation and investigation. *Child Development, 38*, 1079–1088.

Wiesenfeld, A., & Klorman, R. (1978). The mother's psychophysiological reactions to contrasting affective expressions by her own and an unfamiliar infant. *Developmental Psychology, 14*, 294–304.

Wolfenstein, M. (1955). Mad laughter in a six-year-old boy. *The Psychoanalytic Study of the Child, 10*, 381–394.

Wolfenstein, M. (1954). *Children's humor: A psychological analysis*. Glencoe, IL: The Free Press.

Wolfenstein, M. (1951). A phase in the development of children's sense of humor. *Psychoanalytic Study of the Child, 6*, 336–350.

4

Humor, Physiology, and the Aging Process

WILLIAM F. FRY, JR.

INTRODUCTION

This chapter surveys the scientific information available about the physiology of humor, mirth, and laughter. It also considers some of the ways in which that physiology can be important and useful in respect to certain aspects of the aging process—especially ways in which various physiologic effects contribute to furthering a more realistic and fruitful relationship between the aged and the rest of society.

PROBLEMS ASSOCIATED WITH THE AGING PROCESS

The aging process presents a complex picture. It truly creates a paradox as it unfolds in our lives. On one hand, we observe that the growing number of years in life is associated with a growing number of experiences and a growing treasury of wisdom about life: The elderly person is enriched by experience. The aging process gives us all something that is very important to ourselves and to all those about us. We gain as we pass through our lives.

81   Copyright © 1986 by Academic Press, Inc.
All rights of reproduction in any form reserved.

But, paradoxically, at the same time as we gain during the aging process, we also are losing. As it gives, the aging process also takes away. Along with its burgeoning of wisdom and experience, the aging process is also deteriorative. In this sometimes heartbreakingly imperfect world, we find these two opposite forces operating: One is giving and growing; the other is waning and taking away. While experience grows, one finds one is undergoing physical deterioration. Our bodies begin to show signs of physical deterioration during the 20s or 30s and this process continues throughout the rest of our lives. As we are waxing in experience and wisdom, we are waning in various physical parameters.

Humor's Value in the Aging Process

With the various problems associated with aging as a reality in our lives, it is appropriate to emphasize those factors that can diminish, offset, and compensate for the inroads of aging. Such emphasis can result in improving the quality of life of the elderly and of ourselves as each of us enters old age. If any agency can oppose physical deteriorations and impairments and emotional distress, it needs to be recognized for its benefits in improving the comfort and happiness of old age.

Humor, mirth, mirthful laughter recommend themselves for our consideration in this regard, for many reasons which are becoming more widely recognized and respected. The most obvious reason is that humor, mirth, and laughter are universally available. Every human is born with the capacity for developing a sense of humor, and almost all of us realize this capacity. Another important reason has to do with humor's unique power in human life. As one result of his analysis of the findings of the Harvard University longitudinal Grant Study, psychiatrist George Vaillant (1977) designated humor as one of the five mature coping mechanisms available to humans for successfully dealing with disadvantageous circumstances. "Humor is one of the truly elegant defenses in the human repertoire. Few would deny that the capacity for humor, like hope, is one of mankind's most potent antidotes of the woes of Pandora's box." (Vaillant, 1977, p. 116).

In addition to various general values of humor, mirth, and laughter for dealing with problems of the aging process, there are numerous specific values; many of which are just now being recognized, studied, and brought into use by various projects utilizing humor. This book serves as a landmark indicating the progress already achieved in this regard. It also indicates the strong and sincere professional interest in future progress using humor in combatting the unfavorable elements of the aging process. Various chapters of this book explore what is being achieved; others explore future possibilities. A nascent science is being celebrated in these pages. The roles of humor in the aging process constitute a discipline just now being formulated.

THE SPECIAL ROLES OF HUMOR
PHYSIOLOGY IN THE AGING PROCESS

It is satisfying to recognize at this time that particular, specific values are offered by humor physiology for dealing with the problems of the aging process. Humor physiology (or gelotology: the science of laughter) is currently undergoing an expansion of exploration and understanding. It is a young science; its studies are basic science studies, examining the most basic issues of human physiological functioning. But already, despite its newness and its deficiencies of technical sophistication, there is enough information to illuminate its values for the elderly.

Humor physiology, refers to those events occurring in our bodies in association with humorous experiences. We are exposed to humorous stimuli and we perceive and respond to that humor. Within our psyches, an emotion of mirth is stimulated. Mirth is accompanied by or results in various behaviors, such as mirthful laughter. There are three basic elements in this system: the stimulus (humor, comedy, etc.); the emotional response (mirth); and the accompanying behavior (laughter, smiling, chortling, guffawing, tittering, giggling, etc.).

It is axiomatic that various other emotions and attitudes will accompany the humor experience, along with the resultant mirth. For one, if we share a humorous experience with another person, we experience a sense of heightened rapport with that person, along with the mirth. Again, experiencing mirth conveys a sense of hopefulness, as described by Mindess (1971). And there are others. In contrast to Bergson's (1921) view that "laughter has no greater enemy than emotion" (p. 63), several of these associated or accompanying emotions actually enhance or increase the mirth reaction. The well-recognized infectiousness of mirth is greatly assisted by the empathic rapport developed between those sharing a humorous event.

Just as mirth can be accompanied by or found associated with other emotions, it is also evident that many physical phenomena are occurring during the mirthful experience and its accompanying behavior. These phenomena have their own repercussions on the individual's functioning. In other words, the mirth and its behavior are joined by a wide variety of physiological activities, and these activities stimulate other physiological processes as secondary ramifications of their occurrence. This physiologic impact is extensive and sometimes profound. Laboratory study has demonstrated that mirth and its mirthful behavior have impact on most of the major physiologic systems of the human body. Further study should demonstrate that mirth has effect throughout the body, affecting all physiological systems.

Review of Humor Physiology Studies

The history of humor–mirth physiology studies is inconsistent. One would be hard put to unearth references to the physiology of mirth and laughter in the scientific literature of the first half of this century. Only two studies were reported during the 1930s in the United States. Paskind (1932) determined that skeletal muscle tone was diminished during mirthful laughter in muscles not actually participating in the laughter. Lloyd (1938) delineated some respiratory elements of laughter in his research, demonstrating an expiratory predominance and an interaction of thoracic and abdominal musculature.

For several centuries, the dominant view of humor posited that it is essentially a cathartic, or relief, element of human experience. Gregory (1924) provided one of the most extensive discussions of the relief theory. Berlyne (1972) found fault with the exclusiveness of relief theories. During the late 1950s and 1960s, Berlyne (1960, 1972) presented and researched a new theory of humor's impact on the human. He proposed that, although catharsis may take place during humor exposure, more information about the data-processing functions of the central nervous system argue for a view of humor response which incorporates, as its major element, an arousal stimulation, an activation of the organism. He theorized the existence of two-part balance in human response during exposure to humor stimuli. Arousal, with increases of nervous system activity, builds as the humor exposure continues. This arousal is not sufficient for mirth and must be joined by the second component, which amounts to reduction of the arousal tension through resolution of the incongruity stimulation existent in the humor until that moment. This incongruity resolution is usually found in the so-called punchline of humor.

The Berlyne incongruity–arousal theory of humor stimulated considerable interest. Several researchers became involved in providing laboratory information to clarify various aspects of the Berlyne theory. Shortly after the introduction of the arousal theory, researchers were prompted to explore the effects of humor exposure on the human arousal physiologic mechanism. Specifically, humor exposure effects on catecholamine activity were studied.

CATECHOLAMINE–AUTONOMIC NERVOUS SYSTEM STUDIES

Schachter and Wheeler (1962) and Levi (1965) explored the relationship between humor exposure and autonomic nervous system variables. Schachter and Wheeler studied the effect on humor responsivity of pharmacological manipulations of the sympathetic nervous system, administering to their subjects injections of epinephrine, chlorpromazine (a tranquilizer), and placebo saline. They concluded, "overt amusement is directly related to the degree of manipulated sympathetic activation" (p. 126). In interpretation of their findings, epinephrine subjects were more amused by humor stimuli than were placebo subjects who were more amused than chlorpromazine subjects. Levi tested the effects of humor exposure by determining the amount of endogenous adrenalin excreted following exposure to humor stimuli. He reported that urine assays demonstrated increases in both adrenalin and noradrenalin excretion with humor exposure, concluding that "emotional responses rated by the subjects as pleasant may be accompanied by increased sympatheticoadrenomedullary activity" (p. 85).

The Schachter and Wheeler and Levi studies were corroborated by results of a study by Langevin and Day (1972). To obtain reflection of autonomic function, they tested galvanic skin response (GSR) and heart rates (HR) during exposure to humor stimuli. They reported, "GSR and HR both indicate that arousal increase is positively correlated with humor ratings" (p. 140).

Preliminary results of a pilot study being conducted by Fry, Berk, and Tan (personal communication, 1984) indicated catecholamine activatiation can be intense during humor exposure and is correlated with degree of laughter. The data, obtained from direct venous blood sampling during exposure to humor stimuli, suggests a complex autonomic response with each catecholamine element (epinephrine, norepinephrine, and dopamine) having its own individual response pattern.

CIRCULATORY SYSTEM STUDIES

The Berlyne incongruity–arousal theory stimulated another group of studies directed at illuminating what occurs in the circulatory system during mirth, with the hypothesis that psychological arousal produces an increase in circulatory activity. Several studies examined the effects of exposure to humor stimuli on heart rate. Most of the studies found heart rate to be increased during humor stimuli exposure.

These include Averill (1969), Fry and Rader (1969), Jones and Harris (1971), Langevin and Day (1972), Sroufe and Waters (1976), and Godkewitsch (1976). The results of my own study (Fry 1969) led me to believe that the direct correlation observed between humor exposure and heart rate is actually a measure of the degree of laughter generated during the humor exposure and is a manifestation of the activity of a pulmonary–cardiac reflex.

Goldstein, Harman, McGhee and Karasik (1975) had somewhat different results in their investigation of correlation between heart rate and mirth. They reported, "the degree of arousal change (either an increase or decrease) between base rate period and the question portion of riddles was related to funniness ratings in an inverted-U fashion" (p. 66). This variation was attributed to the distinctive use of riddles as the humor stimuli, rather than cartoons, jokes, humorous films, or tapes, which were used in the other studies. A study conducted by Scheff and Scheele (1979) surprisingly demonstrated a decrease in heart rate associated with humor exposure and mirthful laughter. This apparent conflict with other data was resolved by the realization that decreased rate readings were made several seconds following cessation of laughter. This experience was serendipitous in that it focused scientific attention on the period of resolution or relaxation following the stimulatory phase associated with the humor behavior (laughter).

Another circulatory system study, by Fry and Savin (1982), investigated the effects of humor exposure on arterial blood pressure using direct arterial cannulization. During exposure to humor stimuli, mirthful laughter is accompanied by brief, but sometimes large, increases of both systolic and diastolic blood pressure levels. Increases are directly proportional to intensity and duration of the laughter. After laughter has ceased, there is a short period with the blood pressure levels below prelaughter baseline. Thus, this study reveals the stimulation–relaxation pattern.

RESPIRATORY STUDIES

Two respiratory studies have demonstrated this stimulation–relaxation pattern in respiratory activity during mirthful laughter while exposed to humor stimuli. These studies are the early one carried out by Lloyd (1938) and the one conducted by Fry and Rader (1977). Fry and Rader demonstrated that with mirthful laughter there is marked activation and disruption of the physiological respiratory cycle. After laughter has ceased, respiratory activity decreases and does not revert to normal cyclic breathing for a short period thereafter. A study by Svebak (1977) supplied information compatible with the stimulation–relaxation pattern: A high incidence of sighing is correlated with high incidence of laughter.

The Lloyd and the Fry and Rader studies demonstrated a surplus of expiration compared with proportion of inspiration. A study by Fry and Stoft (1971) showed that this expiratory disproportion does not result in arterial oxygen deficiency during laughter of up to three minutes duration in normal subjects. S. Young (1982) reported decreased levels of expired carbon dioxide during laughter.

SKELETAL MUSCULAR SYSTEM

The stimulation-relaxation pattern has also been observed in muscle behavior associated with mirthful laughter during humor exposure. Paskind (1932) reported that muscles not involved in the actual laughter behavior (those of an immobilized right arm) entered a state of relaxation during laughter. Schwartz (1974) had similar results in his study of joy or happiness imagery. During happy imagery, forehead muscles registered a relaxation of tension on the electromyograph. Svebak (1975) demonstrated the stimulation–relaxation pattern from another perspective, showing that a high degree of variance of abdominal respiratory body circumference—being an indicator of abdominal muscle tension level—is directly correlated in women with high frequency and duration of mirthful laughter. A study by Chapman (1976) also found muscle tension to be increased in direct correlation with the degree of mirth response to humor stimuli. The relaxation phase was not demonstrated in some subjects even as late as 20 seconds after cessation of stimuli exposure.

CENTRAL NERVOUS SYSTEM EFFECTS

The central nervous system has been inadequately studied regarding its participation in mirth responses. In an incomplete study with a small number of normal subjects, Fry, Yeager, Henderson and Vreeland (1969) indicated a laughter-timed disruption of alpha rhythm, accompanied by an intensification of fast wave activity during exposure to humor stimuli. Svebak (1982) reported studies revealing electroencephalogram (EEG) data compatible with greater coordination of function between right and left hemispheres during humor stimuli exposure and mirthful response. He found subjects exposed to humor manifested less discordant (right–left hemisphere comparison) alpha rhythm in association with mirthful laughter. This decrease of discordance was specifically derived from alterations of right hemisphere behavior during humor exposure.

These studies, as sketchy as they are, provide information confirming an impact of humor, mirth, and laughter on the central nervous system (CNS). This impression is in line with that derived from a wide variety of clinical reports reflecting CNS participation in humor-related experiences. In susceptible individuals, mirthful laughter can precipitate epileptic seizures (Beneicke, 1967). Laughter convulsions have been observed as major indications of CNS pathology (Cantu, 1966). Furthermore, mirthful laughter is a common precipitant of cataplectic seizures, known to be associated with abnormal brain activity (Fry, 1963).

IMPLICATIONS OF FINDINGS IN HUMOR PHYSIOLOGY

When we consider this scattering of physiologic data in its totality, and, especially, when we compare this data with the extensive information available from studies in other areas of human emotions and behavior, one must agree that there is a great deal more to be done. Nevertheless, even at this early stage of humor physiology, there are certain general implications and impressions that are apparent. One is the demonstration that humor, mirth, and laughter have some impact on most, if not all, of the major human physiologic systems. Another is the recognition that humor physiology is frequently characterized by a pattern of stimulation followed by a period of relaxation. A third implication is that one can expect that the quality of the life of individuals and their relationships with others can be significantly improved as the result of emphasizing humor and encouraging participation in humor, mirth, and laughter. The advantages of humor are jointly emotional, psychological, and physiological and are additive to each other.

Humor Physiology and Life Quality in the Aging Process

With the specific information available about physiologic impact of humor, mirth and laughter and with the general implications of the nature of this impact and its probable benefits, it is time to consider particular aspects of humor physiology and life quality benefits for the elderly. All that has gone before suggests that these benefits can be significant and are of widespread interest.

This is not to say that humor physiology provides a simple solution for all the problems associated with the aging process. Laughter does not make physical deteriorations cease or disappear. Humor is not a magical elixir of youth. We cannot laugh away our natural aging process. However, we can modify the impact of the process in each life through various physical mechanisms associated with humor physiology. People can be emotionally and physically vitalized through humor. Physical deterioration can be made to have less consequence for life quality. Elderly people can take greater control of their life experiences by enhancing the role of humor in their lives.

What are the specifics of humor physiology benefit? This section considers separately several body systems and details, in each case, the positive contributions made by humor physiology. One of the most obvious system activities with humor behavior is the involvement of the skeletal muscle system. The general stimulation–relaxation pattern of humor behavior is especially important here. Stimulation is reflected in the activity of those muscles actually participating in the mirthful response—laughter, chuckling, giggling, smiling, and so forth. Relaxation occurs in other muscles and, later, in those laughter participation muscles after the mirth action is completed.

MUSCLE STIMULATION

Skeletal muscles are activated at all levels of humor response, whether of mild or of profound and extensive intensity. Mild mirth is associated with varying combinations of smiling, chuckling, and chortling. These mild behaviors are accompanied and manifested by varying degrees of activity of muscles of the face, scalp, neck, and shoulders. A graduation ranges from this mild response to the opposite extreme—a full-scale belly laugh. The belly laugh, depending on the individual's style, can involve massive activity of thoracic and abdominal muscles or even muscles of the entire body when the person is kicking and thrashing about and flinging his arms and legs into the air in great hilarity.

Whatever the degree of muscle involvement, it is clear that humor stimulates significant exercise that, in its basic nature, is not different from the exercise derived with any sports activity or calisthenics. With mirth, then, we have an exercise experience which is on line with the large number of very important physical benefits already well defined by research in the discipline of exercise medicine. These benefits are too numerous to detail here, but they range all the way from the most general effects, such as the cardiac rehabilitation value of regular exercise, to very specific and even somewhat obscure effects, such as the stimulation of increased production of plasminogen activator, which helps prevent excess blood clotting and thrombosis. The net picture amassed by exercise medicine in extensive research is that regular exercise has body-wide value for health and general functioning. Mirth behavior provides exercise of greater or lesser degree.

Humor exercise does not compare episode-for-episode with marathon running or Olympic swimming in terms of exercise quantity and intensity. However, running and swimming are concentrated into a certain block of time of their devotees' days, whereas humor exercise can take place intermittently all day long, any day, every day.

No researcher has yet determined the total exercise represented in a day's accumulation of laughter. No study has yet determined the number of calories consumed by mirth exercise during the passage of an average day. However, the potential for frequency of laughter during a day is much greater than that for frequency of more arduous exercise. Keeping that frequency factor in mind, it may be that total mirth exercise during an average day in an average life will be significantly greater than that of the marathon running an average person might ever do. The potential frequency of mirth exercise recommends it for our consideration when thinking of the well-established value of exercise for our health.

That general health value, of course, applies to elderly people as well as to the rest of us. But there is another, more specific issue to consider in the case of the elderly. That is, many elderly people who might profit most from exercise conditioning—people who need stimulation of their circulation, strengthening of their heart muscle, or increase of their thrombosis-preventing plasminogen activator production—are not physically able to run or swim. They may be chairbound or bedridden. Limbs may be paralyzed; joints may be frozen; muscles may be deteriorated. The patients may not be able to run or swim, but most of them will be able to laugh. The doctor prescribes exercise: the patient can't get up out of bed, but the patient can laugh.

MUSCLE RELAXATION

The above are some of the presently recognizable values of humor physiology in muscle stimulation. Muscle relaxation is another beneficial facet of humor physiology. Muscle relaxation occurs in those muscles that relax while other muscles are being stimulated to participate in mirth behavior or in mirth-participating muscles which relax after the laughter is over. This relaxation of muscle tension can act to break up the spasm–pain–spasm–pain cycle that is so much a part of the joint and limb discomforts that commonly increase as the aging process advances—the snap–crackle–pop syndrome, the neuralgias, rheumatisms, Charley horses. Again, the frequent and repetitious nature of mirth behavior is a marked advantage.

CARDIAC MUSCLE EXERCISE

Related to this readily apparent skeletal muscle behavior with mirth is the less apparent cardiac muscle behavior. A major portion of the heart is muscle tissue. Increased heart rate and increased blood pressure during laughter reflect stimulation of heart muscle activity. They reflect cardiac exercise. The clinical implications of this cardiac stimulation are not limited to value for the aged population, but have significance for people of any age. However, the increased tendency for a sedentary life with advancing years brings laughter exercise into greater importance as the years pass.

Both prevention and rehabilitation factors are found to be relevant in the issue of laughter exercise and cardiac muscle. Ample study has demonstrated the association between regular cardiac exercise and lessened vulnerability to coronary heart disease. Briefly, present evidence indicates the importance of high density lipoprotein (HDL), a component of the body's cholesterol fraction. Blood levels of HDL are increased with regular exercise. HDL is recognized as an important cholesterol carrier, presumably combatting the human aging tendency towards developing atherosclerosis.

Also, it has been demonstrated in several studies that regular exercise, when carefully monitored, has pronounced rehabilitation benefit following recovery from the acute stages of a coronary heart attack. It is a modest extrapolation to extend well-established data about the benefits of exercise to a consideration of the possible cardiac benefits of stimulation by mirthful laughter, despite the absence of definitive research on the clinical benefits of laughter. The observation that in contrast to several other types exercise such as jogging, tennis or shoveling snow, when engaged in indiscreetly or intemperately, there is a striking paucity of incidence of heart attack during the stimulation and exercise of laughter suggests a complex combination of exercise benefit and heart attack–sparing factors.

CIRCULATORY VALUES OF MIRTH

The mirth exercise benefit potentialities are not exclusively for the elderly, but can be available for any age. There is another aspect of the stimulation effect of mirth behavior on cardiac activity that has greater specificity for older people: The circulation stimulation resulting from the cardiac stimulation. Arterial circulation is enhanced by the hydrodynamics of increased pump (heart) action and consequent increased pressure head (blood pressure) in the arterial system. Venous circulation is also activated through the milking action of the mirth-active muscles and by the bellows action of the laughing thoracic cavity. The aerodynamics of thoracic cavity have not been specifically studied for laughter, but they have been studied for the related behaviors of coughing and the Valsalva Maneuver. Intrathoracic pressure increases with sharp expiratory behavior, such as coughing or laughter. This increase temporarily diminishs venous return from the periphery to the heart. However, this inhibitory influence is effectively countered by the impact on venous circulation of the often abrupt inspiratory events in coughing and laughter.

Older people tend to be less active than in their earlier years. Along with the muscle wasting and exercise deficiency already discussed, this inactivity has a deleterious impact on circulation. An extreme, familiar, and highly undesirable example of this circulatory insufficiency is the stasis ulcers that frequently develop when people are excessively inactive. What is reflected in such clinical pictures is the vicious chain of diminished activity leading to diminished stimulation leading to diminished circulation leading to pathologic developments which ultimately lead to further diminution of activity. There are, of course, numerous procedures and mechanisms clinically utilized to obviate this undesirable weakening of circulation. No single one is completely satisfactory, and varying combinations are used for each individual case.

Humor, mirth, and laughter, being well favored in many other ways, are available as usually well accepted ancillary elements in the clinical effort against circulatory insufficiency. Laughter not only brings a flush to the cheeks and a glow over the torso but it can also help diminish the vulnerability to blood clot formation resulting from vascular stasis. It can diminish the fading–drowsing of aged hypotensive afternoons in the sun. It can quicken the movement of oxygen and cellular nutrients to tissues existing on the metabolic nutritional poverty line. It can stir the circulation of immune elements and phagocytes in attack against various noxious factors threatening the elderly person's bodily integrity. The circulatory system is, after all, the transport system of the body; humor physiology can expedite its operation.

CLINICAL RESPIRATORY VALUES

Another important part of humor physiology is the participation of the respiratory system. The lungs play significant roles, not only in laughter but also in other mirth behavior—chortling, chuckling, snorting, guffawing, and so forth—which accompany various degrees of mirthful response. There are several clinical implications of these respiratory activities.

As indicated above, expiration is in varying degrees of excess over inspiration during laughter. This prevalence distinguishes laughter from normal cyclic breathing in a clinically valuable way. Normal cyclic breathing is characterized by a more or less equality of expiration and inspiration. This rhythmic breathing produces the passage in and out of the lungs of tidal air. Cyclic breathing leaves behind in the lungs varying quantities of residual air, depending to a large extent on the natural elasticity of the lung tissue. The exchange of residual air with environmental air is slower than the exchange of tidal air. As the residual air continues to remain in place, its oxygen content continues to decrease. More and more oxygen is lost to the metabolic demands of the body, until an osmotic balance is reached where residual air contributes little to the oxygen supply being circulated to body tissue cells. In addition to losing oxygen content, residual air develops a buildup of two body metabolic waste products—carbon dioxide and water vapor. In other words, residual air is characterized by a deficiency of the oxygen required for normal cellular metabolism and by a surplus of metabolic waste products. The excesses of carbon dioxide contributes to the development of acidotic condition and the excess of water vapor provides increased potential for overgrowth of bacterial flora and pulmonary infection. These effects are not desirable for people of any age, but they are particularly unfavorable for the aged, given various physical aging impairments already mentioned.

Humor respiration (laughing, chuckling, etc.), disrupts cyclic breathing, increases ventilation, and, with its expiratory balance, invades the residual air, thus accelerating residual air exchange. Enhanced is the intake of oxygen-rich air. This effect is reflected in the results of the Fry and Stoft study (1971), demonstrating a maintenance of oxygen levels in peripheral blood during prolonged, heavy laughter. Also, with this acceleration of residual air exchange, carbon dioxide and water vapor exhalation is increased. The increased carbon dioxide discharge is reflected in the laboratory study of S. Young (1982). These effects of humor respiration on pulmonary function are identical to objectives of clinical respiratory therapy, which has been administered to 25–30% of all hospital patients during the past decade, according to figures presented by the U.S. Office of Technology Assessment in a recent report to the U.S. Congress.

Another respiratory feature of laughter, involving especially those explosively expiratory components which frequently occur, is its action of freeing and expelling the various discharges accumulated in the tracheobronchial tree. It is a common observation that laughter may turn into or be alternated with coughing, particularly when there is significant mucus or phlegm in the respiratory tract. I know of one respiratory therapist who has developed the practice of telling emphysema patients a joke to get them laughing. As a result, the plugs and globs in their bronchi are expectorated during the laughing and coughing that are their responses to the humor. The patients are more cooperative with this approach than with conventional respiratory procedures because they typically are elderly, weak, tired, and do not much feel like getting involved in the clinical procedure but are happy to hear a joke and to enjoy humor.

CATECHOLAMINES AND ALERTNESS STIMULATION

A further element of humor physiology which has clinical importance in the aging process is the mirth stimulation of catecholamine production. Catecholamine production increases found with mirth are not a simple matter. The physiology is complicated, with various catecholamine fractions reacting with various speeds and intensities. We can more aptly compare catecholamine stimulation to an orchestration than to a shot in the dark. During the past century, it has been widely accepted that catecholamines have generally stimulatory effects. That they are known popularly as alertness hormones and aggressive hormones is an indication of this stimulation. Adrenalin has a motivational role in the flight–fight response behavior. Most standard physiology textbooks provide detailed descriptions of catecholamine studies and their results.

An additional feature of catecholamine effect was demonstrated in research by McGaugh (1983), indicating a special memory stimulation function of adrenalin. McGaugh studied the effect of adrenalin on the memory power of experimental rats, using maze running as the experimental task. Increased administrations of adrenalin resulted in the animals improving their maze-learning abilities. McGaugh interpreted his data as indicating improved memory function. This improvement was found equally in young and in elderly rats.

One of the dismaying characteristics of the aging process is the fading of alertness. These changes are associated with diminished memory and retention and are a common part of the waning side of aging. This tendency can be opposed by the stimulatory effects of humor—presumably, in part, because of its enhancement of catecholamine production and greater alertness. Humor brightens human interaction and intensifies responsiveness. Clinical experience with this humor effect has been reported by the Andrus Foundation of the University of Southern California (1983) summarizing the results of their pilot study of the values of humor in a convalescent chronic care population. "The residents . . . appeared to be more aware of each other, . . . became more and more open to participation, . . . expressed more outgoing positive attitudes, . . . increased socialization among themselves (p. 58)." The alertness-enhancing, memory-benefiting, stimulatory effects of humor have also been studied by several researchers using performance of students in scholastic tasks as the measure of value. These scientists include: Browning (1979), Ziv (1982), W. Young (1982), McGhee (1982), and Goodman (1982). To summarize, they found consistency in enhancement effects of humor on mental functioning with improvements in learning, creative thinking, and memory.

Combining information from these various sources, we can create a synthesis which provides an understanding of one of the mechanisms whereby humor may achieve its recognized benefits for mental functioning. The explanation is based on the foundation that mirth stimulates increases catecholamine circulation; these increases have a salutory effect on mental alertness and memory, through an as yet undelineated catecholamine-brain interaction. As with respiratory patients described above, we can assume that this method of enhancing mental functioning with humor can be generally more acceptable to patients than are several other methods, such as administering synthetic psychostimulatory drugs or various memory-training routines.

CONCLUSION

This chapter reviews present knowledge about humor physiology— what happens in our bodies when we are exposed to humorous experiences, when we react to this humor with the emotion of mirth, and when we participate in various forms of mirth-associated behavior. Some of the more obvious applications of humor physiology are discussed within the context of health considerations, particularly as they apply to the health needs of the elderly. I am sure that there are many more applications that can be considered now and in the future.

I have deliberately limited my contribution to the subject of humor physiology, writing little about the huge and very important contributions humor, mirth, and laughter make to the emotional, cognitive, and interactional functioning and well-being of humans. The classic bedside manner of health professionals has always included a sizable portion of humor; we are, at this stage, in scientific exploration beginning to delineate the specific ways in which bedside manner humor has worked its magic, emotionally and physically, over the ages.

In this presentation, I hope that I have sufficiently underscored one central and highly important point: The remarkably intimate and pervasive impact of humor, mirth, and laughter on human functioning. These elements of human experience have an important impact on our emotional lives. They are important to the relationships between people in many ways. Also, we can now say that humor physiology involves the participation of most, if not all, of the major systems of our bodies in significant and usually beneficial ways.

REFERENCES

Andrus Foundation (1983). *Humor: the tonic you can afford.* Los Angeles: University of Southern California.

Averill, J. R. (1969). Autonomic response patterns during sadness and mirth. *Psychophysiology, 5,* 399–413.

Beneicke, U. (1967). Laughing as a releaser of petit epilepsy fits. *Psychiatry, Neurology, Medical Psychology, 19,* 380–381.

Bergson, Henri (1921). *Laughter: an essay on the meaning of the comic.* (C. Brereton & F. Rothwell, Trans.) London: Macmillan.

Berlyne, D. E. (1960). *Conflict, arousal and curiosity.* New York: McGraw-Hill.

Berlyne, D. E. (1972). Humor and its kin. In J. H. Goldstein & P. E. McGhee (Eds.), *The psychology of humor: theoretical perspectives and empirical issues* (pp. 43–60). New York: Academic Press.

Browning, R. C. (1979). *Classification and behavioral categories of humor, wit and comedy.* Paper presented at the Second International Conference on Humor, Los Angeles.

Cantu, R. C. (1966). Pathological laughing and crying associated with a tumor ventral to the pons. *Journal of Neurosurgery, 24,* 1024–1026.

Chapman, A. J. (1976). Social aspects of humorous laughter. In A. J. Chapman & H. C.

Foot (Eds.), *Humour and laughter: theory, research and applications* (pp. 155–185). London: Wiley.

Fry, W. F., Jr. (1963). *Sweet madness: A study of humor*. Palo Alto, CA: Pacific Books.

Fry, W. F., Jr. & Rader, C. (1969). Humor in a Physiologic Vein. *News of Physiological Instrumentation, July*, 3.

Fry, W. F., Jr., & Rader, C. (1977). The respiratory components of mirthful laughter. *Journal of Biological Psychology, 19*, 39–50.

Fry, W. F., Jr., & Savin, M. (1982). *Mirthful laughter and blood pressure*. Paper presented at the Third International Conference on Humor, Washington, DC.

Fry, W. F., Jr., & Stoft, P. E. (1971). Mirth and oxygen saturation levels of peripheral blood. *Psychotherapy and Psychosomatics, 19*, 76–84.

Fry, W. F., Jr., Yeager, C. L., Henderson, J. & Vreeland, R. (1972). *EEG correlates of mirth*. Unpublished raw data.

Godkewitsch, M. (1976). Physiological and verbal indices of arousal in rated humor. In A. J. Chapman & H. C. Foot (Eds.), *Humour and laughter: theory, research and application* (pp. 117–138). London: Wiley.

Goldstein, J. H., Harman, J., McGhee, P. E., & Karasik, R. (1975). Test of an information-processing model of humor: Physiological response changes during problem-and-riddle-solving. *Journal of General Psychology, 92*, 59–68.

Goodman, J. (1982). *Laughing matters: The magic of humor in the workplace, classroom and home*. Paper presented at the Third International Conference on Humor, Washington, D.C.

Gregory, J. C. (1924). *The nature of laughter*. London: Kegan Paul, Trench, Trubner.

Jones, J. M. & Harris, P. (1971). Psychophysiological correlates cartoon humor appreciation. *Proceedings of the 79th Annual Convention of the American Psychological Association*, (pp. 381–382).

Langevin, R. & Day, H. I. (1972). Physiological correlates of humor. In J. H. Goldstein & P. E. McGhee (Eds.), *The psychology of humor: theoretical perspectives and empirical issues*, (pp. 129–142). New York: Academic Press.

Levi, L. (1965). The urinary output of adrenalin and noradrenalin during pleasant and unpleasant emotional states. *Psychosomatic Medicine, 27*, 80–85.

Lloyd, E. L. (1938). The respiratory mechanism in laughter. *Journal of General Psychology, 10*, 179–189.

McGaugh, J. (1983). *Adrenalin and memory function*. Paper presented at the Annual Meeting of the Western Psychological Association.

McGhee, P. E. (1982). *Children's humor and humor in education*. Paper presented at the Third International Conference on Humor, Washington, DC.

Mindess, H. (1971). *Laughter and liberation*. Los Angeles: Nash.

Paskind, H. A. (1932): Effects of laughter on muscle tone. *Archives of Neurology and Psychiatry, 28*, 623–628.

Schachter, S. & Wheeler, L. (1962). Epinephrine, chlorpromazine, and amusement. *Journal of Abnormal and Social Psychology, 65*, 121–128.

Scheff, T. J. (1979). *Catharsis and arousal: Therapeutic use of humor*. Paper presented at the Annual Convention of the American Psychological Association.

Scheff, T. J. & Scheele, S. C. (1979). Humor and tension: The effects of comedy on audiences. In *Catharsis in healing, ritual, and drama*. Berkeley: University of California Press.

Schwartz, G. E. (1974). *Electromyographic studies during emotions*. Paper presented at the Annual Meeting of the American Psychosomatic Society.

Sroufe, L. A. & Waters, E. (1976). The ontogenesis of smiling and laughter: a perspective on the organization of development in infancy. *Psychological Review, 83,* 173–189.

Svebak, S. (1975). Respiratory patterns as predictors of laughter. *Psychophysiology, 12,* 62–65.

Svebak, S. (1977). Some characteristics of resting respiration as predictors of laughter. In A. J. Chapman & H. C. Foot (Eds.), *It's a funny thing, humour.* Oxford: Pergamon Press.

Svebak, S. (1982). The effect of mirthfulness upon amount of discordant right–left occipital EEG alpha. *Motivation and Emotion, 6,* 133–143.

Vaillant, G. E. (1977). *Adaptation to life.* Boston: Little, Brown.

Young, S. (1982). *The mechanics of human laughter.* Paper presented at the Third International Conference on Humor, Washington, D. C.

Young, W. (1982). *The effect of humor on memory.* Paper presented at the Third International Conference on Humor, Washington, D.C.

Ziv, A. (1982). *Cognitive results of using humor in teaching.* Paper presented at the Third International Conference on Humor, Washington, D.C.

PERSPECTIVES

Part II introduces some of the interesting, even extraordinary vantage points from which we can study humor and aging. Chapter 5, by Palmore, analyzes jokes about aging. In so doing, he uncovers our attitude toward old age. Chapter 6, by Seltzer, discusses timing as a key factor in humor and aging. In Chapter 7, Huych and Duchon note the rapid increase in humorous age-related greeting cards. They use them as a research tool to study fears about aging. Chapter 8, by Datan, explores the humor of the aged, finding an interwoven theme of power and despair.

99 Copyright © 1986 by Academic Press, Inc.
All rights of reproduction in any form reserved.

5

Attitudes toward Aging Shown by Humor: A Review

ERDMAN B. PALMORE

INTRODUCTION

Attitudes toward the aged are crucial for the quality of life enjoyed, or suffered, by elders in our society. Many, if not most of the problems of aging, stem from, or are exacerbated by, prejudice and discrimination against the aged. There is abundant evidence of widespread agism in our culture, including negative stereotypes and attitudes (Palmore, 1982). The majority of aged are often thought to be sick, senile, sexually impotent, unhappy, isolated, lonely, useless, and poor. There are also some positive stereotypes and pro-aged misconceptions that exaggerate such qualities as wisdom and serenity (Palmore, 1977, 1981). One problem with attempts to measure and classify such attitudes with survey research is that most people do not want to admit that they are prejudiced against the aged, or even that they are prejudiced in favor of the aged.

Humor often reveals attitudes that people do not want to admit (McGhee & Goldstein, 1972; Zwerling, 1955). Jokes are often based on unconscious assumptions that would not be admitted on a conscious level. Indeed, one of the major theories of humor is that it functions to bypass the inhibitions of the superego and allows the release of id drives such as sex and agression (Freud, 1905/1960). The

Copyright © 1986 by Academic Press, Inc.
All rights of reproduction in any form reserved.

plea, "I was only joking," is often an exuse for hostile statements or actions. The warning, "You better smile when you say that," indicates that a statement would not be acceptable unless it is excused as humor.

This chapter illustrates how content analyses of humor about the aged can be used to answer the following types of questions. How widespread are negative or ambivalent unconscious attitudes toward aging and the aged? What kinds of fears or anxieties about aging seem to be the most frequent? Which aspects of aging produce more negative or ambivalent attitudes? Does our culture have different attitudes toward aged men compared to aged women? What are the functions of humor about aging? In order to answer these questions, we review three content analyses of jokes about aging, two content analyses of cartoons about aging, two content analyses of birthday cards, one content analysis of jokes by the aged, and a debate over the methods and meaning of content analyses. We also discuss promising possibilities for future research.

CONTENT ANALYSES OF JOKES

Palmore's Analysis

The first content analysis of humor about aging was published by Palmore in 1971. His sample consisted of 264 jokes about aging and the aged collected from 10 popular joke books and from jokes he had heard. He classified these jokes according to four dimensions: subject matter, gender, activity versus disengagement, and positive versus negative view of aging. Table 5.1 presents the results of this multiple classification.

Overall, more than half of the jokes reflected a negative view of aging or the aged; that is, they implied one or more of the negative stereotypes about the aged listed in the introduction. For example, the definition of old age as an incurable disease and Emerson's assertion, "We do not count a man's years until he has nothing else to count," view old age negatively. However, over a quarter were clearly positive in their view of aging. The aged person often turned out to be more capable than expected, as in the following story:

An 80-year-old lady wanted a physical checkup because she noticed she was losing her sexual desires. When asked by her doctor when she first noticed this, she replied, "Last night and then again this morning."

TABLE 5.1
Jokes Classified by Subject, Gender, Activity–Disengagement, and
Positive–Negative Dimensions

	Number	% Positive	% Negative	% Neutral
Joke topic				
Age or longevity	59	30	46	24
Physical ability or appearance	45	9	82	9
Old-timer or old fashioned	44	55	16	29
Sexual ability or interest	31	48	41	10
Age concealment	30	0	93	7
Old maid	18	22	72	6
Retirement	14	29	36	36
Mental ability	13	8	85	8
Happiness or unhappiness	5	40	40	20
Death	5	0	80	20
All	264	27	56	17
Gender				
Men	92	35	51	15
Women	66	14	77	9
Both	106	30	48	23
Activity–disengagement				
Activity	30	67	23	10
Disengagement	45	4	78	18

Another 17% of the jokes reflected neutral or ambivalent attitudes toward the aged. Thus, almost half the jokes showed positive or ambivalent attitudes, which suggests that many attitudes toward the aged in our society are positive or neutral.

The most frequent subject of the jokes was longevity or some other aspect of aging that did not fit in any of the other subject categories; for example, "You're as young as you feel, they say, but seldom as important." These jokes reflect somewhat more positive and less negative attitudes that average, which indicates that longevity may be viewed somewhat more positively than other aspects of aging.

The second most frequent subject was the physical ability or appearance of the aged:

A 70-year-old man who loved to square dance went to a doctor because his right knee began to give him trouble. After a thorough examination, which revealed no specific disease, the doctor carefully explained that as a person ages, the cartilage and connective tissues often shrink and suffer from poor circulation and that his knee trouble appeared to be simply a result of aging. The patient replied, "I still don't understand, because my left knee is just as old as my right knee, and it doesn't give me a bit of trouble."

The frequency of such stories indicates that fear about physical decline in aging is a primary concern in our society. This interpretation is supported by the fact that 82% of the jokes on this subject reflect a negative view of physical abilities among the aged.

Almost as frequent were jokes about old-timers or old-fashioned ways. In contrast to the previous category, the majority of these jokes reflected a positive view of the old-timer of old-fashioned ways, such as the definition of an old-timer as one who can remember when virtue was a virtue and not a vice. Only 16% of these jokes were negative in attitude, indicating that most old-timer jokes reflect a certain respect for old-timers and nostalgia for their old-fashioned ways.

The next most frequent subject was the sexual ability or interest of the aged, such as Oscar Wilde's assertion, "Young men want to be faithful and are not; old men want to be faithless and cannot." (Prochnow, 1969) These jokes are almost equally divided between a positive view and a negative or ambivalent view, which may indicate that many people both fear declining sexual abilities in old age and cherish the hope that their ability will not disappear.

Next in frequency come the jokes about age concealment, such as the man who confided to a friend, "It's terrible to grow old alone—my wife hasn't had a birthday in 6 years." Most of these jokes are classified as negative in attitude because they imply something shameful about aging and a mild dishonesty in attempting to pass as a younger person.

Almost three-fourths of the "old maid" jokes were also classified as negative because the old maids were usually viewed as lonely, frustrated, shriveled, and so forth. For example, an old maid was variously defined as "an evaporated peach," "a lemon that has never been squeezed," "a girl who failed to strike while the iron was hot" and " a woman who is always looking under her bed in hope of finding a burglar." These negative views seem to reflect the traditional social norm that women should marry and those who do not by the time they become aged are to be pitied and censured. It is significant that there were no "old bachelor" jokes.

Retirement jokes were almost equally divided between those with a positive attitude toward retirement (Willie cries because he doesn't like school but has to stay there until he's 15; the teacher replies,

"Don't let that worry you, I have to stay here until I'm 65"); those with a negative view of retirement ("Don't retire; retire problems"); and those with a neutral or ambivalent view ("When a man retires and time is no longer a matter urgent importance, his colleagues generally present him with a clock"). This seems to reflect society's mixed views of retirement with its positive and negative aspects.

In contrast, most of the mental ability jokes were negative and seemed to reflect beliefs and fears of declining mental function in old age such as the four stages of memory loss: (1) forget names, (2) forget faces, (3) forget to zip up fly, (4) forget to zip down fly.

The last two subject categories, happiness (unhappiness) and death have only five jokes each, or less than 2% of the total of each category. An example of the happiness category is the 90-year-old man who was asked on his birthday how it felt to be 90 years old. He replied, "Great, when you consider the alternative." An example of jokes dealing with death is the following story:

A funeral of a comedian in London was attended by many old-time comedians who had gathered to say a last farewell. During the ceremony, one man looked up at his neighbor and asked, "'Ow old are you, Charlie?" "Ninety," replied the old-timer. " 'Ardly worth going 'ome, eh?"

The infrequency of such jokes may indicate that there is less concern about unhappiness or death in old age than about other aspects of being old. There is considerable evidence that shows most aged persons are not especially worried or unhappy nor do they fear death more than younger persons (Riley & Foner, 1968).

More than twice as large a proportion of jokes about men were positive compared to jokes about women. More than three-fourths of the jokes about women were negative. This suggests that our society views aging among women more negatively than aging among men. Two other pieces of evidence support this conclusion. While the term *old maid* generally has negative connotations, there is no corresponding negative term for men such as *old bachelor*. Apparently, old unmarried men are not the object of pity or censure the way old unmarried women are. This may be related to our traditional double standard, which views the extramarital sex relations of men more tolerantly than the extramarital sex relations of women. Even more significant is the fact that nearly all the age concealment jokes refer to women. Perhaps the most likely explanation of this fact is that in our society it is more important for women to keep their youthful appearance because they are more dependent than men on their physical attractiveness for self-esteem and status. Men are more likely to have other bases for self-esteem and status, such as occupation or positions of leadership in various organizations. These bases do not deteriorate as rapidly with aging as does youthful appearance. This may be another result of male dominance in our society. It certainly indicates a double standard of aging in which women seem more ashamed of aging than men.

The tabulation of attitudes by whether the jokes related to an activity or disengagement theory of aging showed that two-thirds of the jokes that implied that the aged can or should remain active reflected positive views of aging, while three-fourths of those implying that the aged do or should disengage reflect negative views of the aged. This suggests that those favoring the activity theory of aging tend to be more optimistic and positive about elders' capabilities and adjustment than those favoring the disengagement theory.

Davies' Analysis

The second content analysis of jokes about aging used a sample of 550 jokes found in six joke anthologies (Davies, 1977). This analysis tabulated the jokes according to three dimensions: subjects, positive–negative views of aging, and gender of the referent. Like Palmore, Davies found that over half (63%) of the jokes were negative toward aging. He also found that jokes about sexual or physical aspects of aging were the two most frequent subjects, just as Palmore found them to be among the most frequent subjects. The frequencies of mental aspects, age concealment, and old maid or bachelor jokes were also similar to the frequencies in Palmore's analysis. Finally, his analysis also agrees with Palmore's finding that jokes about older women were substantially more negative than jokes about older men.

Davies found substantially more jokes about death (over a third of the total). However, this may be because he was specifically searching for jokes about death, while Palmore was primarily looking for jokes about aging in which death may have been involved. Somewhat surprisingly, he found that about the same proportion of the jokes about aging (63%) were negative, as were the jokes about death (57%). This seems to indicate that our culture views aging as negatively as death itself.

Davies recommended that there be various interventions to reduce the negative attitudes toward aging supported by the negative jokes. He recommended courses and programs on aging at all educational organizations and at all levels. At the personal level, he recommended reacting against and refusing to laugh at negative stereotyping of aging in humor. He also recommended that various organizations, such as the National Council on Aging and the Grey Panthers, set up committees to monitor and to object to the use of negative humor about aging and negative portrayals of the aging in the media.

Richman's Analysis

The third content analysis of jokes on aging was published in the same issue of *The Gerontologist* as Davies' analysis. Richman (1977) compared 100 jokes about the aged with 160 jokes about children. He, too, found that over half (66%) of the jokes about the aged were negative, but only one-fourth of the jokes about children were negative. Thus, he concluded that the predominance of negative jokes about the aged could not be explained by assuming that all jokes tend to be negative. This finding is consistent with other evidence that children are viewed more positively in our culture than are the aged.

Richman categorized jokes in terms of both their overt and covert themes. Nevertheless, he, too, found the most frequent themes to be physical or mental aspects, sexual ability, and age concealment. He found that the covert message of the age concealment jokes, as well as many others, was that one must deal with and accept one's developmental stage and the tasks of that stage. These jokes criticize the desire of the old to be other than what they are.

He also found three fairly frequent positive themes. The affirmation of life was illustrated by the story of the old man who threw down his heavy burden and cried out for the Angel of Death to come and take him. However, when the Angel of Death appeared, the man changed his mind and asked the angel to help him get his burden back on his shoulders.

The theme of sex as an affirmation of life was illustrated by the story of the young bull and the old bull. The young bull said he was going to run down the hill and make love to one of the cows in the valley. The old bull said he was going to walk down the hill and make love to all the cows in the valley.

The third positive theme, aging as a value in its own right, was illustrated by the story of the old man who said to his grandson that he wished he could feel like a child again. The grandson replied, "Then why don't you get mamma to spank you?" This joke points out one advantage of old age compared to childhood: greater freedom.

Richman found that a theme common to both jokes about the aged and jokes about children was the *battle between generations*. He speculates that the dynamic basis of some of the negative attitudes toward the aged is derived from the unresolved early conflicts of children with their parents that are continued and maintained throughout the life span.

THE DEBATE OVER METHODS AND MEANING

Criticisms

Weber and Cameron (1978) questioned the conclusions of the previous three content analyses by pointing out that none of them tested the reliability of their positive–negative classifications. They claimed that "it is extremely difficult to make any interpretations of the attitude manifested in a particular joke" (p. 73). They suggested that independent judges should be used in such content analyses to test the reliability of such judgments.

Furthermore, they asserted that so-called negative jokes may serve a variety of positive functions, such as the following:

1. Social satire. Negative jokes about the position of the aged in society might be a means of criticizing and accenting the inequities of our society concerning the way the aged are treated in comparison to other groups. In this case, the joke might be viewed as an agent of social change. For example, they cite the following negative joke:

A small boy was sitting at a curb, crying. An old man passed by and kindly asked, "Why are you crying, Sonny?" "Because I can't do what the big boys do." So the old man sat down and cried too. (p. 74)

Weber and Cameron claim that this joke calls attention to the segregation of both younger and older groups from the mainstream activities of life and makes a covert proposal to include both old and young in the "big boys' " activities.

2. "Healthy" criticism of aged. They cite the preceeding joke as an example of how a healthy criticism is being made of the elderly's desire to be other than what they are. Richman (1977) also noted that some negative jokes "emphasize the importance of self-acceptance and dealing with age appropriate tasks" (p. 213). (However, this raises the question, What are age-appropriate tasks? Sexual activity is not usually inappropriate among healthy aged.)

3. Self-criticism by the aged. They assert that many of these negative jokes were generated by, or at least circulating among, the elderly themselves. This possibility is supported by the research of Richman and Tallmer (1976) reviewed below.

4. Transcendence. Weber and Cameron assert:

> The individual who responds with humor to the realities of growing old may have learned to live with what some perceive to be the "tragedy of aging" without giving it the final word. Laughter, in this case, recognizes the false permanancies [SIC] of trying to 'stay young' and gives one the freedom to look at life with a 'transcendent smile.' (p. 75).

Thus, humor may function to bring about acceptance and transcendence of aging.

Because of these many positive functions, they disagree with Davies' recommendations for various interventions to oppose negative jokes about aging.

Replies

The three authors criticised by Weber and Cameron replied in the same issue of *The Gerontologist* as follows:

Palmore (1978) agreed that it is sometimes difficult to decide on the attitude that a joke is conveying. He encouraged the commentators and others to use independent judges to check the reliabilities of the coding. However, he pointed out that the similarity of findings in all three independent content analyses indicates a kind of reliability of the overall findings. He also agreed that "it appears wise to refrain from making social policy statements about the place of 'negative' jokes about aging in society until we know a great deal more about the functions of such jokes" (Weber & Cameron, 1978, p. 75). However, he asserted, "Just as we have become more aware of and sensitive to racism and sexism wearing the mask of 'humor' about blacks and women, I think a greater awareness of ageism in humor would be a healthy thing for us as individuals and as a society" (p. 76).

Davies (1978) also pointed out that the consistency of negative findings by the three independent assessments of a large number of jokes from different sources gives support to the reliability of the findings. Furthermore, he pointed out that a large amount of supportive data about negative attitudes to aging in our society is referred to in the original articles. He also disagreed that negative humor could have positive effects. He argued that by focusing upon decrements, negative humor has a stereotyping effect that emphasizes liabilities instead of strengths and also creates an ingroup (the young) versus outgroup (the old) effect.

Richman (1978) recognized that there is a subjective element to the analysis of jokes but argued that it is a creative activity, as in the skillful analysis of dreams. He recognized that multiple meanings may be read into them but that differing interpretations need not necessarily mean disagreement. In preparing his reply, he did a test of reliability asking seven colleagues to rate the five jokes discussed by Weber and Cameron as being positive or negative in attitude toward aging. There was 86% agreement with the original ratings, and three of the seven raters agreed 100%. He considered this acceptably high reliability for the purpose of the analysis. However, he did agree with Weber and Cameron that there should be no movement to censor or criticize jokes about the aged.

CONTENT ANALYSES OF CARTOONS

Smith's Analysis

Smith (1979) analyzed 2217 cartoons from eight magazines with large circulations. He found that elders appeared in less than 5% of these cartoons and appeared in only 1.5% of the women's magazines. He suggested that this relative absence in women's magazines "may reflect an attempt to insulate female readers from images of aging, due to societal norms which especially devalue and denigrate the aging process among women" (p. 409).

As for the attitudes toward elders conveyed by the cartoons, he found that over half were ambivalent or neutral. Only 21% were positive (which is similar to the analyses of jokes) and 26% were negative (which is substantially less than in the analyses of jokes). Cartoons about non-aged adults and about children were predominately neutral (over 85%). Smith did a formal test for reliability of the ratings among the independent coders and found a reliability coefficient of .80.

He found that themes most often associated with negativism toward the aged were those of sexual dysfunction and ultraconservatism. Positive themes were primarily depicted through unusual roles for the elderly. This type of humor depends on perceived incongruities or departure from the expected. An example given was of an older man walking away from an apparent mugger who is lying on the street tied in knots. "Senior Power" is the elder's parting comment.

Smith found no difference between the genders as to proportion negative or positive (in contrast to the analyses of jokes) but did find men substantially overrepresented in the cartoons (in agreement with the analyses of jokes). He concluded that both the rarity of elders in cartoons and the tendency toward a negative view of elders (when there was a viewpoint) provides further documentation of the pervasive agism in our society.

Polisar's Analysis

Polisar (1982) did a content analysis of 500 cartoons from the *New Yorker* (1982). She found that somewhat more of these cartoons dealt with the elderly (10%), but the proportions of pro-aged (25%), anti-aged (28%), and ambivalent (47%) were similar to the proportions found by Smith. The most frequent themes were conservatism/old-fashioned (20%), physical appearance (20%), and best time of life (18%). The themes of old maid/dirty old man (10%) and age concealment (10%) were moderately frequent. She also analyzed the portrayal of elders in commercials, situation comedies, movies, and talk shows on television. She concluded that attitudes toward aging shown in the media tend to be ambivalent, but this ambivalence often leans toward the negative as a result of agism fostered by negative stereotypes.

Birthday Card Analysis

Two content analyses of birthday cards are included here because these cards usually contain some kind of cartoon or picture. Two sociologists (Demos & Jache, 1981) analyzed a sample of birthday cards and found that over half of them portrayed aging as negative, and this was especially true for women. The majority of them pointed out a decline in appearance: wrinkles, gray hair, and loss of sexual attractiveness.

The other analysis (Dillon & Jones, 1981) found that most of the birthday cards with an aging theme (27% of the total cards) were negative and dealt with physical or mental loss (56%), age concealment (25%), sympathy (3%), or not showing one's age (6%). Only 9% were positive and implied that things get better with age or that aging is just a matter of mental attitude.

JOKES BY THE AGED

The only published analysis of jokes by the aged used 144 jokes told by older people (aged 60–90) living in the community, some from nursing homes and some enrolled in a college course (Richman & Tallmer, 1976). They cite the following as a typical joke about sexual decline told by a 75-year-old man.

There was a little old Jewish man who went to the doctor for a checkup. The doctor checks him over and says, "You are in fine physical shape, so what is bothering you?" The little old man says, "I still have the desire to have an active sex life, but I can't." The doctor says, "I just came back from a symposium where we discussed this problem. The cure is to eat 20 pounds of pumpernickel bread." The old man thanks the doctor and leaves. He then goes to a bakery and asks for the 20 pounds of bread. The woman behind the counter says, "Are you having a party, Mr. Goldberg?" He answers, "No." She says, "But Mr. Goldberg, it will get hard." "In that case," says Mr. Goldberg, "I'll take 40 pounds." (p. 5)

When they analyzed jokes by major themes, they found that by far the most frequent theme was sex, with one-third placed in that category. This was true of jokes told by all ages. They concluded from this that sex is an enduring topic that maintains its interest, if not its possibility, throughout the life span. However, among those over 70, 43% of the jokes told by males were sexual, in contrast to only 20% of the jokes told by females. The researchers were not sure whether this meant that sex is less a concern of older women than older men or that women were less likely to discuss sex with the male researchers. The latter possibility should be examined in future studies by varying the gender of the interviewer.

Furthermore, they found four major attitudes evident in these sexual jokes:

1. an awareness of decline, with an ability to laugh at oneself,
2. an affirmation that while there's life, there's sex,
3. an association of sex with fertility, pregnancy, birth control, and birth, and
4. a vicarious identification with the sexual activities of the young.

The second most popular theme was death (17%), sometimes containing an affirmation of life. Some of these jokes represented both anxiety over death and an ability to laugh at this anxiety. For example, this joke was told by a 92-year-old man:

While a minister was recovering from an operation, the nurse pulled down the shades. "Why are you doing that?" asked the wife. "The house next door is on fire," said the nurse, "and I don't want your husband to wake up and think the operation was a failure!"

The third theme was personal, physical, or mental decline (15%). When one adds several of the sex and death jokes, about one-fourth of all the jokes touched upon decline or loss. But it was also true that a sizeable majority were concerned with life and activity, not death and senescence. All of the jokes in which age is associated with a loss of attractiveness were about women, which reflects the stereotype that women are more concerned with age declines in appearance and attractiveness than are men.

Another frequent theme was orality and drinking (16%). An example of orality as a substitute for sex was the woman whose doctor advised her to take orange juice as a birth control device. She asked if she should take it before or after sex, and he replied, "Instead." Less frequent themes were anality, marital dissatisfaction or infidelity, and work. The latter two themes were told mainly by persons under age 70.

Two major differences in the frequency of themes in jokes told by the aged in contrast to jokes about the aged are the following.

1. There were no jokes told by the aged about age concealment, while that was one of the most frequent themes of jokes about the aged. It is unclear whether this means that older people rarely lie about their age or that they do but don't like to joke about it.

2. Only 3% of jokes told by the aged were about loss of attractiveness, in contrast to the frequency of this theme in jokes about aging. Again the interpretation is unclear: Are the aged rarely concerned about loss of attractiveness, or are they so concerned that they do not joke about it? Jokes are considered funny only when they do not produce too much anxiety.

One of the frequent pronouncements implied by these jokes is that vicarious pleasure in the young is consistent with appropriate goals of aging. The difficulty comes if one attempts to *be* young rather than to appreciate and to enjoy the young. A second frequent pronouncement is that forced retirement at age 65, when the healthy individual is still very much involved and not ready to retire, is very questionable and even ridiculous. Finally, the authors note that most of these joketellers "are not about to disengage," and so they suggest that if they want to remain engaged, they must preserve their sense of humor. (This raises the question of how one can preserve a sense of humor. Does one need to practice? Does one need to "use it or lose it"?)

FUNCTIONS OF HUMOR ABOUT AGING

It may help to clarify the various functions of humor about aging if we review the basic concept of humor and classic theories about humor in general. A basic definition of humor would be communication using incongruity and its resolution with the intention of producing mirth. (This definition was worked out by the following participants in the Conference on Humor and Aging: Eli and Marcy Cohen, Eve and Lennard Gottesman, Brydie and Erdman Palmore.) This definition clarifies that humor is an intentional communication (not an accident or something funny that just happens); that it must contain some incongruity and its resolution (a joke has no point unless both elements are present); and that the intention of humor is to produce mirth (whether or not it succeeds). Thus, the basic function of humor is to produce mirth, but there are various theories about why mirth is produced and its effects.

Perhaps the oldest theory is that humor is based on the surprising contrast between expectations and actuality. Plato saw this as the basis for classical comedy in the general form of impotence masquerading as fate. The typical situation is that a terrible fate arises from which there appears to be no escape; but suddenly, the fate turns out to be not a fate after all, since it is not able to put its threat into effect (Feibleman, 1939). This theory was later reflected in Kant's statement (1911) that laughter is "an affection arising from a strained expectation being suddenly reduced to nothing" (p. 10).

This theory is illustrated by the story of the 80-year-old lady who was complaining to a friend that she had a lot of trouble during the night because a man kept banging on her door. When her friend asked, "Why didn't you open the door?" the lady replied, "What? And let him out?" Here the expected trouble is reduced to a potentially enjoyable adventure.

Many of the jokes with positive attitudes toward the aged have the theme that fears about aging are unwarranted because the aged person is not so bad off after all. The following example probably reflects fears of disability in old age:

An old lady who lived on the second floor of a rooming house was warned by the doctor, as he placed a cast on her broken leg, not to climb stairs. After several months he took off the cast. "Can I climb stairs now?" she asked. "Yes," he replied. "Good. I'm sick and tired of shinnying up and down that drainpipe!"

Jokes that fit this theory function to challenge the stereotypes about aging and thus may have a healthy effect on attitudes toward aging.

Another classic theory of humor advanced by Jamblichus, the Greek philosopher, was that comedy emphasized the ugly in order to demand a change for something preferable (Feibleman, 1939). The following criticisms of old people seem to fit this theory:

As people grow older, they often confuse being careful with being wise.

Old Age: that period of life in which we compound for the vices that we still cherish by reviling those vices that we no longer have the enterprise to commit.

Many a man who can't direct you to a corner drugstore will get a respectful hearing when age has further impaired his mind.

One might argue that jokes that fit this theory are a kind of social criticism and serve a useful function in bringing about desired social change.

A more recent theory of humor is stated by Hobbes (1839), "The passion of laughter is nothing else but sudden glory arising from some sudden conception of some eminency in ourselves, by comparison with the infirmity of others" (p. 101).

When applied to jokes about the aged, this theory would say that we often laugh at the infirmity or incapacity of the aged because it makes us feel superior by comparison. This is illustrated by the following definition of old age: that time of life when a man flirts with girls but can't remember why. Or by this description of the sexual life cycle of man: tri-weekly, try weekly, try weakly. It seems clear that jokes that fit this theory function to reinforce negative stereotypes about aging.

The final theory we consider is Freud's (1905/1960): Humor is pleasurable because it outwits the inhibitions of the superego and allows the release of id drives such as sex and aggression. Clearly, many of the jokes about the aged are sexually titillating, such as the one about the 90-year-old man who married a beautiful 18-year-old girl. It seems he only lasted 5 days, but it took the undertaker 3 days to get the smile off his face. In a similar vein is the story of the old lady who was held up by a robber who proceeded to frisk her for money. After a thorough search all over her body, he gave up; but she exclaimed, "Heavens, young man. Don't stop now—I'll write you a check."

As for jokes that would release aggressive drives against the aged, there seemed to be few clear examples, if any. Of course many jokes show negative attitudes toward the aged in varying degrees. The following two semihumorous quotations seem to reveal hostile, if not aggressive, impulses toward the aged:

Age is no cause for veneration. An old crocodile is still a menace and an old crow sings not like a nightingale.

Some old women and men grow bitter with age; the more their teeth drop out, the more biting they get.

A variation of this Freudian theory is that humor allows us to deal with repressed fears, such as fears of sexual impotency, disability, and death.

The value of humor in releasing such inhibitions appears quite debatable and may depend on which inhibitions are released and how they are released. Releasing inhibitions against the sex drive, as long as the expression of the drive is limited to telling jokes, seems fairly harmless. Releasing aggressive drives may have more negative effects. Releasing repressed fears may be positive or negative depending on how they are dealt with.

In summary, it seems clear that humor about aging has many functions, some positive and some negative. No blanket statement is justified. The function of each joke should be judged individually and by each of us as individuals. This is also true of a joke's *basic* function: Does it make us smile or laugh? Clearly, the question of whether a joke is funny or not is highly subjective and a matter of personal taste. While we might all agree that "bad" jokes should be discouraged, we would probably have great difficulty agreeing as to which are the bad jokes.

FUTURE RESEARCH

Content analyses of humor published during various periods in the past could be used to trace changes in attitudes toward the aged. For example, if attitudes toward the aged were more positive before the Industrial Revolution, as some historians have suggested (Achenbaum, 1979; Fischer, 1978), then more of the humor on aging published before the Industrial Revolution should be positive toward the aged.

Similarly, humor about aging could be compared cross-culturally. If attitudes toward aging are more positive in Oriental and other more traditional societies, then more of the humor on aging in those societies should be positive compared to such humor in this country.

The causes and consequences of a sense of humor about aging would be another promising field of research. Such research would first have to develop a reliable and valid measure of a sense of humor about aging. A sense of humor about aging could be defined as the ability to understand and enjoy humor about aging. A scale to measure this sense might distinguish between positive and negative subscales. The positive subscale could be based on enjoyment of jokes with a positive view of aging, and the negative subscale on enjoyment of jokes with a negative view. Then one could do cross-sectional surveys to find the correlates of the overall sense of humor about aging and of the positive and negative subscales. Such surveys could answer questions such as the following, Is there a greater sense of humor about aging among the aged than among the young and middle-aged? Is the humor about aging among the aged more positive than among younger persons? Is the humor about aging among women more negative than among men? Do higher socioeconomic groups have a greater sense of humor or more positive humor about aging? Do healthy active people have more humor and more positive humor about aging?

The next step would be longitudinal surveys to find out what prior characteristics predict a greater sense of humor, or more positive humor, and what consequences result from more, or more positive, humor. Does a greater sense of humor result in better physical or mental health, better adjustment to aging, or greater longevity?

Another method of research would be experimental, in which one attempted to change the sense of humor through some kind of training program. If one could change the sense of humor, then one could experiment to see the effects of the changes.

In other words, sense of humor about aging could become a standard variable for gerontological research just as life satisfaction, physical and mental health, income adequacy, and so forth, are standard variables. It could be used as an independent variable to examine its effects, as well as a dependent variable to examine its antecedents. All the standard methodologies—cross-sectional, longitudinal, and experimental—could be used to study it. The possibilities seem limited only by our creativity and the resources available.

CONCLUSIONS

Despite a diversity of methods and materials, fairly consistent findings emerge from these analyses of humor about or by the aged. The majority of this humor shows negative attidutes toward aging, and little of it shows clearly positive attitudes. Certain themes tend to predominate, such as longevity, physical or mental ability, appearance and attractiveness, sexual ability or interest, and age concealment. Jokes about old women tend to be more negative than those about old men. Humor about aging has many functions, some positive and some negative, and judgments about such functions are at present highly subjective. Additional research, using cross-sectional, longitudinal, and experimental methods, is needed to understand the causes and consequences of such humor. In the meantime, perhaps we can all agree that humor about aging is one of the most entertaining and interesting topics in all of gerontology.

REFERENCES

Achenbaum, W. (1979). *Old age in a new land.* Baltimore, MD: Johns Hopkins Press.
Bohn, J. (Ed.). (1939). *The English work of Thomas Hobbes* (Vol. 4). London: Clarendon Press.
Davies, L. (1977). Attitudes toward old age & aging as shown by humor. *Gerontologist, 17,* 220–226.
Davies, L. (1978). Mr. Davies replies. *Gerontologist, 18,* 76–77.
Demos, V., & Jache, A. (1981, September 22). Return to sender—please! *Woman's Day,* pp. 20–21.
Dillon, K. & Jones, B. (1981). Attitudes toward aging portrayed by birthday cards. *International Journal of Aging & Human Development, 13,* 79–84.
Feibleman, J. (1939). *In praise of comedy.* London: Allen & Unvoid.
Fischer, D. (1978). *Growing old in America.* New York: Oxford University Press.
Freud, S. (1960). *Jokes and their relation to the unconscious.* In James Straches (Ed. & Trans.), *The complete psychological works of Sigmund Freud* (Vol. 8). London: Hogarth Press. (Original work published 1905).

Kant, E. (1911). *Critique of aesthetic judgement.* Oxford, England: Chanadon Press.

McGhee, P. & Goldstein, J. (1972). Advances towards the understanding of humor. In J. Goldstein & P. McGhee (Eds.), *The psychology of humor.* New York: Academic Press.

Palmore, E. (1971). Attitudes toward aging as shown by humor. *Gerontologist, 11,* 181–186.

Palmore, E. (1977). Facts on aging: A short quiz. *Gerontologist, 17,* 315–320.

Palmore, E. (1978). Dr. Palmore replies. *Gerontologist, 18,* 76.

Palmore, E. (1981). Facts on aging quiz: Part 2. *Gerontologist, 21*(4), 431–437.

Palmore, E. (1982). Attitudes toward the aged. *Research on Aging, 4*(3), 333–348.

Polisar, D. (1982, April). *Figurative aging.* Paper presented at Southern Sociological Society Meeting in Memphis, TN.

Prochnow, H. (1969). *A treasure of humorous quotations.* New York: Harper & Row.

Richman, J. (1977). The foolishness and wisdom of age: Attitudes toward the elderly as reflected in jokes. *Gerontologist, 17,* 210–219.

Richman, J. (1978). Dr. Richman replies. *Gerontologist, 18,* 77–79.

Richman, J. & Tallmer, M. (1976, November). *Jokes by the aged.* Paper presented at 29th Annual Meeting of the Gerontological Society, New York, NY.

Riley, M. & Foner, A. (1968). *Aging and society: Vol. 1. An inventory of research findings.* New York: Russell Sage Foundation.

Smith, M. (1979). The portrayal of elders in magazine cartoons. *Gerontologist, 19*(4), 408–412.

Weber, T. & Cameron, P. (1978). Humor & Aging—A response. *Gerontologist, 18,* 73–76.

Zwerling, I. (1955). The favorite joke in diagnostic and therapeutic interviewing. *Psychoanalytic Quarterly, 24,* 104–115.

6

Timing: The Significant Common Variable in Both Humor and Aging

MILDRED M. SELTZER

INTRODUCTION

There is an old joke about an interview with the most famous comedian in the world:

Q: They tell me you're the most famous comedian to the world.
A: That's right.
Q: To what do you attribute——
A: Timing.

One is tempted, in response to this joke, to ask, "What's funny about the joke?" The answer is, "Timing, and who knows?" The contributors to this volume focus on various aspects, perspectives, and components of the relationships between aging and humor. This chapter focuses on the time and timing aspects of both humor and aging.

Those writing chapters for this book, as well as authors of other publications, discuss some of the difficulties in defining humor and its essence. People may agree that something is humorous but have difficulty in identifying the basis for their agreement. Boskin (1979),

Copyright © 1986 by Academic Press, Inc.
All rights of reproduction in any form reserved.

McGhee (1979), and others (e.g., Chapman & Foot, 1976) refer to the range of humor behaviors, the functions of humor, and its categories. McGhee, for example, compares humor to beauty saying that it "exits[s] only in our minds and not [in] the real world" (1979, p. 6). To paraphrase another, earlier scientist, We think, therefore humor exists.

Humor has been the subject of psychological analysis, approached primarily from either a psychoanalytic or cognitive perspective. The limitations in laboratory studies of humor are self-evident: In vitro humor lacks the spontaneity that is so large a factor in real life humor. Moreover, because subjects for research projects are often chosen from the available pool of school or college age students, findings apply to only a small part of the life span. An exception is Schaier and Cicirelli's study (1976), which used a Piagetian framework to compare humor comprehension in three age groups (50–59, 60–69, and 70–79). They found that those in the older group did not understand the jokes as well as did the younger ones but that the older people thought the jokes were funnier than did the younger ones.

While there is a considerable body of literature about the psychology and social psychology of humor, a cursory review of life span development textbooks suggests that humor is a neglected aspect of middle and late life. Birren, Cunningham, and Yamamoto, in the 1983 *Annual Review of Psychology*, "Psychology of Adult Development and Aging," devoted two sentences to the subject of humor. These authors noted that "humor is beginning to be discussed in relation to age" and that it may be "one of the strategies that individuals use in adapting to the stresses of life" (p. 561).

While for the most part sociologists have not devoted as much attention to humor as have psychologists, a number of them have dealt with the topic. They have focused on humor's role in conflict, as a mechanism of social control, as a way of strengthening ingroup relationships or of expressing tension between groups, and as a form of communication (Klapp, 1950; Obrdlik, 1942). Myrdal (1944) called attention to the role of humor in black–white relationships. He pointed out its social functions "as symbolic excuse for imperfections, a point to what would otherwise be ambiguous. It also gives compensation to the sufferer. The 'understanding laugh' is an intuitive absolution between sinners and sometimes between the sinner and his victim" (p. 38). Further, jokes serve to make those telling them feel superior to those who are the butt of the jokes. Jokes also serve as a means of creating collective and covert approval for what cannot be overtly approved because of our moral standards (p. 38).

Martineau (1972) in his chapter, "A Model of the Social Functions of Humor," reviews the development of a sociology of humor until 1972. He notes the universality of humor in all social systems and in human interactions. Others have dealt with specific aspects of humor (Atchley, 1971; Coser, 1959; Emerson, 1969; Zijderveld, 1969). There are also periodic calls for an increased interest in a sociology of humor. Koller (1978), for example, called for the development of a sociology of humor that would examine social variables related to humor and for the development of a network of sociologists interested in the study of humor.

It would be inappropriate to leave even a brief discussion of the social aspects of humor without acknowledging the early contributions of works of Radcliffe-Brown (1952). Early in the twentieth century, he described the "joking relationship" as a relationship between two people, "one in which one is by custom permitted, and in some instances required, to tease or make fun of the other, who in turn is required to take no offense" (p. 90). Joking relationships can be either symmetrical or asymmetrical. The former are those in which the teasing or joking is mutual, while the latter are characterized by little or unequal reciprocity. A more complete discussion of a sociology of humor can be found in Rosenberg (Chapter 9, this volume).

A perspective of humor that cuts across both psychology and scoiology is the matter of timing. Consideration of the relationship between timing and humor as both relate to aging is the concern of the balance of this chapter.

PSYCHOLOGICAL TIMING

As we all know, our appreciation of humor is seriously affected by timing, both in the introduction of humorous material and within the material itself. "I'm not in the mood now" is an almost impenetrable barrier to the would-be comedian. Even when the time is right, effective timing in presentation is what distinguishes the successful jokester from the party bore. The professional stand-up comic's cadence is the product of years of trial-and-error practice to achieve the effective pace for presenting material, for instance, the now-classic lengthy pause of Jack Benny in answer to the holdup man's, "Your money or your life."

Watching the masters, we as an audience are aware that humor is creative (Berlyne, 1972; Koestler, 1964). In fact, Atchely (personal communication, March 18, 1983) suggested that humor is the poor peoples' creative art.

Timing distinguishes tragedy from humor as Holland (1982) points out, "A tragedy is just a comedy slowed down, you could say. Conversely, if we speed tragic 'serious' things up they get funny." In a broader sense, time and timing and their meaning, measurement, and dimensions are highly individualized concepts. In *Patterning of Time*, Doob (1971) points out that time permeates every arena of human existence and that, regardless of what we may be able to change in our lives and social systems, we are unable to "affect the passing of time; at the very most we make only suitable adjustments to it" (p. 5).

Kastenbaum's (1982) chapter, "Time Course and Time Perspective in Later Life," contains a discussion of the complexities in dealing with the meanings, perceptions, and perspectives of time. He points out that "human aging involves a complex relationship with the fourth dimension. . . . We create our own time frameworks as well, however, as individuals and as a society" (p. 80). He goes on to observe that, unlike most topics covered in the *Annual Review of Gerontology and Geriatrics*, time is still unshaped as a field of study. Other topics have "reasonable coherent histories that can be updated" (p. 81). Aside from the fact that it is extraordinarily difficult to define time, one is faced with other problems: How do individuals measure and deal with time? Does one's perspective change throughout the life cycle? If there are changes, are these developmental or situational or are other factors involved? Equally, if not more important, Kastenbaum raises the question about what time perspective is. Our memories are our time machines and our language its mechanism. Some people live in the past (the Sunset Boulevard complex), while others are future oriented. Elsewhere (1983) I have referred to old people as temporal immigrants, people who have immigrated from the past to the present. Mead referred to "a new figure, migration in time" (1970, p. 48). As we age, we create and recreate our pasts, our presents, and our expected futures. These themes persist in life-span books, articles, developmental theorists' works, and in sociological and social psychological analyses of aging (see, for example, Bortner, 1979; Hendricks, 1982; Neugarten & Hagestad, 1976; Troll & Seltzer, in preparation).

SOCIAL TIMING

Industrialized societies are, to a great extent, shaped by calendars and clocks. The integration of the social system is dependent in part upon the temporal coordination of peoples' activities through such devices as airline schedules, class schedules, work shifts, and public transportation systems. Similarly, the allocation of many positions in social systems is based on chronological age (see, for example, Atchley, 1975; Cain, 1981; Neugarten, 1981). Legislation, such as the Social Security Act, Older Americans Act, Anti-Age Discrimination in Employment Act, and the Age Discrimination Act, attests to the importance of chronological age as an impersonal, legal criterion for eligibility for services and as a basis for or protection against discrimination. It is virtually impossible to discuss social organization without reference to temporal dimensions and equally impossible to discuss social organization without reference to the aging of individuals and populations.

As individuals we are affected by social time. Our built-in social calendars (Hareven, 1982; Neugarten & Hagestad, 1976; Neugarten, Moore, & Lowe, 1968) inform us when to marry, produce children, attend school, retire. Age-related norms function as standards against which to measure whether we are *on time* or *off time* for life events. The college student of 55, the bride of 14, the mother at 12, the father-for-the-first-time at 60 are nonnormative or atypical for their ages. Their *age* and *stage* of life do not match. People who are off-time in relation to other people of their ages and stages often experience time-disordered relationships (Seltzer, 1976) because the various spheres of their lives are not synchronized. They may be on schedule in their careers and off-time in their parenthood. The most significant aspect of an event may be its timing rather than its occurrence. *When* something happens (birth, death, unemployment) may be more important than the fact that it happened. Becoming a widow at age 25, for example, is thought to be more stressful than becoming one at 75, when one might, at least statistically, be expected to be widowed, given the fact that almost 70% of women 75 and older are widowed. All of these themes are temporal ones, and we see their persistence in life span books, articles, developmental theorists' works and in sociological and social psychological analyses of aging.

Without belaboring the point, then, time and timing are crucial elements in social and personal life as well as in the creation and transmission of humor. The balance of this chapter therefore, focuses on the interrelationships of time, aging, and humor specifically in two broad areas: (1) selected intraindividual age-related temporal changes that could relate to humor behavior, and (2) off-timing, cohortcentric, and timelessness as social aspects of humor. A final section deals with speculations, questions, and potential research topics related to possible interrelationships of humor, aging, and time–timing.

SELECTED INTRAINDIVIDUAL AGE-RELATED TEMPORAL CHANGES THAT COULD BE RELATED TO HUMOR BEHAVIORS

Three topics and the relationship of each to humor behaviors are covered in this section: (1) age-related slowing of behavior, (2) age-related changes in arousal, and (3) age-related changes in time perspectives.

Slowing of Behavior and Humor

Data strongly suggest that a slowing in behavior is a universal concommitant of aging (Birren, Woods, & Williams, 1980). The findings of Canestrari (1963) suggest that older people require more time to learn material than do younger. Usually, there is some slowing under some circumstances for some tasks (Birren *et al.*, 1980).

What, then, are the relationships among the slowed behavior of aging, humor, and time? Is there an age-related decrement in responses to humor? Do older people take longer to *get* the point of a joke or to *get to* the point of a joke? Do older people have a changed threshold for humor stimuli so that the joke has to be more obvious or "stronger" in order for them to respond to it? Are there age-related changes in responses to the different media of humor: art, music, written words, cartoons, recorded language, silent movies, talking moving pictures, or television? Do older people respond to these different media differently because of general slowness of behavior or because of decrements in different sensory receptors?

Some have concluded that the slowness of response in older subjects is the result of cautiousness (see, for example, Botwinick, 1978, Chapter 8). Does this factor affect an individual's responses to jokes? Are older people reluctant to laugh at jokes because they are cautious about whether a joke was intended? Is their cautiousness related to uncertainties, in turn related to a slowness in processing humor information? Do people who are telling jokes to older people have both to shift their timing and to increase their emphasis to deal with the slowness and changed threshold?

The Law of Parsimony in humor may have a curvilinear relationship with age: For the young, simple humor stimuli are best; for those in midlife, complex stimuli are more desirable; for the elderly, simplicity may once again be preferred. Perhaps we should note that all of the foregoing comments are speculations and hypotheses in search of research.

Arousal Changes and Humor

While there are a variety of studies related to the role of arousal on the behaviors of older people (see, for example, Smith, Thompson, & Michalewski, 1980), in general those working with older people have found that very high and very low arousal levels result in less effective performance of tasks. In his work on the psychology of humor, Berlyne (1972) uses the terminology of arousal, stating that a buildup and release of tension are related to responses to humor. He suggests that humor is related to a moderate level of arousal, which engenders positive affect, while very high or very low arousal levels result in negative affect.

Berlyne also discusses cognitive aspects of humor that involve a temporal dimension, the collative properties of stimuli, which also affect arousal levels. When presented with humor stimuli, individuals collate or compare information about the stimuli and their experiences, involving recollections of the past and anticipations of the future, thus affecting behavior. In humor as in other activities, we respond to present stimuli both in terms of memories of the past and of anticipations of the future. Such collative variables affect arousal levels.

Finally, Berlyne calls attention to the importance of cues to help people define situations or stimuli as humorous. He notes that arousal can be counteracted by reassuring cues which define a situation as harmless, a joke, or play. This reminder emphasizes the point that such cues could be even more important in mediating jokes for older people with slower arousal and increased cautiousness in responses.

Data showing that older people take longer than do younger ones to become aroused also indicate that older people take longer to return to their base level (Powell, Buchanan, & Mulligan, 1975). This finding suggests further relationships between levels of arousal and humor responses in old age. An audience of older people may well need a longer warm-up time and longer intervals between humor stimuli. Older audiences listening to the rapid-fire delivery of contemporary stand-up comics may experience the reality of a cognitive overload. Older audiences may also react to the Anglo-Saxon language of contemporary comedians with a high level of arousal; this also affects their responses to humor.

The need for external stimuli to define a situation as humorous, the pacing of stimuli, the increased cautiousness of older people, suggesting that they will risk errors of omission rather than commission and consequently not laugh at jokes, all suggest that the styles of comics may well differ when dealing with older as compared with younger audiences. Timing, thus, continues to be a major variable in response to humor. It is also a variable in need of more research.

Age-Related Changes in Time Perspectives and Humor

Doob (1971) suggests that changes affecting temporal behavior are both biological and cultural. Both kinds of changes are experienced individually, with each giving rise to other possible changes in temporal behavior. Several writers have suggested that some time in midlife we begin to measure distance from death rather than time from birth (Butler, 1963; Cumming & Henry, 1961; Neugarten, 1979). There is not, however, support for the belief that time seems to go faster as we age (Wigdor, 1980). Nonetheless, there are some questions about how our changed measuring system can affect our behavior in the realm of humor, both as the creator and recipient of humor.

For example, as we increasingly recognize our mortality, do we move toward eliminating the extraneous in our lives and take a more active role in structuring what time is left? Findings on survivors in nursing homes suggest that the more assertive live longer (Lieberman, 1975). One can speculate that in late life, internal locus of control is more adaptive than external locus of control. Certainly these findings reinforce the adaptive importance of mastery of one's environment in order to survive.

Nahemow (personal communication, May 2, 1983) suggests that because we realize that we are mortal, we begin to be more selective in what we decide to do and not to do. As we age, we take increased responsibility for structuring our days, months, and years, particularly during retirement. In earlier life we are more at the call of our calendars. Schools structure the hours and seasons; employers, our days and years. In retirement and subsequently in our old age, we become more responsible for the structuring of time. Our role model in old age perhaps should be the orchestra conductor, whose interpretations of tempo influences how the orchestra plays.

If Nahemow is correct about our perceptions of time, do we perceive the tempo of life as speeding up because of the age-related slowing of our behavior? Do we live in a Charlie Chaplin–like world in which the assembly line moves at an increasingly rapid pace? If this is the metaphor of old age, what then happens to our sense of humor? Do some older people fail to respond to humor, not because of slowness of behavior, sensory decrement, caution, or lack of cues, but simply because, like Queen Victoria, they are not amused? If the answer to these questions is yes, it suggests that styles of humor and humorists would change according to their audiences. Comedians, to be more successful with older audiences, would pace differently, provide multiple cues in order to define the beginning, middle, and end of jokes, define the existence of jokes, and give additional reassurance about the appropriateness of responses. These are matters of style rather than of content. We now turn to the content of humor. The focus will be on off-timing, timelessness, and cohortcentricity in humor. In changing the focus, we also move from issues of individual time and timing to those of social time and timing.

OFF-TIMING, TIMELESSNESS, AND COHORTCENTRICITY IN HUMOR

Off-Timing as a Source and Butt of Humor

From a life span perspective, the issue of timing enters into virtually every aspect of adult development and aging from that of research designs to the consideration of the different kinds of time that affect us as individuals: social, historical, and life. Each cohort defines and experiences social time differently; but all define, through age norms and life course mapping, the appropriateness of behavior for "a person of that age" (Atchley, 1975). Behavior is defined as on-time or off-time. What is on-time for one cohort may change for the next one. It is the on-time and off-time activities that often become the focus of humor. The humor may arise out of the incongruity of the situation or the element of surprise arising from the unexpected, nonnormative age-related behavior. Such jokes are not new. For example, the Book of Genesis tells us that both Abraham and Sarah were old and "it had ceased to be with Sarah after the manner of women." Nonetheless, Sarah conceives and bears a son named Isaac, which in Hebrew means joke.

Often the on-time and off-time activities that become sources of humor are sexual in nature as the following jokes illustrate:

A man sees his doctor. The doctor finds the man in excellent condition for a person of 80. [Notice it is usually a man in these jokes.]
Doctor: How old was your father when he died?
Patient: Who said he's dead?
Doctor (taken aback): He's still alive? Then, how old was your grandfather when he died?

Patient: He's still alive.
Doctor: Alive?
Patient: Oh, yes, He just got married.
Doctor: A man that age wants to get married?
Patient: Who says he wanted to?

There are a series of such jokes that implicity speak to the sexual prowess of old men as off-timing activities. There is a female counterpart of such jokes, although implicitly, this joke also speaks to a man's sexual and reproductive potential, and interestingly enough, the man is defined as the woman's husband!

An old woman learns from her physician that she is pregnant. She calls her husband.
Woman: Jake, I'm at the doctor's office and he says I'm pregnant.
Jake (after a lengthy pause) [timing]: Who's calling?

Of course, there is the story about the old woman who goes to the doctor to complain that she's losing her desire for sex.

Doctor: When did you first notice this?
Woman: Twice last night and then again this morning.

Another variation on this theme is the story of the old count who marries a young woman. They have separate bedrooms as befits royalty. The first night of their marriage, he goes to her room once, then again, and then a third time. She comments on his performance by commenting, "You are quite a man. This is the third time tonight." "Oh," he says, tapping his head, "senility."
A final variation on the theme relates to the older man involved with two 20-year-old women. Finally, he breaks off both relationships telling one of his friends, "I'm not wired for two-twenty."

The Timelessness of Some Humor

Given the social aspect of humor, one can expect some common themes in humor—themes that reflect some of the persistencies and tensions in social organization. For example, all societies are age graded; deal with males and females differently; and have some form of family, religious, economic, and political institutions. Often the social structure is characterized by a hierarchical structure, structured inequalities, and invidious distinctions. As noted earlier, humor serves, under these circumstances, as a means of dealing with the resultant conflicts, tensions, and intergroup relationships. While the specific content of the joke may change, its basic structure is heard throughout an individual's life and, often, throughout a culture's history. In the United States, what were once jokes about the Dutch eventually became jokes about the Poles or Appalachians. One becomes sufficiently familiar with the essential nature of some jokes that one does indeed "stop me if you've heard this one." Another way of dealing with overly familiar jokes is told in a joke itself:

A number of people had lived together a long time and had shared the same jokes an equally long period of time. They decided, because of their familarity with one another's jokes, to shorten each joke to a number. One day, Jim told Pete "23." Pete did not laugh and Jim asked why. The response was, "You told it better last time."

While at one level the jokes in the previous section dealt with off-timing situations, at another, more timeless level, they may be expressions of intergenerational tensions. The most common arenas in which such tensions are and have been expressed are sex, power, and economics. Some old people have formidable economic power, which is envied by the young. A way of expressing this envy is through the mocking, making fun of, and joking about the possession of such attributes by the aged and their reluctance to give them up even when they no longer can deal with them as competently as can the young. Thus, the sexuality of the aged has been the focus of humor for generations, as is evidenced in the comedies of Aristophanes.

If such jokes can be interpreted as expressions of intergenerational tensions, then they can also be viewed as timless expressions of anxieties about aging. We may feel about aging as we do about death—it is not being old that is frightening, rather it is the associated processes and how we will experience them. Thus, the joke about the two old men who watch beautiful women but don't know why is an expression of anxiety about being old as well as an expression of derision by the young against the old (Davies, 1977; Kalish, 1979; Palmore, 1971; Richman, 1977).

Cohortcentricity of Humor

Some humor is time bound. Jokes related to current events, political figures, and scientific discoveries, for example, are very time bound just as aging is time bound. This section focuses primarily on the cohortcentricity of humor. This topic is closely related to off-timing and timelessness as aspects of humor but is conceptually distinct from each. Cohortcentric humor has two aspects: (1) the time-limited aspect of some humor, and (2) humor as evidence or predictor of ongoing social change.

Boskin (1979) writes, "Humor is invariably connected to a time frame" (p. 3). Fadiman (1974) also reminds us that our perception of what is funny is affected by a number of social variables: age, class, race, place, and time. He further characterizes humor as having two aspects: a social or folk aspect and an artistic one. The former is more permanent than the latter, which is transitory and thus tends to become dated. He further suggests that "all humor has a high obsolescence rate" (p. 20). The obsolescence rate is particularly high in a technological society, with its remarkable system of virtually instantaneous mass media. While some of his comments may be debatable, his emphasis upon the temporal nature of humor is consistent with the approach taken in this chapter.

Humor about the off-time of events may be a social precursor of changes in age norms. When columnists write humorously about the not-so-empty nest, suggesting how parents can deal with the problem of children who return home, as Erma Bombeck (1981) did some time ago, they called attention to the return-to-the-nest behavior before social scientists did. When there is a persistence of humor about aging fathers, the jokes may anticipate topics of research. It is suggested, then, that the prevalence of jokes about a particular topic are indicative of changing age—or other norms in the joked-about area. In a sense, Neugarten's (1968a) reference to "the pause that refreshes" was an early example of the phenomenon being discussed here. In that instance, the humor about menopause was incorporated in a scientific article reporting how women feel in contradistinction to what physicians believed women should feel. If, as Mintz (1977) suggests, humor *reflects* cultural change, what he might just as easily have said is that people's humor *anticipates* the change.

Fadiman (1974) pointed out that the humor of one generation is not funny to another generation. The joke about "le capeau noire" needs explaining to a cohort that grew up with the pill rather than condoms as contraceptives. Topic humor has a short shelf life as graffiti of the late 1960s and early 1970s attest: "Spiro Agnew, the human Edsel," or, "Mace the nation. Beat the press." (Reisner, 1971, pp. 161, 152). Do shared old jokes reinforce a cohort cohesiveness? Do we have favorite old jokes—a form of nostalgia—as we have favorite old tunes? Certainly a history of humor such as described by Mintz (1977) suggests that there have been some changes in our national humor. What about a history of humor about aging? It would be interesting to examine more carefully the nature of persistent themes. The clothing of a joke may change, but its essential meaning remains the same. There are, for example, humorous variations on the mnemonic devices of different occupations. For orchestra conductors, the left hand is marked *violins* while the right has written on it *cellos*. Accountants show left hands on which is written *debits* and the right represents *credits*, while for sailors, the left side is *port* and the right *starboard*. From a broader historical point of view, rebellion against leadership can be expressed in jokes about leaders, while jokes about those waiting in the wings to assume positions of power may be repeated historically with only the names of the players changed.

SUMMARY

In summary, then, it is suggested that a focus on off-time events and behaviors in old age become the source or content of humor and that such jokes reflect intergenerational tensions and anxieties about aging. Similarly, some jokes about old age and old people are timeless, again possibly reflecting difficulties and anxieties in intergenerational relationships. One need only examine Greek and Roman literature— as well as Boccacio, Chaucer, Shakespeare—to be reminded that the behaviors of the old have often served as a butt of humor.

If there is a timelessness to some themes, there may also be cohort differences in humor behavior, both in the creation of humor and in responses to it. And, finally, jokes may serve as a unobtrusive measurement of changing age norms as well as provide us with a rich source of research hypotheses about ongoing social changes.

CONCLUSIONS

The temptation in dealing with the three topics of humor, timing, and aging is to raise a myriad of questions, not all of equal significance but of almost equal interest. In general, the questions fall into two major categories: those dealing with the style both of comedians and of their audiences and those dealing with the content of humor. Earlier, a series of questions was raised about characteristics of aging that might affect older peoples' responses to humor. In reviewing the psychophysiological data, questions were raised about changes in arousal patterns, cautiousness, the need for mediating cues, and related issues, and how these might affect the humor responses of older people. The other side of this particular issue of style relates to what comedians might take into consideration in performing before older audiences. It was suggested that a less frenetic, slower, "cleaner" act might be more effective with an older audience. There were also some suggestions about the older joke teller him- or herself. Such individuals when telling jokes may take longer to get to the point of the joke. There are all, of course, speculative questions in search of data.

As noted earlier in this chapter, there are few gerontological theorists and life span authors who have dealt with any of these issues extensively or who have discussed more than peripherally a sense of humor as an adult developmental phenomenon. It would be interesting to learn, for example, at what stage of life or ego development can one begin to direct jokes at oneself? If developmental tasks exist, then one would think the development of a sense of humor would be one of the tasks if for no other reason than that it would be fun.

From the viewpoint of content, it has been suggested that, on the one hand, the content of humor may change to reflect social changes and topical concerns, while, on the other hand, there may be a timelessness to some themes, particularly those relating to intergenerational tensions. The humor of a people can serve as a rich source of information about that society's attitudes, values, and beliefs, not only about aging but about many other aspects of social life.

A number of questions have been raised about potential areas of research—in fact, more questions than answers. There is an apocryphal story that on her deathbed, Gertrude Stein asked Alice Toklas, "Alice, Alice, what is the answer?" When there was no response, Stein said, "Then what is the question?" This chapter has, perhaps, raised more questions than it has answered, but then, "Why not?"

REFERENCES

Atchley, Robert C. (1971). In Atchley, R. (Ed.). *Understanding American society* (pp. 309–310). Belmont, CA: Wadsworth.

Atchley, Robert C. (1975). The life course, age grading, and age-linked demands for decision making. In N. Datan & L. H. Ginsberg (Eds.), *Life-span developmental psychology: Normative life crises* (pp. 261–278). New York: Academic Press.

Berlyne, D. E. (1972). Humor and its kin. In J. G. Goldstein & E. McGhee (Eds.). *The psychology of humor: Theoretical perspectives and empirical issues* (pp. 43–60). Academic Press: New York.

Birren, J. E., Woods, A. M., & Williams, M. V. (1980). Behavioral slowing with age: Causes, organization and consequences. In L. W. Poon (Ed.), *Aging in the 80s*. (pp. 293–308). Washington, D.C.: American Psychological Association.

Birren, J., Cunningham, W., & Yamamoto, K. (1983). Psychology of adult development and aging. *Annual Review of Psychology, 34*, 543–577.

Bortner, R. W. (1979). Notes on expected life-history with introduction by Daniel J. Levinson. *International Journal of Aging and Human Development, 9*(4), 291–294.

Boskin, J. (1979). *Humor and social change in twentieth-century America*. Boston, MA: National Endowment for the Humanities Learning Library Program, Boston Public Library.

Botwinick, J. (1978). *Aging and behavior: A comprehensive integration of research findings*. New York: Springer.

Bombeck, E. (1981, February 4). Mom finds a solution to in-and-out offspring. *The Chicago Sun Times*, p. 70.

Butler, R. N. (1963). The life review: An interpretation of the reminiscence of the aged. *Psychiatry, 26*(1), 65–76.

Cain, L. D. (1981). Age distinctions and their social functions: A critique of the Age Discrimination Act of 1975.

Canestrari, R. E., Jr. (1963). Paced and self-paced learning in young and elderly adults. *Journal of Gerontology, 108*, 3.

Chapman, A. J., & Foot, H. C. (Eds.) (1977). *It's a funny thing, humor*. Oxford, NY: Pergamon Press.

Coser, R. L. (1959). Some social functions of laughter. *Journal of Human Relations, 12*(2), 171–182.

Cumming, E., & Henry, W. (1961). *Growing old: The process of disengagement*. New York: Basic Books.

Davies, L. J. (1977). Attitudes toward old age and aging as shown by humor. *The Gerontologist, 17*(3), 220–226.

Doob, L. W. (1971). *Patterning of time*. New Haven, CT: Yale University Press.

Emerson, J. (1969). Negotiating the serious import of humor. *Sociometry, 32*, 169–181.

Fadiman, C. (1974). Humor as a weapon. *American humor: An interdisciplinary newsletter, 1* (Spring), 20–22.

Hareven, T. K., & Adams, K. J. (1982). *Aging and life course transitions: An interdisciplinary perspective*. New York: Guilford.

Hendricks, J. (1982). Time and social science: History and potential. In E. H. Mizruchi, B. Glassner, T. Pastorello (Eds.), *Time and aging*. pp. 1–11. New York: General Hall.

Holland, Norman, N. (1982). *Laughing: A psychology of humor*. Ithaca, NY: Cornell University Press.

Kalish, R. (1979). The new ageism and the failure models: A polemic. *The Gerontologist, 19*, 398–402.

Kastenbaum, R. (1982). Time course and time perspective in later life. In Carl Eisdorfer (Ed.), *Annual review of gerontology and geriatrics* (vol. 3), pp. 80–101. New York: Springer.

Keith-Spiegel, P. (1972). Early conceptions of humor: Varieties and issues. In J. G. Goldstein & P. E. McGhee (Eds.). *The psychology of humor: Theoretical perspectives and empirical issues*, pp. 4–42. New York: Academic Press.

Klapp, O. (1950). The fool as a social type. *American Journal of Sociology, 55*, 157–162.

Koestler, A. (1964). *The act of creation*. New York: Dell.

Koller, M. R. (1978). Workshop: Developing a sociology of humor. *Sociological Ab-*

stracts (Suppl. 81). Presented at the 1978 Annual Meeting of the North Central Sociological Association.

Lieberman, M. (1975). Adaptive processes in later life. In N. Datan & L. H. Ginsberg (Eds.), *Life-span developmental psychology*, pp. 129–160. New York: Academic Press.

Martineau, W. H. (1972). A model of the social functions of humor. In J. H. Goldstein & P. E. McGhee (Eds.), *The psychology of humor*, pp. 101–128. New York: Academic Press.

McGhee, P. (1979). *Humor: Its origin and development*. San Francisco: Freeman.

McGhee, P. E. (1972). On the cognitive origins of incongruity humor: Fantasy assimilation versus reality assimilation. In J. G. Goldstein, & P. E. McGhee (Eds.), *The psychology of humor: Theoretical perspectives and empirical issues*, pp. 61–80. New York: Academic Press.

McGhee, P. E., & J. H. Goldstein, (1972). Advances toward an understanding of humor: Implications for the future. In J. G. Goldstein and P. E. McGhee (Eds.). *The psychology of humor: Theoretical perspectives and empirical issues*. pp. 243–262. New York: Academic Press.

Mead, M. (1970). *Culture and commitment: A study of the generation gap*. Garden City, NY: Natural History Press/Doubleday.

Mintz, L. E. (1977). American humor and the spirit of the times. In A. J. Chapman & H. C. Foot (Eds.), *It's a funny thing, humor*, pp. 17–22. Oxford: Pergamon.

Myrdal, G. (1944). *An American dilemma* (Vols. 1 & 2). New York: Harper, 1944.

Neugarten, B. L., Moore, J. W., & Lowe, J. C. (1968). Age norms, age constructs, and adult socialization. In B. Neugarten (Ed.), *Middle age and aging: A reader in social psychology*, pp. 22–28. Chicago: University of Chicago Press.

Neugarten, B. L., Woods, V., Kraines, R. J., & Loomis, B. (1968). Women's attitudes towards the menopause. In B. Neugarten (Ed.), *Middle age and aging: A reader in social psychology*, pp. 195–200. Chicago: University of Chicago Press.

Neugarten, B. L., & G. O. Hagestad. (1976). Age and the life course. In R. H. Binstock & E. Shanas (Eds.), *Handbook of aging and the social sciences*. pp. 35–55. New York: Van Nostrand Reinhold.

Neugarten, B. L. (1979). Time, age and the life cycle. *American Journal of Psychiatry*, *136*, 887–893.

Neugarten, B. L. (1981). Age distinctions and their social functions. *Chicago Kent Law Review*, 57(4), 809–826.

Obrdlik, A. J. (1942). Gallows humor—A sociological phenomenon. *American Journal of Sociology*, *47*, 709–716.

Palmore, E. (1971). Attitudes toward aging as shown by humor. *The Gerontologist, 11*, 181–186.

Powell, D. A., Buchanan, S., & Mulligan, W. (1975). Relationships between learning, performance and arousal in aged vs. younger V.A. patients. Paper presented at the Gerontological Society meeting, Louisville, KY.

Radcliffe-Brown, A. R. (1952). *Structure and function in primitive society*. Glencoe, IL: The Free Press.

Reisner, R. (1971). *Graffiti: Two thousand years of wall writing*. Chicago: Henry Regnery.

Richman, J. (1977). The foolishness and wisdom of age: Attitudes toward the elderly reflected in jokes. *The Gerontologist, 17*(3), 210–219.

Schaier, K. W., & Cicirelli, V. G. (1976). Age differences in humor comprehension and appreciation in old age. *Journal of Gerontology, 31*, 577–582.

Seltzer, M. M. (1983). Unstarted projects, unused paragraphs, and unfinished business. *The Gerontologist, 23*(2), 120–122.

Seltzer, M. M. (1976). Suggestions for the examination of time-disordered relationships. In J. F. Gubrium (Ed.), *Time, roles, and self in old age*, pp. 111–125. New York: Human Services Press.

Smith, D., Thompson, L. W., & Michalewski, H. J. (1980). Averaged evoked potential research in adult aging: Status and prospects. In L. W. Poon (Ed.), *Aging In the 1980's*, pp. 135–154. Washington, DC: American Psychological Association.

Troll, L. E. (1982). *Continuations: Adult development and aging*. Monterey, CA: Brooks/Cole.

Troll, L. E. and Seltzer, M. *Further thoughts on the expected life history* (in preparation).

Wigdor, B. T. (1980). Drives and motivations with aging. In J. E. Birren & R. B. Sloan (Eds.), *Handbook of mental health and aging*. pp. 245–261. Englewood Cliffs, NJ: Prentice Hall.

Zijderveld, A. C. (1968). Jokes and their relation to social reality. *Journal of Social Research, 35*(2), 286–311.

7

Over the Miles: Coping, Communicating, and Commiserating through Age-Theme Greeting Cards*

MARGARET HELLIE HUYCK
JAMES DUCHON

INTRODUCTION

This chapter explores the use of greeting cards as a strategy for coping with anxieties associated with aging. Our preliminary research suggests that younger American adults, at least, recognize age-theme birthday cards as vehicles for expressing and diffusing anxieties about changes linked to age. In particular, greeting card humor seems uniquely suited to dealing with tensions generated in close interpersonal relationships. While most individuals acknowledge common card themes, they also easily adapt or even distort their perceptions to convey an intended unique message. Even when the card is not actually sent, many individuals seem to obtain relief and pleasure from contemplating the intended message and the recipient's response.

* Prepared for the *Humor and Aging* Conference, sponsored by the Gerontology Center, West Virginia University, May 10–14, 1983, with the assistance of students in Introductory and Developmental Psychology courses, particularly Rose Serrano.

139 Copyright © 1986 by Academic Press, Inc.
All rights of reproduction in any form reserved.

Thus, responses to greeting cards may indeed reveal important aspects of coping with anxieties associated with aging.

HUMOR AS A COPING MECHANISM

Humor has long been recognized as having the potential for serving individual and social needs. It is evident that humor serves to release tension safely and thus promotes a sense of well-being in the individual. Members of a group may gain solidarity by disparaging outsiders.

Freud (1905/1960), in one of the most thorough examinations of humor yet undertaken, proposed that most (if not all) jokes are *tendentious*, or purposeful. Humor, like dreams, serves as an outlet for inner tensions and anxieties. A number of analyses of humor posit that anxiety provokes the use of humor. Aggression is one way of responding to anxiety; Feinberg (1978) went so far as to hypothesize that humor in all forms is an act of aggression directed against individuals, groups, institutions, God, fate, nature, and death. Several of these themes are evident in greeting card humor. The vagaries of fate, particularly those accompanying aging, threaten disruptions in self-esteem or patterns of connectedness; the cards provide ways of communicating and relieving the consequent distress.

According to Freudian theory, potentially dangerous aggressive and sexual impulses are converted into benign or socially acceptable interactions through a process of "jokework," analogous to dreamwork. The techniques used to represent symbolically the covert feelings and wishes are similar to those in dreamwork: condensation, where a fragment of an image, word, or sequence stands for the whole; substitution, where something that evokes the *real* wish appears in the overt version; and even reversal, where one says the opposite of what is intended. Dreamwork, in analytic theory, involves elaborate camouflage of meaning. According to Zillmann's (1983) insightful reinterpretation of Freud's writing on humor, the disguises involved in jokework are intended more as embodiment or embellishment than as camouflage and thus are more obvious than most dreams. One reason that the purposeful aspects of humor are less disguised is that, as Freud pointed out, humor also contains nontendentious, or nonpurposeful elements, which generally arouse a response of mirthful pleasure. The combination of tendentious and nontendentious elements in any particular joke or stimulus (such as a greeting card) means that we can respond humorously to the stimulus as a whole, without having—or being able—to determine whether we are finding pleasure in the tendentious or nontendentious elements.

The disguises of humor are evident especially in contemporary greeting cards, which are the focus of this analysis. For example, one greeting card features a picture of a very wrinkled dog with that could be regarded as an expression of whimsical resignation; inside, the message reads, "Oh, well. Another year, another wrinkle. Happy Birthday!" A 27-year-old woman looked at this card, laughed, and said it was a "cute card." When questioned further about her responses, she said she would send it to her 58-year-old aunt, intending to tell her aunt that "wrinkles could be cute." Thus far, it would appear that the appeal of the card lies in the cute dog. However, it does not seem farfetched to suggest that the underlying message is also appealing to the young woman: "You, may my old aunt, have wrinkles, just like this dog." This is a rather disparaging observation, one that gives the young sender a boost but at the expense of her aunt. The underlying disparagement is, in fact, recognized by the young woman when she says that, if the card were sent, the aunt would "be glad I remembered her birthday"—a frank avoidance of the card message altogether; and "she may also get a laugh from it." That is, the humorous enjoyment accrues to the sender, not the recipient, and, unless the perceptions are probed, the enjoyment can be attributed to the least tendentious elements of the stimuli, the cute dog.

The example above illustrates one of the common ways in which humor is used to cope with anxieties. By laughing at the vulnerabilities or misfortunes of another, we feel superior. Most of the research on disparagement, or put-down, humor, investigates the relative enjoyment of disparagement humor directed at targets varying in similarity, sentiments, and status (see Wolff, Smith & Murray, 1934; LaFave, Haddad & Maesen, 1976; Zillmann, 1983; Zillmann & Cantor, 1976). Some of the research seems contradictory or unclear as to whether we can enjoy a joke that disparages someone we like. Psychoanalytic theory or any theory that allows for normal ambivalence in close personal relationships would posit no incongruence between envy and admiration both directed at the same individual. Persons who are close to us and who have the power to make us feel better or worse about ourselves, to increase or alleviate our sense of anxiety, are obvious targets of rage whenever they threaten to make us feel worse. Direct expressions of rage and threat are considered inappropriate and offensive; a card can provide some expression of the more negative sentiments, combined with a counterbalancing message. The niece says, to her aunt, in effect: You may have more experience and more of other things that I admire and want—but you have more wrinkles. She also says, I remind you not of wrinkles, but send this cute dog on your birthday as a token of my affection.

We discuss other ways in which humor can be used to cope with anxieties as we examine more closely the use of greeting cards.

Greeting Card Humor

GENERAL CHARACTERISTICS

Greeting card humor is distinctive in that it is more obviously and intensely interpersonal: One selects a card to send to a particular recipient. It is different, then, from a private appreciation of a cartoon appearing in the *New Yorker*, bathroom graffiti, or the television comic's jokes. The selection and transmission of a greeting card is an act of communication, transmitting a message from the sender to the recipient. However, unlike many forms of communication, it is not delivered personally and does not require a response. It is thus an excellent mode for transmitting messages that may be difficult to deliver face to face. Such messages may be those that express sentiments typically considered threatening or inappropriate in a relationship, such as envy or sexual desire. In addition, the sending of cards provides an excellent medium for projecting the anxieties of the sender onto the recipient; such projections are more likely to be challenged if introduced into face-to-face communication.

We thus expect "humorous" cards to convey messages that are important to the sender (e.g., that include tendentious elements) but that require or benefit from some embedding or embellishment with non-tendentious elements. The contemporary greeting cards are ideally designed, since they typically contain several elements that together constitute *the card;* individuals who send or receive them may focus on one or another of the elements. The shape, colors, and figures of the artwork typically suggest pleasurable and/or humorous responses using contemporary conventions of exaggeration and stereotyping. In addition, the verbal message typically follows fairly classic forms of jokework, involving brevity, surprise, and plays on words.

AGE-THEME BIRTHDAY CARDS

The cards selected for analysis in our research were chosen on the assumption that cards designed for individual occasions (rather than holidays) are chosen by the purchaser in accord with his or her own concerns as much as or probably more than an informed sensitivity to the recipient's interpretation of the card. In particular, birthday cards were expected to be particularly good vehicles for dealing with feel-ings about advancing age. Typically, the individual is confronted with a variety of standardly sentimental, whimsical, and witty cards. Select-ing a card to mark someone else's birthday presumably rouses anxie-ties about aging. The presumption guiding this investigation was that contemporary age-theme birthday cards evoke complex responses in individuals and help them to deal with potentially troubling feelings. This research was initiated when the senior author collected over 100 such cards from a variety of stores and began speculating about what each card might mean. Several ways of coping with issues of aging seemed to be conveyed by the cards. These included (1) projecting personal anxieties (and problems) onto the recipient and often reas-suring the recipient that things aren't all that bad; (2) supporting de-nial or avoidance of age changes; (3) puncturing denial or illusions, often in a sadistic way; (4) sharing fate, where a negatively valued age change is identified but shared; and (5) pointing out compensations. This initial list of strategies was subsequently modified as part of the systematic development of methods used to understand individual's responses in this study, as summarized below.

RESPONSES TO AGE-THEME BIRTHDAY CARDS

Procedures

In order to explore the communications transmitted through birth-day cards, individual adults were shown selected age-related greeting cards. They were asked to whom they would send such a card and what message they thought it would convey to the recipient.

THE STIMULI

Over 100 *contemporary* birthday cards were purchased in neigh-borhood drugstores, bookstores, newspaper shops, and a downtown department store. As indicated above, an initial perusal of these birth-day cards suggested several plausible coping strategies to the senior author. While these categories seemed reasonable, the object of this study was to assess how the respondents themselves experienced the cards. Thirty-two cards that expressed diverse, representative mes-sages were selected for analysis.

THE RESPONDENTS

Fifty-eight individuals aged 23–70, with a mean age of 41, were interviewed. Twenty-seven were male and 31 were female.

THE SETTING

Interviews were conducted in environments that were akin to those in which individuals would customarily buy or receive greeting cards or would consider doing so. These settings included private homes, a cafeteria, a shopping mall, and a public library. Academic environments were avoided.

THE INTERVIEWERS

Fifteen students served as interviewers for this study. A series of brief training sessions were conducted by the authors in order to develop their interviewing skills, especially their probing techniques. They were trained in a group to facilitate a consistent and homogenous approach to the respondents and to the questionnaires.

THE INTERVIEW

A questionnaire was developed in which each respondent was presented with a greeting card and asked to think of someone to whom they might send that particular card. In the event that no one came to mind, the respondent was required to imaging an appropriate person. Respondents were asked to describe their relationship to that person, such as sister, friend, and so forth; how close they felt to the intended recipient (rated 1–5); and the recipient's age and sex. Respondents were then asked the following:

1. what they would be trying to say to the recipient by sending that particular card, for example, what the intended message would be;
2. how they thought the recipient would feel when receiving the card; and
3. how the respondents would feel if they received such a card.

Interviewers asked questions about one to four cards. Answers were queried routinely, and it required 10–15 minutes to ask questions about a single card. Ten respondents were shown only one card, 5 respondents were shown two cards, 38 respondents were shown three cards and 5 respondents were shown four cards. Because the unit of analysis was the response to the message communicated by a particular greeting card and was not focused upon individual respondents, an unequal number of responses per person was allowed.

Data Analysis 1: Tabulating the Responses

VARIABLES TABULATED

Responses were coded for: (1) coping style, (2) aggressive components, (3) respondent demographic data (age and sex), and (4) information about the relationship between the sender and the intended recipient (age, sex, and closeness).

COPING STRATEGIES

Seven categories of coping strategies were derived from the data by reviewing all interview responses to the question, "What would you be trying to say by sending this card?" Responses having similar messages were grouped together. The second author developed a coding manual describing each coping category. This manual was used to train two independent research assistants to classify each response into one of the seven categories. If they were unable to code a response, they were instructed to label it uncodable.

One category, *shared fate,* is illustrated by two responses: "Together we're growing older," and, "I'd be laughing with her about getting older." These and others like them had the shared theme of growing older together. Another respondent put it bluntly, "We're in this thing together."

A second category was named *positive reframing.* This group of responses contained the message that one should look at growing older from a different perspective, one that is more positive, and/or less painful or discouraging. Responses such as the following were included in this group: "I would make her think about what she has to be grateful for, rather than looking back in the past," and, "I would like to say that getting older is not getting old and decrepit, but we're getting better."

A third category was *punctured denial/forced sharing.* The message in this group carried the communiqué that the recipient should not live under the illusion of continued youthfulness. It is an aggressive response, a forceful attempt to get recipients to admit that they are getting older. Examples of this type of message are, "He is getting older and must realize that," and, "I'm trying to make him see the truth about his age."

A fourth category is referred to as *detachment*. This group of responses is intended to reassure the recipient that he or she is not among the "old folks" group. It differs from positive reframing because positive reframing agrees that the respondent is a member of the older group: the focus in detachment is on distancing from that age-group identification. It represents detachment from or denial of such a membership. One respondent said she would send a particular card in order to "remind him that he is not *that* old." Another stated that she "would be trying to say that . . . he is not over the hill yet."

A fifth category contains the idea of *trivializing* the seriousness of becoming old. In a sense, it makes light of a serious matter. One respondent said that the message he would intend from a particular card was "not to . . . take getting older seriously; it's not that big of a deal." Another respondent said that the card is a "rueful laugh at getting older."

A sixth category is *neutralizing by confronting one's fears*. These responses shared the message confronting fears head-on, apparently in order to neutralize or disarm them. The intent is to regard openly the fears of getting old and then laugh at them. Examples of this type of response include, "to paradoxically exagerate their attitudes (of getting older) and to get them to laugh at their fears," and, " to make someone realize their silliness at being afraid of being old."

A seventh category is *complimenting the recipient with the intent to increase closeness*. Examples of this message are, "She's young and healthy and in a way I'm saying that I wish I was as young as she is," and, "Lucky you, you're still young and healthy."

MISSING DATA

Thirty percent of the responses obtained to the question, "What would you be trying to say by sending this card," were uncodable for coping style category, either because the respondent could not articulate their intentions or because the responses were inadequately probed for clarification. These were included in the calculation of reliability.

RELIABILITY

Two independent raters agreed on 80% of the judgments for coping category. Agreement in this case means that the raters put the responses into the same coping category or both agreed it was uncodable. For the cases in which there was disagreement, the two investigators discussed the case and reached consensus in order to assign a category.

AGGRESSIVE COMPONENTS

In order to explore further the use of aggression within the humorous context, each message was coded for its aggressive components. This was accomplished using two dichotomous (present or absent) measures: (1) *aggressive intents* (AI) and (2) *aggressive anticipation* (AA). If the respondent indicated that the message carried an aggressive, hostile, or insulting message, it was coded for aggressive intents. An example of a response coded as AI is, "I'd be rubbing it in that he's getting older and those wrinkles are starting to show" If the respondent indicated the message would be *interpreted* by a recipient as being aggressive, hostile, or insulting, then it was scored as containing aggressive anticipation. One instance of this type of response was, "She would feel teased. She would feel the sting. I think she would get the message."

Two raters trained by the investigators independently coded for these components. Again, if there was not enough information to make a decision, it was left uncoded. Only 7 of the 154 responses were uncodable for AI and 8 were uncodable for the 154 AA responses. Interrater agreement was 86% for AI and 93% for AA. The responses that lacked consensus were finalized by a third judge.

Data Analysis 2: Case Examples

In order to explore the ways an individual may use a particular greeting card to express and deal with anxieties in a specific relationship, response records were analyzed holistically. Each interview was treated as a case; interpretaions were based on overt statements made by the respondents and on an understanding of common dynamics of the relationship discussed. The cases presented below are illustrative of the themes that emerged from this approach to the data.

RESULTS

Relationship between Respondent and Recipient

Sex. There was a highly significant (p. < .001) tendency for respondents to identify a same-sex target recipient. Seventy-one percent

of the women would send the card to another woman, and 63% of the
males would send it to another man.

Age.   Respondents were likely to send the cards to someone near
their own age. The mean age of the intended recipients was 43.6 (*SD*
= 15.1), not significantly different from the sender's mean age of 41.2
(*SD* = 12.5). The correlation of .27 between respondent and recipient
ages was statistically significant (*p* = < .001), but the relatively low
correlation indicates that respondents do not necessarily identify
someone near their own age.

Kinship.   Many types of formal relationships with the sender were
indicated, including brothers, sisters, children, parents, in-laws,
friends, and (occasionally) work supervisors. When responses were
grouped, 45.2% of the respondents said they would send the card to a
relative, while 54.8% would send it to a friend.

Closeness.   In general, respondents said they would send such a
card to someone with whom they had close relationship. The respondents indicated on a scale of 1–5 (when 5 was most intimate) just how
close they felt to their recipient. The mean rating was 3.8 (*SD* ± 1.3). A
few respondents spontaneously indicated that the cards should only
be sent to people who are very close. Males and females did not differ
signficantly on this measure. Respondents only identified eight cards
that they could not imagine sending to anyone; five of these respondents were women. (Obviously the relationship between sender and
recipient could not be appraised for this set, although the respondents
did respond to other questions about the cards.)

     The importance of closeness was also revealed in answers to the
question of how the respondents would feel if *they* were the recipient
of the card. Several people indicated that they would appreciate the
card only if sent from the "appropriate" person, usually "a close
friend." An example of this was expressed by the reply to a card with a
window on the front cover, revealing a pair of woman's legs on the
inside; the message inside read, "Don't let anyone tell you you're
getting old, pal—notice how fast you opened the card." The respondent said, "How I feel would depend on who the sender was. If the
message the sender was trying to get across was that I am getting
older, I'd feel depressed. If the sender was implying that I could still
be considered young, I'd feel very happy." Another respondent's reply to a different card was, "It would depend. If it was someone that
was older or my age, then mildly amused; if younger, annoyed." At
least some of the messages, then, have more than one meaning, and

the interpretation depends upon the relationship between the sender and the recipient.

Coping Styles

Relative Frequencies. The frequency (number and percentage) with which each codable coping style was rated is presented in Table 7.1. The most frequently identified coping style was punctured denial, with 38.7% of the responses. Next most common was positive reframing, with 22.6%. Thirteen percent of the responses were scored as shared fate, 11.3% as detachment, 5.7% as trivializing, 5.7% as complimenting, and 2.8% as neutralizing by confrontation. The last three (trivializing, complimenting, and neutralizing) had only six, six, and three coded responses, respectively. Therefore, any conclusions about these responses should be regarded with caution.

Aggressive Components. Overall, approximately half of the respondents acknowledged some aggressive intents in sending the cards included in this study. Aggressive intents related differently to the particular coping styles; results are shown in Table 7.2. at one extreme, all of the messages scored as neutralizing by confrontation had aggressive intents (although only three responses were of this type). Nearly all (90.2%) of the respondents who used punctured denial messages also acknowledged aggressive intents. The least aggressive messages appeared to be positive reframing (12.5% AI) and detachment (16.7% AI). These results confirmed that some of the coping styles were more hostile than others.

TABLE 7.1
Frequency and Percentage of Coping Styles[a]

Coping style	Percentage	Frequency
Punctured denial	38.7	41
Positive reframing	22.6	24
Shared fate	13.2	14
Detachment	11.3	12
Trivializing	5.7	6
Complimenting	5.7	6
Neutralizing	2.8	3
	100.0	106

[a] Overall interrater agreement on coding was 80%. Forty-eight of the total 154 responses were uncodable on this measure.

In general, the aggression or hostility that the respondent anticipated the recipient to perceive, assessed as anticipated aggression (AA), is less than that acknowledged by the sender. While nearly half of the respondents acknowledged some aggressive intent, only 36.3% anticipated an aggressive interpretation by the recipient. As shown in Table 7.2, this pattern holds true for punctured denial, trivializing, neutralizing, and complimenting. For positive reframing, shared fate and detachment messages, about the same (small) proportion as acknowledged aggressive intents anticipated the recipient would interpret it as hostile. It may be speculated, then, that in many cases the aggressive message buried within a humorous context lessens the hostility. The senders in this study seem to be aware of this process.

Gender Differences. Chi-square tests of independence revealed no differences between male's and female's use of coping styles. However, men (61.9%) were more likely than women (43.8%) to acknowledge aggressive intents ($p < .04$). There was a trend for men, more than women, to anticipate a hostile interpretation by a recipient (41.3% vs. 25.3%, $p < .06$).

Age Differences. Age was dichotomized into a younger (40 years old or less) and older group (41 years or more). A Chi-square test of independence between age and coping styles was significant ($p < .05$), as shown in Table 7.3. The largest difference between age groups was with the coping style of detachment. In the younger group, 18.5% of the responses were coded as detachment, while only 3.8% of the responses from the older group were so rated. The younger respondents apparently use humor to detach themselves from the "old

TABLE 7.2
Percentage of Each Coping Style Coded as Aggressive
Intents and Aggressive Anticipation

Coping style	(N)	Intents (%)	Anticipation (%)
Punctured denial	(41)[a]	90.2	62.5
Positive reframing	(24)	12.5	20.8
Shared fate	(14)	21.4	28.6
Detachment	(12)	16.7	16.7
Trivializing	(6)	50.0	16.7
Complimenting	(6)	50.0	00.0
Neutralizing	(13)	100.0	33.3
	(106)	50.9	36.2

[a] One response was uncodable for aggressive anticipation.

TABLE 7.3
Percentage of Young and Old Respondents Coded for Each Coping Style[a]

Coping style	Younger than 40 years		Older than 40 years	
	%	(N)	%	(N)
Positive reframing	16.7	(9)	28.8	(15)
Shared fate	7.4	(4)	19.2	(10)
Punctured denial	38.9	(21)	38.5	(20)
Detachment	18.5	(10)	3.8	(2)
Trivializing	7.4	(4)	3.8	(2)
Neutralizing	5.6	(3)	0.0	(0)
Complimenting	5.6	(3)	5.8	(3)
	100.0	(54)	100.0	(52)

[a] $\chi^2 = 13.1$, $df = 6$, $p < .05$.

folks." The older group tends to use positive reframing (28.8%) and shared fate (19.2%) to a greater extent than do younger respondents (16.7% and 7.4%, respectively). That is, the older group more often attempted to reframe or rationalize the drawbacks of old age into something more positive. The older group, too, sought comfort by sharing their fate of growing older with others. The other coping styles showed little or no differences between age groups.

Cases Illustrating Coping Themes

MAINTAINING THE AGE SYMMETRY

In addition to tabulating the response frequencies for the sample, interviews were examined holistically, using a case study approach. Each interview was evaluated to deduce the underlying themes in terms of that respondent and the particular relationship discussed.

One theme that emerges from such a case study perspective is that one's own aging becomes meaningful largely when it threatens to disrupt an established balance in an important relationship. Many close relationships seem to be predicated upon established relative ages; one is the younger, the elder, or peer in a dyad (or set) and aging is acknowledged and managed in the context of such relationships. The contemporary age-theme birthday cards seem to evoke anxieties about the difficulty of maintaining a delicate balance, particularly when the intended target is trying to deny aging.

As we indicate above, the most commonly coded coping strategy was that of punctured denial. The essence of the messages included in this category is, "You, too, are aging, not only I." If one person denies aging and the other does not, the effect is to increase the distance between them. Thus, the messages seem to be directed at maintaining an established relative relationship, whether it is a peers or older–younger dyad. Many of the cards set the recipient up for a compliment (supporting a denial of aging), which is followed by an insulting disparaging observation. An example is the card of an attractive woman saying, "I don't think you're getting old," and snickering inside as she says, " I think liver spots are sexy." A 31-year-old woman would send it to her fairly close 35-year-old woman friend to tell her that she's not as young as she used to be. She recognizes the hostility implied: "She'll laugh and maybe want to kill me." When asked how she would respond if she were to receive it, she replied, "At first I'd laugh, then the more I'd think about it the madder I'd get."

Other cards evoke the envy felt for someone who is successfully passing for younger, as well as the desire to change the situation. The most blatant example of this is revealed in a card presumably designed to express envy: "You're young, you're healthy, you're in the prime of life. . . . You "little shit." A 40-year-old man would send it to his 30-year-old brother because "he's 10 years younger than me and he always teases me about my age; I have to admit sometimes I do feel jealous. I wish that I could have stayed 20, but I have to learn to accept getting older. I can't wait until my brother starts getting older and starts showing it." If *he* received the card, he would feel pepped up for a while, but "once I faced reality again I'd feel depressed again." A 65-year-old woman would send it to her 45-year-old son-in-law; she clearly resents his successful efforts to stay in shape: "I don't care for people that try to be something that they're not. I think he doesn't want to accept that he is getting older." She imagines her son-in-law would "laugh it off" but would be mad deep down. If *she* received the card it would make her think of when she was young, healthy, and beautiful. "I feel happy while I'm thinking of the past, but after I'd think about it and come back to reality, I get all shook up to face my responsibilities now."

One group of cards "pulling" for punctured denial coping strategies are those dealing with the transition from age 29 to 30. As noted by other investigators (Dillon & Jones, 1981; Levinson, 1978; Sheehy, 1976), this is evidently a transition that evokes considerable anxiety. Card manufacturers have responded by providing a colorful selection of birthday cards, nearly all of which suggest that the recipient is denying moving beyond age 29. Four of the cards used in this research featured the following messages: (1) "Them years sure whip by, don't they dearie. You wake up one mornin' and you're 29! And a few years later you wake up and you're . . . 29 again!": (2) a cartoon of a man lighting candles in the shape of 29 on a cake: "Again this year, eh?"; (3) "You're 29? . . . Oh, Goody! I just love pretend games, too!"; and, (4) a picture of a rooster and a bull putting up a poster that says, "Happy Birthday! Only 29 today!" but inside the card informs us "Same ol' cock and bull story!"

Many of the respondents indicated they would send such a card to inform the recipient that the sender knows the secret, and thus the recipient cannot pretend to have a competitive advantage by pretending to be younger than he or she is. This use presumably maintains a previously established age–status relationship, which might be threatened if one partner in the relationship ages less quickly than the other. For example, a 34-year-old woman would send it to her 32-year-old sister to tell the sister that she knows she is trying to lower her age or exaggerate her youth. "Thirty is a turning point in life. I'd be saying she's claiming to be younger than she actually is." Another 34-year-old woman would use it in retribution for her 29-year-old sister teasing her about getting older: "It implies that if she wants to pretend she's young and I'm old, she'll need to pretend. She's losing her status as young."

REASSURANCE

A theme closely relating to the envy and competitiveness tapped above are the responses that inform the recipient that he or she is growing older and then offers reassurance about the specified change. Some of the responses clearly state that the recipient has a problem, while the sender presumably does not. For example, a 60-year-old man would send this card warning, "Ready or not, Dearie . . . here comes another one!" to his "very close" 55-year-old sister. The overtones of sibling rivalry are clear in his intended message: "Whether she likes it or not, she's a year older. She says she can't stand the idea of her being 60 . . . so I'd send her this card telling her that she's nearing it." He acknowledges that the card would really sadden her, since "when she turned 20 she felt old already." He claims *he* would feel happy if he received the card because he wants to live to be 80. Implicitly contrasting himself with his worried sister, he says, " I don't let anything bother me on my birthdays." He also claims, "I don't look for hidden messages in cards—I just take cards at face value," but he clearly sees their potential for evoking anxiety. This looks like a personally useful system whereby he resolutely evades anxiety on his birthdays but would love to make his sister "face up to the fact she's getting older." Presumably, she expresses enough anxiety for both of them, thus allowing big brother to feel calm and superior.

SHARED FATE

An alternative way of handling anxieties about aging is to identify a potential problem but present it as a fate shared by the sender and recipient. The general coping strategy seems to be to convey that *we* are growing older. At the least, it implies that a peer relationship is maintained as both age over time. For example, a card depicting a woman pointing out, "Now that we're getting older we have something we never had before . . . thigh wrinkles," pulls for a shared fate response. Some respondents see the card as conveying a positive, cherishing message affirming long and deep affection. A 35-year-old woman would send this card to a close woman friend the same age: "I'd be laughing with her about getting older—we've known each other a long time. They've chosen something funny. When you get old, things start falling apart, but thigh wrinkles is low on things that bother you. It trivializes what is going to happen. She'd laugh. It makes fun of the symptoms of age that we share."

One of the many cards with sexual-aging themes shows a keyhole revealing shapely legs; inside is the message, "Don't let anyone tell you you're getting old, pal . . . Notice how fast you opened this card!" A 70-year-old man would send the keyhole card to his close male friend of the same age. The message would be "not to despair—that we were still the same boys we used to be when we were in college . . . . Sometimes we get together and feel sorry for ourselves because we're 70, but this card would affect us both in the same way. We're still very much alike."

COMPENSATIONS

Another use of such cards to maintain a relationship is to point out compensations for each age. Presumably, the reassurances about aging are intended for the senders as well as for the recipients. For example, a card offering, "A birthday tip: Every time you start to wish you were younger . . . think about pimples," pulls for this message. A 28-year-old man would send it to a 44-year-old male friend to say, "Think how good you've got it now!" If he received it, he would laugh and think, "Good point!" A somewhat less benign version is offered by a 60-year-old father to his 23-year-old daughter; the father is trying to deal with his daughter's anxieties about growing older. "I'll be trying to tell her she is getting older but to look on the bright side. She should think of when she was younger and had a bad acne problem, which she didn't like either. I'm actually saying that either way she won't win—she doesn't want to be young again because of pimples." He thinks she would laugh "because it's a cute card and she'd understand what I'm trying to say." In addition to feeling like a good father, this man seems to be using the card to affirm his own strategy of aging; he "doesn't wish to be younger" in part because he focuses on the liabilities of past ages.

DISTANCING

Another father, age 38, seemed to use this "pimples" card to deal with anxieties about his attraction to his 11-year-old, "very close" daughter and to master an earlier insult. In this case, his daughter's aging presumably threatens the existing relationship. He would send her the card to tell her "that pretty soon she's going to have a face like that—pimples and blemishes—and she's not going to like it. Real soon." Presumably he would rather not admit that his daughter is moving into womanhood and sexual maturity; given his very close relationship with her, the change may arouse erotic fantasies. An emphasis on the unattractive features of pubescence may help him keep a safe distance. An additional meaning became clear when he recalled that when he was 17, a 15-year-old girl sent him a card card like this; he felt bad because he had a lot of pimples on his face. Sending a card like this to an adolescent female would be one way of compensating for that old hurt. This aspect illustrates, again, the ways in which family members provide a projective ecology, with the daughter substituting for the father's former girlfriend. Humorous cards such as this may, clearly, express multiple complex feelings.

DYNAMIC DISTORTIONS

The complex meanings of the cards are most clearly seen in cases that seem to involve dynamic distortions. In reading over the interviews, it seems clear that some respondents were quite able to perceive selectively, to reinterpret, or even to distort the card stimulus, presumably in the service of their own internal needs. This reality is, of course, perfectly congruent with the theories about thematic apperception tests and other projective stimuli. The results of this research support the initial premise that humorous greeting cards may be used as projectives and that gross distortions or idiosyncratic interpreteations emphasize the potential of the card responses for understanding individual motivations.

For example, the card stating, "We're not old, we're just mature! This morning I was so mature I could hardly get out of bed," clearly pulls for a shared fate message. However, a 28-year-old man would send it to an aunt or uncle over 50 to inform them, "Although you've lost your youth, you are wiser now." If *he* received the card he would "tear it up immediately." Denying the shared fate stimulus, he says, "I'd be angry because it doesn't apply to me. I'm only 28 years old." The threatened losses of aging are apparently so strong he even introduces the compensations of wisdom into the card, but he distorts the stimulus in order to avoid any share in the process.

Another example of motivated distortion of the stimulus was provided by a 70-year-old woman, sending an "over 30" card to her 67-year-old woman friend. The card depicts an older woman saying, "Don't feel so bad about having a birthday—lots of people over 30 lead happy, useful lives." The cartoon images are of old people sitting on the park bench feeding birds, begging, sweeping the street, playing horseshoes, drinking in the park, looking through binoculars at a young woman sun bathing. The respondent would mean to tell her friend sarcastically, "we are not over the hill, even though we're way past 30. She'd probably laugh because we joke, year after year, about being too old for fun even though we both know it isn't true." In this case, the respondent has changed *useful* into *fun*, presumably a verb that describes something more available to them.

The picture of two old men in wheel chairs, with large type, "HAPPY BIRTHDAY! Just wanted to be sure you heard me," evoked what is probably a projective response from a 41-year-old man. He would send the card to his 69-year-old uncle-in-law to say, "He has a hard time concentrating. He ought to know it's his birthday. He's too preoccupied with his job . . . . He ought to do something with the rest of his life except work hard. He has all of his senses and everything." Although he feels his uncle would be happy to know he's being thought of, if he himself received this card he would "ball it up and throw it away," which is, in fact, what he does with his midlife concerns when he puts them onto his uncle (who is probably delighted to have such absorbing work).

DISCUSSION

Overall, the results of this research support Freud's (1905/1960) contention that humor allows the expression of otherwise hidden feelings. As he said, "Jokes . . . make possible the satisfaction of an instinct (whether lustful or hostile) in the face of an obstacle that stands in its way. They circumvent this obstacle and in that way show pleasure (p. 101)." Freud was particularly interested in analyzing the relationship in which a joke was told in order to understand how the joke served to communicate thoughts and feelings which would otherwise be denied direct expression. It seems that some contemporary greeting cards serve a similar purpose for some Americans. Lust and hostility, from mild chiding to sarcastic insults, were evident in the communications which our respondents admitted they would want to convey throught the cards.

It is notable that males in this study were more likely than females to intend aggressive messages and to anticipate that a recipient would experience the card as aggressive. These findings fit with McGhee's (1979) observation that sexual and aggressive humor is more popular among men.

This research helps clarify the ways some individuals respond to potentially stressful themes couched in a humorous idiom. However, it is not clear to what extent the responses reflect the card stimuli, the personality characteristics of the respondents, or particular relationships described. We have suggested that these cards can be viewed as a projective assessment, similar to thematic apperception test cards. However, in order to extend this line of research, larger samples of adults should be interviewed about a standardized set of cards in order to assess the latent stimulus demand (LSD) of the card (Henry, 1956). While some cards seem to pull for particular issues (e.g., anxiety about sexual potency or loss of young-female beauty), without good normative data it is difficult to assess the ways in which cards are used. Without normative information about the LSD of cards, it is impossible to assess the ways in which individuals project personal, idiosyncratic meanings into the cards. It would be useful to assess how various senders and recipients interpret cards and to relate these interpretations to aspects of personality and the relationship between sender and recipient.

At this point, it is reasonable to assume we have demonstrated that individuals do, in fact, modify or even distort LSD themes in favor of more personalized messages. The fact of individual interpretation suggests that we must be very cautious about analyzing the messages of cards, cartoons, or other humor in terms of what experts decide to be the underlying message or anxieties conveyed. Rather, the research focus should shift to inquiries into how such humorous stimuli are received and interpreted and into the factors affecting the perception–interpretation processes.

In addition to clarifying the stimulus value of such cards, we need to understand better whether, what, and how individuals use humorous cards as coping strategies. While nearly all our respondents could identify someone whom they might send each card to, we do not know whether, in fact, they send such cards. Other researchers have reported that jokes are more likely to be initiated by higher status than lower status individuals; that joketellers have a history of social assertiveness, including physical and verbal aggression; and that self-disparagement humor is more common among women than among men (McGhee, 1979). It is not clear whether similar distinctions would be found for the use of humorous cards such as those used in this research.

Furthermore, it would be interesting to assess more clearly how this kind of humor may serve positive functions for the individual sender or for the relationship. As McGhee (1979) pointed out, the relationship between early distress and conflict and the greater use of humor during childhood is ambiguous, although they tend to co-vary. McGhee suggested that the appropriate question is whether a child who is subjected to unusual distress is better adjusted as a result of using humor than he or she would otherwise be. Similar questions might well be asked about the use of humor to deal with anxieties and real distresses associated with aging: Do those who enjoy and send birthday cards like these cope better than those who don't? And, What are the consequences for a relationship and for different kinds of relationships?

Our bias is to endorse humor as a coping device and to encourage further research in order to understand this strategy. At the most personal level, it can be a relatively mature defense mechanism, providing perspective through self-irony and confrontations with personal or shared human foibles or even tragic flaws. In addition, we agree with the importance of humor as a social lubricant as a scholar of humor described it, "We have just begun to understand the social functions of humor, but it is already apparent that humor is commonly used as a "lubricant" for social interaction. It is difficult to imagine a substitute device that would be equally successful at promoting smooth and comfortable social interaction" (McGhee, 1979, p. 245).

We have contributed a bit more data to this inquiry. However, much more must be explored in order to decode the kinds of ambivalent messages often carried through the mails in the guise of contemporary birthday greetings. Does she who laughs, last?

REFERENCES

Dillon, K. & Jones, B. (1981). Attitudes toward aging portrayed by birthday cards. *International Journal of Aging and Human Development, 13*(1), 79–84.

Feinberg, L. (1978). *The secret of humor.* Amsterdam: Rodop.

Freud, S. (1960) Jokes and their relation to the unconscious. In J. Strachey (Ed. and Trans.), *The complete psychological works of Sigmund Freud* (Vol. 8). London: Hogarth.

Henry, W. E. (1956) *The analysis of fantasy.* New York: Wiley.

LaFave, L., Haddad, J., & Maesen, W. A. (1976). Superiority, enhanced self-esteem, and perceived incongruity humor theory. In T. Chapman & H. C. Foot (Eds.), *Humor and laughter: Theory, research, and applications* (pp. 116–131) New York: Wiley.

Levinson, D., with Darrow, C., Klein, E., Levinson, M., & McKee, B. (1978). *The seasons of a man's life.* New York: Knopf.

McGhee, P. E. (1979). *Humor: Its origin and development.* San Francisco: Freeman.

Sheehy, G. (1976). *Passages: Predictable crises of adult life.* New York: Dutton.

Wolff, H. A., Smith, C. E., & Murray, H. A. (1934). The psychology of humor: I. A Study of responses to race-disparagement jokes. *Journal of Abnormal and Social Psychology, 28,* 341–365.

Zillmann, D. (1983). Disparagement humor. In P. E. McGhee & J. H. Goldstein (Eds.), *Handbook of humor research:* Vol. 1 *Basic issues* (pp. 85–107). New York: Springer-Verlag.

Zillmann, D. & Cantor, J. R. (1976). A disposition theory of humor and mirth. In T. Chapman & H. C. Foot (Eds.), *Humor and laughter: Theory, research, applications* (pp. 26–42). New York: Wiley.

8

The Last Minority:
Humor, Old Age, and Marginal
Identity

NANCY DATAN

INTRODUCTION

Conventional wisdom regards laughter as the best medicine: *Reader's Digest* stocks this wisdom in its monthly table of contents. However, many of my colleagues regard the theme of this volume, humor and aging, as an oxymoron: What's funny about aging? they ask in disbelief. Perhaps my colleagues believe that laughter, the best medicine, will never cure—no matter what—the last universal terminal disease of the life cycle. In this they are, of course, correct. However, when I am in doubt, I ask an expert: in this case my friend Leland Taylor, who celebrated his ninetieth birthday at the end of April with a private publication of a portion of his collection of obscene limericks (1983). "Aging is unbearable without humor," Leland told me. I am grateful to Leland for permitting me once more to bring his poetry to a gerontological audience.

This chapter is a first step toward a heuristic ethnography of humor and aging; and Leland, as he has so often done before, is serving as my principal informant. This chapter proceeds from the premise that humor serves two purposes: It regulates social boundaries, and it deflects painful truths. My thesis is that the humor of aging can be compared to ethnic humor. I have previously suggested that the life cycle carries with it a temporal equivalent of ethnocentrism, which I term

Copyright © 1986 by Academic Press, Inc.
All rights of reproduction in any form reserved.

the *narcissism of the life cycle*. Put simply, this concept suggests a survivor's disdain for the past, which has already proven to be endurable, however terrible, and ignorance of the future as unknowable. A popular slogan will serve as brief illustration: "Never trust anybody over thirty," the rallying cry of a cohort that was unable to envision its own passage into adulthood. Despite the relaxation of age norms that Neugarten (1982) has described and notwithstanding the multiple possible age gradients in an age-pluralistic society, ours remains an age-graded culture that pits one generation against another when school bonds compete against increases in social security, as though the well-being of the elderly had nothing to do with well-educated youth. I am proposing, in short, that age confers identity and that old age in particular can best be understood as the last minority, a status we should expect to attain, yet one to which we remain selectively blind, as much of our humor on aging will demonstrate.

The conceptual foundations of this chapter lie in psychoanalysis and in cultural anthropology: Freud (1960) was the first (and remains among the few) to suggest that wit serves to deflect the painful truths of life, while Radcliffe-Brown (1965) introduced the concept of the joking relationship into the study of social organizations and Warner showed how the use of humor could be viewed as an indicator of social status (Warner & Lunt, 1941). The humor of aging serves both intrapsychic and social-structural purposes. Humor by and about old people can be seen to deflect the painful truths of biological decline and inevitable death and thus, as Freud suggested, to convert the unbearable into the humorous—and so to master, in the mind at least, that which eventually will prove to master us.

The social use of humor is a double-edged sword. Humor may serve two functions: First, it may reassure the young that the old are distant from themselves—an unwholesome purpose, as this chapter suggests, that parallels the use of racist, sexist, and ethnic humor to define the *other* as inferior and so to preserve the self-esteem of the ingroup by maintaining some form of social segregation. Second, humor may serve the outgroup, the marginal group, or the stranger to strengthen a sense of internally defined identity, whether through the humor of self-disparagement or through the humor of power.

Studies of humor and disparagement (McGhee & Duffey, 1983a; 1983b; Zillman, 1983) demonstrate the distancing function of humor among children, who enjoy the disparagement of the other, showing that white children are amused by the disparagement of nonwhite victims, boys by the disparagement of girls. These studies suggest that one of the earliest lessons in laughter is humor at the expense of the socially disadvantaged relative to oneself. The growth of a humor of self-defense may parallel the emergence of an internally defined identity, as the present chapter suggests through its heuristic model of aging as a form of ethnic identity, and the humor of aging may parallel the humor used against and by ethnic groups in the service of self and social boundaries.

I consider three categories of ethnic humor and show how these serve the dual purpose of regulating social boundaries and deflecting painful truths. I then explore the applicability of these categories to the humor of old age. The first category I call *imposed humor*, the humor that is used by one group to denigrate another. In this category we find racist, anti-Semitic, sexist, and ageist humor. The purpose of such humor is to exclude its targets from access to power; it is basically an outgrowth of the ridicule children employ on the playground to show the world who is part of the group and who is not. The apparent paradox of agist humor is that, logically, it is humor denigrating one's future self. If, however, my notion of temporal ethnocentrism, the narcissism of the life cycle, is accepted, we see that it becomes possible to deny an unknowable future self and, in so doing, to deflect the painful truths of biological decline.

The second purpose of humor is that of self-defense: I call this second category *the humor of the resilient underdog*. The Jews of Eastern Europe provide a vast fund of shtetl humor, a prototypical example of humor in this second category. Humor of this sort deflects the painful truths of powerlessness. It is not imposed from the outside but generated from within the group itself: Although the group does not thereby gain public power, it attains the private power of self-definition. My friend and resident expert, Leland Taylor, confirmed the utility of this second category, noting, "You laugh at yourself, not at others."

The humor that comes from strength is based on strength and not on the wry acceptance of weakness. In light of my opening claim that laughter, the best medicine, offers no cure for aging and death, it may be expected that this third category, *the humor of power*, will require a different power base for the elderly humorist than for the ethnic powerhouse. As I shall show, it might sometimes be argued that the old have the last laugh.

ETHNIC HUMOR

Imposed Humor

The first category of ethnic humor is *imposed humor*—jokes by a majority or ingroup about a minority or outgroup. The B'nai B'rith

Anti-Defamation League has learned from history that jokes about Jews are often a prelude to the destruction of the Jews, and the vigilance of this group keeps anti-Semitic jokes out of the public domain. Racist jokes, too, are disappearing from the public domain, in the wake of the newly perceived danger of insulting a no longer powerless minority. To illustrate this category of humor I must turn to sexism: jokes that serve to keep women in their place, safely away from power. It is a paradox that women have none of the prerogatives of numerical majority and much of the powerlessness though little of the cohesiveness of the minority. Unlike humor based on the assumed inferiority of a race or an ethnic group, humor predicated on the assumption of the inferiority of women enjoys national syndication. Thus Art Buchwald (1979), despite statistics and insurance rates that demonstrate that women are safer drivers than men, produced the following description of women drivers:

"Have you ever caught a hit-and-run parker?" I asked Inspector Renfrew.
"No, but . . . we're getting closer all the time," he said. "For example, we now have a profile of the average hit-and-run parker. She's either a man or a woman, middle class, respectable, and usually votes for the law-and-order candidate. Her weakness is getting into a parking space without going over the yellow lines. She has trouble backing up, and panics easily when she sees anything moving in front or behind her. . . ."
"You keep saying 'she.' Does this mean the hit-and-run parker is usually a woman?"
"I wouldn't say that, but a recent survey of automobile body shops around the country indicates that more women than men are sneaking in to have their cars repaired."
"But they have more time."
"That's true, but we find a majority of them tell the body shop owner they'll pay in cash on condition that their husbands never find out about it."

As we shall see, much of the humor about old age falls into this category and serves to assure us that the old are not persons like ourselves.

The Resilient Underdog

The second category of ethnic humor is that of the resilient underdog. This is the humor of which Freud (1960) speaks when he says that wit can translate a painful truth into laughter. The examples from Jewish humor are numerous. For instance:

> A little old Jew was stopped in the street by Nazi soldiers, who grabbed him and asked him, "Tell us, Jew, who began this war?" He replied: "The Jews and the bicycle riders."
> And the soldiers asked: "Why the bicycle riders?"
> And he answered, "Why the Jews?"

Our laughter springs from our secret knowledge, shared with the little Jew, that neither the Jews nor the bicycle riders began the war: The Nazis did. But there laughter ends, and the little Jew is still in the hands of the soldiers. I like to think, though nothing but optimism supports this belief, that this is a transitional stage in the development of humor and identity, intermediate between the humor in which others laugh at one's powerlessness and the humor that proceeds from power.

The Humor of Power

Contrast the bitter humor of Jews in Germany with the humor of Jews in Israel.

It is said that David Ben-Gurion met with his Ministers of Defense and Finance to discuss Israel's newest crisis. His ministers claimed they had a surefire plan to achieve lasting peace and prosperity: Israel would declare war on the United States, and after Israel had been defeated, the Americans would bring military and economic aid and strengthen Israel as they had Japan and Germany.

"Yes," said Ben-Gurion, "and what if we win?"

When the Jews left powerless minority-group status behind them and achieved nationhood, such jokes as this one, predicated on power, were born.

HUMOR AND AGING

Imposed Humor

The earliest gerontological conversation I can recall on the topic of humor and aging yields an age-graded equivalent of imposed humor.

In 1972, at the first convention in my professional life, Erdman Palmore mentioned his interest in humor and aging to Morton Lieberman, who later remarked to me that he had been interested in the topic once but only found a single joke with a million variants. The basic story is as follows:

An elderly man took a young wife and after a couple of years went to the doctor, worried because his wife had not become pregnant. The doctor advised the couple to take in a young boarder. Some months later the doctor encountered the couple and remarked that the wife looked happy and pregnant. "I'm so glad things worked out," he told the two of them, "and how's the boarder?" "Just fine, doc," said the old man, "and she's pregnant too."

Get it? The young boarder was supposed to be a *guy*. *He* was supposed to impregnate the young wife, because old men are supposed to be impotent. But the joke was on the doctor, because the old man impregnated *two* young women. Thus he proved himself as potent as the doctor, maybe twice as potent as the doctor, and incidentally not quite human, since men characteristically experience a decline in sexual potency as they age (Weg, 1983).

This joke serves many purposes. It turns the tables on the medical profession as well as the biological life cycle; it denies not only biological decline but physical vulnerability and dependency. Last but not least, through the exclusion of old women, this joke denies a very bitter truth: Men die sooner than women, and those old persons in need of sexual companionship in later life are—statistically speaking—women, not men.

We might ask finally: Who tells this joke, and who laughs? Who takes comfort from the punch line? As I shall show by contrast with the next category of humor, I do not believe this to be an old man's joke. Old women are not part of the joke and thus, I would argue, are not part of the audience either. This, then, is a joke for young and middle-aged men. While it deflects anxieties about old age and sexual decline, it also denies the future.

The Resilient Underdog

What are the jokes the old men tell about sex, sensuality, and the fear of biological decline? I rely on my resident expert, Leland Taylor, whose obscene limericks reflect the category I have termed *the resilient underdog*.

The verse that follows, which was written by Leland in his 80s, samples the possibilities of humor in late life.

> I'm in my ninth decade, alas,
> And I fear it has now come to pass:
> The lead from my pencil
> (Decrepit utensil)
> Has now settled down in my ass.

That this claim was somewhat premature is shown by a pair of limericks written in the same month, July 1975, when their author was 82:

> To her bedmate she said with a curse,
> "I've laid many better, none worse:
> In your sad condition
> You need a mortician
> To get yourself laid in a hearse."

And:

> She said, "There's no shadow of doubt
> That at your age you're simply played out;
> That pendant deflection
> You call an erection
> Shows your wherewithal is without."

The final limerick in this brief sample was written in 1979, when Leland was 86:

> A sensuous, dried up old hag
> said, "Dirty old men aren't my bag.
> I much prefer young—
> who are strong and well hung—
> with organs unlikely to sag."

Let me approach the task of analysis by asking about these limericks the question I asked of the prototypical joke in the preceding section. Who wrote these poems? The author was a man in his 80s. The voice proclaiming sexual decline in men was that of a dissatisfied woman. Who laughs? Young men might be just a little less likely to laugh at these verses than at the joke of the preceding section; women of any age, including old women, might be more likely to laugh. "Laugh at yourself, not at others," Leland offered as his guideline for humor and aging. Relying on his expertise once again, I suggest that this selection of verse represents the category I term the *humor of the resilient underdog.*

The Humor of Power

To suggest that there can be a humor of old age that is in some sense a counterpart of the humor of ethnic power is to ask: What power do old people have? Knowledge is power, and one of the strengths of the old is that each old person knows, as no young person does, something about old age. As I was soliciting his assistance for this paper, Leland Taylor asked me what I would do for answers after he died, and I told him I would be in the position of an anthropologist whose tribe had migrated to the big city—I would simply have to take up another speciality in developmental psychology until I grew old myself. He rubbed my inadequacies in as I tried out my ideas: "You'd better be gathering your material, because I won't be around to geront for you much longer."

That is a powerful threat, and my final selection from the poetry of Leland Taylor is an example of the humor of power. Secure in a good old age for the moment—Leland was approaching eighty as he wrote this poem 1972—he let his own knowledge of an uncertain future become the power of this final poem, a warning to all younger poets who tell romantic lies about the blessings of old age.

THE SENIOR CITIZEN GETS IT ALL TOGETHER

by
Otto Genarius

Grow old along with me,
  As hair becomes quite thin
  And rheum drools down the chin;
  With ringing in the ears
  And eyelids oozing tears;
The best is yet to be.

Grow old along with me,
  Your leopard-spotted skin,
  Great sacs of fat therein;
  With paunch and sagging jowl
  And breath ungodly foul;
The best is yet to be.

Grow old along with me,
　　Your eyesight weak and blurred;
　　Your speech, a mumbled word;
　　The foot that does not land
　　True to the brain's command.
The best is yet to be.

Grow old along with me,
　　Your breathing hard, with gasps;
　　Your coughing, hacking rasps;
　　Great weight upon the chest;
　　The need to stop and rest.
The best is yet to be.

Grow old along with me,
　　Your anal sphincter loose,
　　Leaking colonic juice.
　　While pissing really hurts
　　And urine comes in spurts;
The best is yet to be.

Grow old along with me.
　　Your digits gnarled and bent,
　　Your vital juices spent;
　　Hair growing white and sparse
　　Except on ear and arse.
The best is yet to be.

Grow old along with me;
　　To mutter and to grumble
　　And at your zipper fumble;
　　Your peter hard to find
　　And sex confined to mind;
The best is yet to be.

Grow old along with me;
　　With varicose leg veins;
　　With fleeting, stabbing pains;
　　And ballocks dead and cold,
　　Relics of tail untold;
The best is yet to be.

Grow old along with me;
　　The best is yet to be.
　　As I lie here in bed,
　　With signals flashing red
　　And bottles for IV,
　　A plastic tube for pee;
　　A mask on mouth and nose,

In pain from head to toes;
Both legs in plaster casts;
P A's emitting blasts;
The jugs of bloody waste
And nurses, anxious-faced;
The flaccid bags of blood
Releasing wasted flood.

Grow old along with me;
The best is yet to be.
  Where is the ape that wrote
  This often quoted quote?
  Was he a youthful fool,
  His ears still wet from school?
  Or middle aged nit wit
  Who flung this pot of shit?
  What dried up senile fart
  Sold this tripe on the mart?

Grow old along with me;
The best is yet to be.
  Now if you find that bard,
  Please give him my regard;
  Then melt ten pounds of brass
  And pour it in his ass;
  And shove his precious nuts
  Clear up into his guts.
  But leave his ears intact
  And let his brain react.
  Then play this loud refrain,
  Again ! Again ! Again !
Grow old along with me;
The best is yet to be.

David Gutmann (personal communication, May 5, 1983) has proposed that the privilege of the stranger empowers the aging humorist. Perhaps this poem is a song of vengeance: The narcissistic wounds of an uncertain old age await the poet, but he has the victory of the preemptive strike: He has humiliated the younger generation—which is doomed to succeed him into old age—before old age can humble him. Armed with the power of the survivor and the stranger, he achieves what Gutmann suggests might be the last victory of the aged: The refusal to accept the posturing and pretenses of youth. Anthropologists have shown that the jester is granted social license to bring the unacceptable, even the unconscious or the socially taboo, into the open light of day for the discharge of cultural as well as intrapsychic tensions (see Vecsey & Lorenz, Chapter 10, this volume). Perhaps the "greying" of American society will expand the social license of our aging humorists and thus break down the social barrier of age-grading and the intrapsychic barrier of the narcissism of the life cycle, freeing us all to accept the fears and thus experience the blessings of a good old age.

THE POWER OF MARGINAL IDENTITY

This chapter has offered the reader a heuristic framework in which to consider the humor by and about the old. The model of humor proposed here rests on conceptual foundations laid by Freud in psychoanalysis and by Radcliffe-Brown and Warner in cultural anthropology. Freud (1960) proposed that wit may serve to deflect the sting of a painful truth; in this chapter, it has been suggested that old age forces the recognition of more than one painful truth. The young fend off the knowledge that old age awaits them, too, through a humor that disparages the old and denies the continuity of the life cycle, thus replicating the values of our age-graded society and its overevaluation of youth. The old enjoy the power of knowledge and perhaps the freedom songwriter Kris Kristofferson defined as "just another word for nothing left to lose." The special status of the aging humorist, combining marginal identity with the immunity of the jester, enables the old person to voice the painful truths of aging through the medium of a humor of power—the power of the survivor.

REFERENCES

Buchwald, A. (1979). Syndicated column, *The Washington Post.*
Freud, S. (1960). *Jokes and their relation to the unconscious.* New York: Norton.
McGhee, P. E., and Duffey, N. S. (1983a). Racial–ethnic differences in the onset of children's appreciation of humor victimizing different racial–ethnic groups. *Journal of Cross-Cultural Psychology.*
McGhee, P. E., and Duffey, N. S. (1983b). The role of identity of the victim in the development of disparagement humor. *Journal of General Psychology.*
Neugarten, B. L. (1982, August). *Successful aging.* [Invited address] American Psychological Association Public Lecture Series, Washington, DC.
Radcliffe-Brown, H. R. (1965). *Structure and function in primitive society.* New York: Free Press.
Taylor, L. (1983). Selected limericks and poems. Morgantown, WV: The Permutation Press.
Warner, W. L., & Lunt, P. L. (1941). *The social life of a modern community.* New Haven: Yale University Press.
Weg, R. B. (Ed.). 1983. *Sexuality in the later years.* New York: Academic Press.
Zillmann, D. (1983). Disparagement humor. In P. E. McGhee & J. H. Goldstein (Eds.). *Handbook of humor research: Vol. 1. Basic issues.* New York: Springer-Verlag.

Part III

DEATH AND DYING

Recently, aging has become firmly associated in our minds with death and dying. In ancient times, death occurred at all points in the life cycle. At the turn of the century, life expectancy for men in the United States was a mere 47 years, although the potential life span was no different than it is today. Children died routinely of infectious diseases. However, today death is seen as an event that occurs to the aged. Consequently, a book on humor and aging would not be complete without a consideration of the humor of death. Chapter 9, by Rosenberg, deals with the normally grim profession of funeral directors in our society, and Chapter 10, by Lorenz and Vecsey describes a very different society in which humor is institutionalized in the form of ceremonial clowns who perform to commemorate rites of passage, including death.

 Copyright © 1986 by Academic Press, Inc.
All rights of reproduction in any form reserved.

9

Humor and the Death System: An Investigation of Funeral Directors

EDWIN ROSENBERG

> *It was just a funeral parlor and the man asked me
> who I was.*
> *I repeated that my friends were all in jail, with a
> sigh.*
> *He handed me his card. He said, "Call me if they
> die."[1]*
>
> (Bob Dylan)
>
> *Life does not cease to be funny when people die any
> more than it ceases to be serious when people
> laugh.*
> (George Bernard Shaw in Peter & Dana, 1982)
> *You have to be careful in public. After all, everyone
> you meet is a prospective client.*
> (a Pennsylvania funeral director)

INTRODUCTION

There are myriad jokes about funerals and funeral directors. We hear that business is dead, that becoming a funeral director is a grave undertaking, that the proprietor of a vandalized cemetery has lost his marbles, that the profession is characterized by a certain "esprit de corpse," and that the modern funeral-directing family has his-and-hearse cars. But there is little, if any, information on the humor employed by the funeral directors themselves, particularly job-related humor. However, humor is one shield we often employ to deny or soften our exposure to death, and funeral directors are as human as the rest of us. In addition, a major element of humor is incongruity, and since the very nature of the funeral directing profession provides

---

[1] © 1965 Warner Bros. Inc. All rights reserved. Used by permission.

 Copyright © 1986 by Academic Press, Inc.
All rights of reproduction in any form reserved.

strong incongruities (e.g., treating a human being as an object), it is logical to conclude that the profession of funeral directing has its own brand of humor.

This chapter combines occupational sociology and thanatology to focus on what can be called the death-related professions. Merging this with the study of humor (most of which has been psychologically based), we arrive at the investigation of the form and function of humor in the death-related professions. The funeral-directing profession has been chosen, since few professions are so intimately involved with death.

Most models of humor are psychologically based and give social factors but a minor role. Thus, while social factors do indeed play a role in the nature and function of humor, they comprise but one of many subcategories of investigation and in fact have not been adequately researched. In the case of funeral directing, we might hypothesize that the sensitive nature of the profession coupled with mandatory professional training could generate structural influences on the type and amount of humor used by funeral directors regardless of variations in personality or other psychological traits. Thus, this chapter hopes to delineate social influences on humor in a death-related profession. In doing so, we should gain insight into the function of humor for those constantly dealing with death and add to the literature on the sociology of humor.

REVIEW OF LITERATURE

The Social Study of Humor

Within the range of factors that determine whether or not a statement or event is humorous, perhaps the one most frequently mentioned is incongruity. This has also been referred to as bisociation (Koestler, 1964) and discontinuity (Fine, 1983). As early as the sixteenth century, people began to pinpoint suddenness, unexpectedness, and surprise as indispensible prerequisites to laughter. The idea of incongruity (and, usually, the resolution of the incongruity) pervades most definitions and theories of humor. In fact, a nutshell definition of humor could be incongruity, and usually its resolution, which has mirthful intent or effect.

The social context in which an event takes place, all else being equal, can determine whether or not the event is judged humorous. While a comprehensive study of humor must include the comic (i.e., what it is that makes something inherently funny), the humorous stimuli, the psychological perceiving and processing of humor, the physiological reaction to humor, and the hypothesized cathartic effect of humor, we cannot ignore the social setting in which the event takes place. A pie in the face is funny in a circus clown act but not in a fancy restaurant when one is trying to hit up the boss for a raise—there's a time and place for such just desserts.

The literature on humor is scattered with references to the social nature and role of humor. Radcliffe-Brown (1940) viewed humor as an appropriate topic for comparative sociology and focused on the joking relationship as a standard feature in many societies. Obrdlik (1942), drawing on his experiences in Czechoslovakia during the Nazi occupation, wrote that humor emerged because of the social situation and influenced the group characteristics of the Czechs and Nazis as well as relations between the two groups. Mydral (1944) noted the social functions of humor in race relations. Klapp (1950) showed that the role of *fool* has a definite place in social organization. Blau (1955) and Bradney (1957) both wrote on the social functions of humor in bureaucracies, finding that humor enhanced social cohesion by relieving tension and reducing conflict.

While a number of sociological articles and a handful of dissertations on humor appeared in the 1960s, there was not a sufficient body of systematic analysis to herald the emergence of a new subfield called the sociology of humor. If a sociology of humor develops, wrote Martineau (1972), "it should be directed toward incorporating such knowledge into more general explanations of social interaction patterns and the dynamics of group structure and group process" (pp. 102–103). Thus, a sociology of humor should be able to show how humor functions within such dominant orientations as structural functionalism, conflict theory, or symbolic interactionism. The focus of early sociological analysis of humor on the relation of humor to conflict, social control, and social cohesion is on the right path. As Martineau (1972) writes:

> To identify the study of the social functions of humor in this fashion highlights the major contribution it has to offer—that is, to serve as an aid to the comprehensive understanding of group structure and group processes. Humor is part of every social process affecting the system; humor occurs in nearly every type of human interaction and can be analyzed as to how it influences each interaction pattern and the social structure emerging from it. (p. 103)

Fine (1983) notes that sociologists still lag far behind their psychology colleagues in the formal study of humor. He points out that since 1959 neither of the two major sociology journals (*American Sociologi-*

cal Review and *American Journal of Sociology*) has published an article with humor as the central focus. This is especially surprising since, says Fine, "Within most societies there are roles or positions that are conducive to the display performance of humor. Some people are allowed to joke and others are even expected to joke" (p. 161).

Thus, while acknowledging the psychological theories, the next task is to describe some functions of humor and some factors which influence humor, particularly to the extent that those functions and factors are social or are influenced by social structural constraints.

Functions of Humor

Humor has a number of different functions for individuals. Through laughter, we can release internalized tensions. Humor helps us cope with difficult circumstances by allowing us to laugh at our misfortune. It allows for the articulation of ideas or feelings which, without humor, would be difficult, impossible, or dangerous to express.

Another function of humor is to provide feelings of superiority by allowing us to joke about others or about a situation in which we find ourselves. Through humor we can feel above those who are seen as stupid, ugly, incompetent, and so on. (Note, however, that feelings of superiority are mediated by our relation to the target of the humor; for example, a pie in the face may be funny if it happens to one's mother-in-law but not if it happens to one's mother.)

Stephenson (1951) and Martineau (1972) have proposed social conflict and social control as the two major social functions of humor. Martineau (1972) developed a model of the social functions of humor whereby the conditions that determine the functions of humor can be specified. Martineau proposes three intra- or intergroup structural settings. Within these three settings we find various combinations of four variables: (1) the actor, or initiator of humor, (2) the audience, or recipient of humor, (3) the target, or butt of the humor (dichotomized as ingroup or outgroup), and (4) the judgment of the humor (dichotomized as esteemed or disparaged).

The model shows that humor can take on many forms, and the function and effect of humor will vary with the varying social processes that we find in different structural situations. Martineau's model begins to handle these variations systematically and, as opposed to other humor models, decidedly sociologically. The model provides a basis for generating research hypotheses as well as additional theoretical formulations on the social functions of humor.

The basic premise underlying his model is that humor is a social mechanism with definite social functions. As structural settings vary, so will the form and function of humor. Thus, to paraphrase W. I. Thomas (1928), if people perceive events as humorous, they will be humorous in their consequences.

Kane, Suls, and Tedeschi (1977) noted that Martineau's model cannot explain why humor is used in situations where nonhumorous praise or criticism would be just as effective. Still, they conceptualize humor as a tool of social influence and note that humor's power lies in its ambiguity. For instance, if the response to a statement we make is "Smile when you say that, stranger," we can do just that. ("Hey, I was just kidding!") Humor, unlike declarative criticism, allows for face-saving and social recovery.

Martineau's model is a comprehensive one. It is sociological in that the unit of analysis is the group rather than the individual. Also, though Martineau rarely states this explicitly, his model accommodates extremes in sociological theory (e.g., both conflict and structural–functional orientations to the analysis of human social behavior). Even the compromise position of conflict functionalism finds a home in certain parts of the model.

It also incorporates elements of reference group theory. Researchers (e.g., La Fave, 1972) have observed that "jokes tend to be judged as relatively funny by individuals whose reference group was esteemed and whose out-group was disparaged, and conversely, not funny by those whose reference group was disparaged and out-group esteemed" (Fine, 1983, p. 172). This echoes Martineau's ideas. Fine adds that "there is general agreement that reference group theory . . . helps explain the evaluation of group-directed humor" (p. 172).

Yet another function of humor—a function related to considerations of social conflict and social control—is the cathartic experience it may provide (e.g., Mindess, 1971). Humor as catharsis has its advocates and detractors. The former believe that by expressing otherwise forbidden or dangerous thoughts through humor, we alleviate frustration and restore ourselves to a socially normative state. This represents a social control approach to the function of humor.

The opposite approach is more in line with social learning theory. Here the argument is that, through the humorous expression of taboo ideas, we become accustomed to articulating those ideas. From humorous expression will follow serious expression, from which may follow action. Thus, through the catharsis provided by humor, we can either blow off steam harmlessly and maintain conformity to social norms, or we will become accustomed to nonnormative thoughts and expressions that might well lead to deviant behavior. These interpretations are so divergent, and the research so inconclusive, that Holland (1982) was forced to conclude that "the comic catharsis thus enables us to achieve a duality of acceptance and rejection. . . . In other words, we could say the comic catharsis is either transcedence of or submission to or the acceptance or rejection of society, the body, earthly life, religion, or transcendence itself" (p. 102).

This is revelation? It reminds one of the First Law of Sociology: Some do, some don't. Elegant, perhaps even accurate, but not very enlightening. But Holland is not to be faulted for covering all bases. Perhaps the nature of comic catharsis, and other ambiguities of humor as well, can be better specified by considering the social context in which the humor occurs.

Contexts of Humor

In a book-length treatment of humor, Holland (1982) writes about a defense function of humor that is most frequently utilized under certain conditions. That is, the structure of the situation in which one finds oneself will influence the emergence and function of humor. Here's an argument for a sociology of humor if ever there was one. Yet Holland's chapter on conditions is but four pages long, further evidence that while the influence of the social environment on humor is recognized, not a great deal of attention has been paid to that relationship.

Still, the arguments are there. In 1911, Henri Bergson (quoted in McGhee, 1979) wrote that "to understand laughter, we must put it back into its natural environment, which is society and above all we must determine the unity of its function, which is a social one (pp. 26–27). McGhee (1979) notes that other writers comment on factors that influence humor regardless of the associated mental processes or behavioral reactions. Thus, motivation and personality may influence humor but "similarly, the social context in which humor is experienced (or initiated) may influence both the level of appreciation and the functions served" (p. 4). That is, the amount and type of joking vary with social context. Compare, for example, the amount and type of humor in a sales talk versus a night club act versus a wedding.

Many writers perceive a major function of humor to be relieving tension. Further, it seems that the more sacred, revered, or taboo the topic, the greater the impact of humor aimed at it. Thus, to the extent that direct contemplation of death and dying makes us uneasy, there is potential for using humor to alleviate anxiety. Since contemplating death does in fact make many of us uneasy, it is not surprising that much humor involving aspects of death has emerged. Therefore, concludes Vernon (1970), in a sociological analysis of death, "Through humor, problems which may be too frightening to look at directly can be brought into the open and symbolically resolved" (p. 327).

Theories of society and culture give insight into the social uses of humor. Certain cultural, racial, religious, and occupational groups tell certain types of jokes. As mentioned earlier, Radcliffe-Brown (1940) recognized the social value and institutionalization across cultures of the joking relationship. This permits, and on occasion requires, joking or teasing someone with societally guaranteed impunity. Thus social friction can be defused through humor and family or group solidarity maintained. But while informal joking relationships characterize friend and collegial interaction and are particularly characteristic of males, we do not find such humor in the predominantly male funeral-directing profession. Because joking relationships appear to be relatively rare among funeral directors, we can hypothesize some social structural constraints, some type of formal or informal norms regarding humor, which differ from most other professions.

METHODOLOGY

Nine funeral directors were interviewed in the spring of 1983. Three were interviewed at their places of business, the others at the annual meeting of the Pennsylvania Funeral Directors Association. Purposive sampling was used. All funeral directors approached agreed to be interviewed.

In all interviews a semistructured format was used, and confidentiality promised. Guideline questions were the following:

1. Do most funeral directors have a sense of humor about their profession? How would you characterize this sense of humor, if it exists?
2. Is a professional sense of humor important for a funeral director? Why or why not? That is, what is the function of humor in your professional role performance? Does your professional training consider humor at all?
3. Do you think a funeral director who frequently jokes about his work is well adjusted (can see the light side of a serious situation) or poorly adjusted (uses humor to avoid directly confronting serious issues; has poor coping ability)? Why?
4. What or who is the target of the profession-related jokes and

humor of funeral directors? The public? Corpses? Funeral directors? Why do you think this is?

5. Are there jokes about funerals or funeral directors or jokes that funeral directors tell about their work that you think are not funny? Which ones? Why don't they appeal to you?

6. How many trade journals do you receive? Which ones? Do any have a regular humor feature? How do you feel about that?

7. How does your perception of public attitudes toward your profession influence your humor (a) among other funeral directors? (b) in public interactions?

8. Why are the humor and jokes used by funeral directors so sensitive an issue? After all, we sometimes use humor as a shield against direct confrontation of death.

9. Any favorite stories or incidents you would care to relate?

In addition, interviewees were asked their age, how many years they had been licensed, and whether they took over the family business.

The state conference was like any other conference, except that where an academician is accustomed to seeing publishers' displays of texts and instruction aids—the tools of the scholarly trade—one found instead the tools of funeral directing. A representative list of displays would include Ever-Kare, Inc. (bereavement counseling), Muzak, Pittsburgh Institute of Mortuary Science, Homespun (wooden urns), and exhibits of hearses, clothing, chemicals, and caskets.

Pennsylvania currently has about 1500 licensed funeral directors, of whom approximately 1% are female. It is predicted that in 10 years there will only be about 500 practicing morticians in the state. Inflation, net outmigration, and low profits (about 8% of total sales according to the Funeral Service "Insider," a newsletter) will take their toll. There is also great inequality in the distribution of business: About 10% of the state's funeral homes handle 50–80% of the volume. It is the directors of the smaller, lower-volume homes who will fold or retire during the coming decade.

Virtually all Pennsylvania funeral directors are white males. Of the nine funeral directors interviewed, all are white and seven are men. Their ages range from 27–55 (with a median of 34), and the number of years they have been licensed practitioners ranges from 2 to 32 (with a median of 8). Five are first-generation funeral directors; there was one second-, one third-, one fourth-, and one fifth-generation funeral director, indicating a tendency to keep the business in the family (this type of vocational inheritance is stronger among professions than occupations). Some had their practices in towns of fewer than 10,000 people, while others came from the state's largest cities.

RESULTS

The Existence and Nature of Funeral Director Humor

Funeral directors feel that their humor mirrors that of the general public. If ethnic, racist, or sexist jokes are making the rounds, they say, you will hear them among funeral directors, too. As with the general public, there are funeral directors with extremely keen senses of humor, and there are also those who say, as did one funeral director, "I can't even retell a joke I just heard without messing it up."

Two funeral directors mentioned urban–rural differences in opportunities for profession-related humor. Said one rural funeral director, "Most of us work in isolation." Doctors, lawyers, and dentists, he said, mingle with others in their profession on a daily basis. While larger urban firms may have two or more licensed funeral directors on the premises, rural morticians work alone. Aside from national and state conventions, he said, there is little face-to-face interaction. Of humor, he said, "When you're alone, there really is no one to share it with."

The second funeral director agreed: Spontaneous humor is more likely in urban areas where the funeral homes are larger and likely to employ more than one licensed mortician. In a small town, he said, everyone knows everyone else. What goes on in funeral homes in large cities? "Most anything, yes, as long as the boss isn't around."

During work, spontaneous humor—witticisms and one-liners—tends to prevail. One funeral director recalled hearing, amid the bustle of scalpels and stitches at a large funeral home where three preparations were going on simultaneously, "Change heads on one and two!"

Aside from such spontaneous humor, most funeral director humor is anecdotal. When asked for examples of profession-related humor, funeral directors offer not stock jokes but rather real-life incidents which—fortunately, they all agree—happened to someone else.

Professional Socialization and Humor

What impact does the aspiring funeral director's formal training have on his sense of humor? Is gentle humor cultivated, the better to ease the grief of bereaved clients, or is all humor discouraged to avoid offending mourners? To shed light on this, interviewees were asked about humor during their mortuary science college days.

Responses were mixed, but funeral directors generally agree that, while students are students, their mortuary science instructors, as part of the training routine, discouraged humor. One funeral director said none of his mortuary science teachers had a sense of humor nor would any tolerate it in their students. Even potentially humorous incidents were treated seriously. Another indicated that one of the lessons learned is that funeral directing is a serious profession with no place for occupational humor. Incongruous incidents that occurred during training were not treated lightly by the college preceptors. A third concurred that training is "serious, didactic—there's no humor there."

But some instructors do have a sense of humor and are not above showing it on occasion. During one examination, recalled a funeral director of his mortuary science college days, students had to identify by sight various parts of the body, pieces of which had been placed on display tables. There were four or five items per table, and students had 1 minute per table to identify all the parts before moving on to the next table. On one table, next to a piece of the liver, an instructor had placed a balled-up, blood-soaked piece of cotton. Only two students were not fooled. Nervous because of the time pressure, the interviewee failed to identify it correctly. "It looked like a bit of the pancreas to me," he admitted.

One of the women interviewed recalled being known as the class clown while in mortuary science college. Another funeral director recounted pranks that spilled over into the social lives of the aspiring morticians. Like other college students, several would economize by renting a house together. Sometimes they would bring home lab specimens for parties. Eyes were a favorite, for instance, an eye in a drinking glass. "Highball!?!? Oh, I thought you ordered an eyeball!" Or they would set some in a dish on the buffet table, said the interviewee. "Put them there with the other condiments. You know, the ketchup, the mustard, the eyes."

Another funeral director remembered clay and plastic, used for restorative surgery, being fashioned into genitalia to tease the female students. "I don't remember anything being harmful to anybody," he said. The men would also tease the women who were working on male bodies with such lines as, "Are you afraid to touch his tool?" The reverse wasn't reported, however, suggesting—as in other professions—a sex-based double standard of humor, at least among mortuary science college students.

From these and other incidents recounted in the interviews, it seems that mortuary science students are, with few exceptions, increasingly pressured to mask any natural sense of humor behind a somber professional facade. The students take their cues from their instructors, who tend not to participate in, condone, or tolerate much humor. This implies a belief within the profession that humor is not a functional part of the funeral-directing role; in fact, it could be quite dysfunctional.

The Function of Humor in Professional Role Performance

This led to questions regarding the humor used, if any, in professional situations. Several agreed that good funeral directors, whether they are naturally humorous or not, are serious in the funeral home. "It's so serious a thing to the family," said one. "Also, we work in a time frame. I don't have time for humor. I have to get the job done."

Another funeral director felt it is neither important nor beneficial to have a professional sense of humor. "To me, that's wasting valuable time," he said. In funeral directing, another added, "there's no levity involved. If you start it, where do you draw the line? The answer is not to let it start."

Other funeral directors are not so dogmatic. One had no objection to humor "if it was in the right context." He, as did others, worried about public objections.

Still others advocated a more flexible approach. "You kind of go with the families and see how far you can go to ease them," one said. Added another, "If you can bring a little lightness into the situation, it may help a grieving family."

Humor is often present at memorial services, particularly during reminiscences of the deceased. But it is the part of the funeral director neither to initiate nor to participate in these lighter moments. "If someone's telling a story and I'm listening," said one interviewee, "I'll walk away. If there's laughter, I don't want them to look around and see me standing there."

When an incongruity does occur—when something goes wrong on the job—the response is unlikely to be humorous. When a mishap takes place, said one funeral director, you "try to correct it in as tactful a manner as you can." He elaborated his rationale. "Most people have an idea that ties the funeral director to death." There is "a kind of hate relationship" between the family and the funeral director, "an obvious hostility" in some families. You cannot be funny when you are the target of displaced anger. "Sometimes after the funeral they'll come back and apologize for their behavior," he said.

The younger funeral directors were generally more accepting than their elders of humor in a professional situation. One highly esteemed funeral director said that, all else being equal, he would hire the funeral director with a sense of humor. He feels that humor, as in the telling of a gentle anecdote, "has a tendency to bring the family more out into the open. And I think they appreciate that, that you're helping bring them out of guilt or sorrow. And that's happened on many occasions." He was quick to add, however, that he does not view humor as an unmistakable sign of a well-adjusted funeral director. A mortician who constantly jokes about his profession with colleagues and in public, "I think, is hiding an inadequacy."

Intraprofession Humor

Funeral directors are at a loss to come up with stock in-house jokes, in sharp contrast to the myriad jokes about them and their profession. The National Funeral Directors Association's executive director acknowledged that "nothing in NFDA's library includes material dealing with in-house humor which related to funeral directors or funerals" (Raether, personal communication, July 2, 1983). Nor do the professional journals show any formal acceptance of professional humor. The three or four trade journals most funeral directors receive contain no standard humor items. Even the "recollections" columns seem to be serious. "They don't even tell of humorous incidents that happened," said one funeral director.

Another partially disagreed. While recalling nothing specific, he said that the trade journals may contain, on occasion, an article that comments on "something funny that happened years ago." He concurs that there is no regular humor (or humorous) feature and added, "If there was, I wouldn't read it anyway."

One funeral director opined that either nothing funny ever happens in the profession or there is an editorial policy against profession-oriented humor in the trade journals. The latter seems the case. Many funeral directors leave trade journals out for clientele to browse through. Thus, while the general feeling on the lack of humor in the professional press is summed up by one mortician's "I don't see why there isn't any," most agree with the funeral director who said, "I woudn't want to see humor in a journal that people outside the profession might read."

Public Humor

The professional humor of funeral directors is decidedly different from public humor about them and their work. Two of the funeral directors interviewed were piqued by popular jokes about morticians and funerals. "They don't have an understanding of what goes on," said one. And how should one respond, asked the other, when you're talking with someone on the street and a passerby says, "You'd better watch out! He's measuring you!" Especially if you have already heard the line eight times that day. Or in a lounge when a stranger enters and those who know the funeral director say, "Hey, Joe, measure him!" and toss the mortician a measuring tape. "See," said the interviewee, "they don't realize they're putting you on the spot."

"I try to be diplomatic," said another funeral director, referring to public joking about him and his profession. But he is offended by the jokes, by the snide questions about what happens to the jewelry or gold fillings of the deceased; he feels, as do others, that these barbs call his professional integrity into question.

Does the funeral director with a sense of humor rein it in in public? Yes. Is the funeral director concerned about his public image and the impact a reputation as a joker might have on it? Of course. The contemporary mortician is conscious of his personal and professional reputations—which overlap to a great extent—with a sensitivity bordering on defensiveness. "You have to be on your guard all the time," said one regarding the effect of his job on his public deportment. "People are watching you all the time in the funeral business."

One's reputation and the importance of word-of-mouth publicity to the funeral director are reasons for eschewing public—and often private—carousing. Another is that the funeral director is on call 24 hours per day. "Would you want to be prepped by a drunk?" one pointedly asked.

For this reason, many funeral directors feel the state, regional, and national meetings are as essential socially as professionally. "Most funeral directors like to drink," commented one. Hotels love to host funeral director meetings because "they always know there'll be a good bar bill. It's a time for them to let loose." Among their own kind, away from their public and their beeper phones, funeral directors can finally let their hair down.

One funeral director described his efforts to sensitize the public to the insensitivity of its mortician-directed humor. To the standard query, "How's business?"—the expected response being "Dead"—

he answers, "Fine." This defuses the joke, he feels, and makes the
joker consider the underlying tactlessness of the humor.

He also described his variation on an old theme. While in a bar
recently, one of his acquaintances pointed to someone who had just
entered and said to the funeral director, "Which pocket's your tape in?
Measure him."

"Well," replied the mortician, "don't you think I'm a good funeral
director?"

"Sure. Why?"

"I don't need a tape. I have a trained eye."

The funeral director concluded, with a satisfied smile, "It makes
people think a bit."

Most funeral directors, despite their dislike for the public's joking,
go along with it as good-naturedly as they can. No one else mentioned
trying to combat public jokes; if nothing else, funeral directors are
aware of the value of good public relations. "Word of mouth is how we
get our business," said one, "and one word of bad is worth a thousand
words of good."

Funeral directing is indeed a sensitive profession but, in the opinion of another interviewee, morticians "are too concerned about the
reaction of the public." They are afraid the public will misunderstand
the funeral director's laughter. Yet this funeral director said he does
not laugh at public jokes, even if he thinks they are funny. And while
he agreed that a sense of humor makes one a better funeral director
and one's job easier, he claimed you will never find a funeral director
telling a profession-oriented joke at a nonprofessional social gathering.

Grave—but Lighthearted—Stories

As mentioned earlier, when asked for examples of profession-related humor, funeral directors tend to provide anecdotes. The following are encapsulated versions of a representative sampling of such
anecdotes, with the funeral directors' comments where appropriate.

On the way out of the funeral home following a service, a handle on
the casket breaks and the casket crashes to the ground. It was terrible
at the time, said a funeral director who was assisting at the service, but
"later on you might laugh at it, because it happened to the other guy."

At the cemetery, the straps used to lower the casket into the grave
break. Into the open grave fall the casket and a pallbearer, who dislo-

cates his shoulder. The family insisted on opening the casket "to be sure Grandma was OK. OK, hell, she was dead!"

A female funeral director, prepping a body, shaved off the man's stubble only to be informed by the family that it had been his moustache. She painstakingly restored it using hair from the deceased's head. The family complained that the moustache was now the wrong color and would have to be dyed. Half an hour before the viewing, they again changed their minds and demanded that the "moustache" be removed. The funeral director said it all seems funny now but, at the time it happened, "if you'd've gone 'poof,' I would've fallen over."

A funeral director was recalled to the gravesite to supervise the disinterring of a body because the bereaved family felt the deceased's tie was too tight.

During his internship a funeral director was waiting at the gravesite as the procession drove into the cemetery. As the cars pulled up, the bereaved widow's son leapt out of his car, ran to the open grave, and jumped in. Despite the pleas of the funeral director, clergy, and friends, he stayed put, refusing to allow the burial to take place. Finally, a ladder was brought and lowered into the grave, and the distraught young man wrestled out. On the return trip from the cemetery, the interns laughed about the incident. "Should've thrown some dirt on him," said one. "That would've gotten him out."

Following a service, a female mourner reentered the funeral home from the parking lot. "Do you mind if I have a moment alone?" she asked the funeral director. "Of course not," he replied. Curious, he inconspicuously watched as she walked over to the open casket, leaned over . . . and punched the deceased squarely in the face! Unaware that she'd been observed, she turned and walked out, pretending to wipe away a tear as she passed the funeral director, who could barely hide his shock and astonishment.

These incidents display two tendencies of funeral director humor. First, it is largely anecdotal. Second, the perception of the incident as humorous came later—there was nothing funny about these events at the time they happened. In other words, there must be incongruity for humor; and there must be a resolution of this incongruity; and in most cases, the resolution must be relatively harmless. Often the only differences between the comic and the tragic are the degree of pain inflicted on the target and our relation to the target.

"Mistakes are funny," confided one funeral director, "but nothing to make light of." The standard humor of funeral directors, if there is such a genre, is the tragicomic anecdote. It is more tragic when it occurs, less so as the event—the incongruity—is resolved in a relatively harmless fashion, and more comic upon later reflection when the funeral director is temporally, spacially—and legally—removed from the situation. Much of the humor seems to flow from perceived superiority in the form of being grateful it happened to someone else. There is no doubt that any funeral director can empathize with a colleague's past predicaments. Indeed, the most common response obtained when asking other funeral directors if they had experienced such mishaps was, "Oh no, thank the Lord. . . . I shudder when I think of that happening to me."

DISCUSSION

There is an old story about an old Englishman who wanted to find the real America. He journeyed to this country and wound up in the middle of a gigantic cornfield in the middle of a farm in the middle of Kansas which, as we know, is in the middle of America. "Whatever do you do with all this corn?" he asked the farmer. "Well," said the farmer around the stem of his corncob pipe, "we eat what we can, and what we can't, we can!" And he threw back his head and laughed uproariously, to the puzzlement of his foreign guest.

Upon returning to England, the old fellow recounted his odd adventure. "And when I asked what became of the corn," he told a friend, "the farmer said, 'We consume as much as we are able, and that which we are unable to consume we put up in tins.' And he laughed and laughed, and I never found out why."

One has a similar response upon entering a professional subculture, except that in this case we hope to find out why. Abrahams (1978) noted the emergence of special ingroup terms (i.e., jargon) and situated joking (p. 23). Fine (1983) writes that "the power of the group culture can be recognized by anyone who enters a group that has been in existence for some time. Most groups . . . develop a set of joking references that may be unrecognizable to those outside the group" (p. 170).

Thus, to an outsider some subculture humor may be repulsive, some—as in the anecdote above—incomprehensible, at least until it is explained, and sometimes even then the humor is not so evident. There are no shortcuts to the *Verstehen* needed to truly delve into the psyche of the subculture.

For example, one funeral director related how he had been "subbing" for a vacationing colleague when a late-night call brought him to the colleague's place of business to do a preparation. It was the typical dark and stormy night, and he was in a strange facility when suddenly the aspirator clogged, blowing a hose, its fuse, and the fuses in the rest of the house. End of story. My blank face not being the desired response, he went on with some exasperation to explain what an aspirator is, what it does, and how a hose might clog, overheating the machine to the point where the hose bursts and the fuses blow, simultaneously plunging the house into total darkness and covering the funeral director with things that usually stay inside people. To those of us unfamiliar with such machines, the tale takes some explaining. Funeral directors, however, immediately identify with the story and, especially since it did not happen to them, find it quite funny.

Nonetheless, some general patterns to the humor of funeral directors can be discerned. First, particularly among younger funeral directors, there is a preference for hiring morticians with, rather than without, a sense of humor. It is felt that such persons would be more sociable, better minglers, and more comfortable with strangers.

Second, there is a feeling among members of the profession that the public image of the funeral director is changing for the better, that today's public realizes that funeral directors are human beings. "The image of the funeral director as a guy in a dark suit and a smug look on his face is gone," said one funeral director.

Still, funeral directors are extremely sensitive to what they perceive as a tenuous public image. "Whatever we do has to maintain respect and dignity," one mortician said. This must seem especially true given the industrywide feeling of unfair persecution. Funeral directors feel state and federal policies are based on shoddy or unsubstantiated evidence. Many complaints about the funeral process are, in fact, directed at cemeteries or crematories and not at funeral directors. One mortician said that the industry average was one complaint per 1000 cases: "Any business would be happy with that." But, as a profession, funeral directors are—perhaps justifiably—highly defensive and thus hypersensitive to any perceived questioning of their integrity. In such a situation it is no surprise they keep a lid on their humor, at least insofar as public awareness is concerned.

Fourth, unlike the finding of Fox (1959) that aspiring physicians learn, during their medical schooling, that humor is an effective, appropriate way to handle their reactions to death and other stressful situations, funeral directors do not joke, or do not admit to joking, about death. Humor seems to be not merely not condoned but actively discouraged during the prospective funeral director's formal training in a college of mortuary science. The funeral director's job is ironically like the lifeguard's. If he does his job well, he's largely unnoticed; if he fails when called upon to perform, it is glaringly obvious, and the consequences may be severe. Just as Emerson (1963) noted that humor in the hospital rarely crossed status lines, it may be that the funeral director feels his humor has no direct function, and could easily be dysfunctional, in interactions with his clientele. Therefore, with humor not guaranteed to help and with its perceived potential to jeopardize the funeral director's effective performance of his duties, no wonder it is formally downplayed during the training period.

Fifth, funeral directors complain about the tendency of the public to joke about their relation to death and corpses. Bowman (1959) noted that morticians were very defensive regarding public joking about funerals and funeral directors. This reinforces the subcultural prediction that many funeral and death-related jokes that are funny to the public (dominant culture) are not funny to funeral directors, being perceived instead as disparaging to the profession. More than one mortician mentioned the dreadful repeated encounters with the question, "How's business?" and the expected response, "Dead." Needless to say, this and similar exchanges were rated by funeral directors as less than hilarious.

Finally, the funeral directing role is rife with potential for incongruity. The odds are that many more incongruous events occur than meet the public eye, but these are handled with the utmost concern at the time of occurrence. Only afterward, when the incongruity has been successfully resolved and sufficiently distanced, do the funeral directors allow themselves the luxury of humorous reflection. Thus their humor tends to be anecdotal. Funeral directors laugh after the fact, especially if they were not involved in the incident, and especially *because* they were not involved in the incident.

CONCLUSIONS

The sociological analysis of humor is concerned with how social structures, statuses and roles determine or constrain the emergence, genre, and uses of humor. Shakespeare wrote, "A jest's prosperity lies

in the ear of him that hears, never in the tongue of him that makes it"
(see Munro, 1957); none would argue that humor, like beauty, exists in
the mind of the beholder. To a large extent, our personalities are
socially determined. It makes sense, therefore, to focus part of the
analysis of humor on social influences. "Certainly humor is not entirely determined by social forces," writes Fine (1983), "but without a
social referent, humor would make no sense" (p. 176).

Little is known about humor in the death-related professions. There
is some information to be gained by surveying research on the health
care professions. Even so, health care research that has yielded insight into the role of humor in those settings has done so not as a goal
but fortuitously, in the course of a larger investigation (e.g., Coser,
1965; Fox, 1959). Other research (e.g., Emerson, 1963) set out to study
the relationship of social structure to humor and happened to choose a
health care setting because of its clear status hierarchy and highly
structured interaction patterns. But in none of these cases was the goal
specifically to study humor in the health care professions. This is to
some extent understandable; as Robinson (1977) noted, "Humor is not
considered to be a formal communication mode. . . . Because health
and illness are 'serious' business, humor is not an expected occurrence" (p. 39).

The purpose of this chapter has been to investigate the humor of
funeral directors to see whether and to what extent a sociological
approach can shed light on humor in the death-related professions. It
seems, based on this limited investigation, that there is indeed a genre
of humor unique to this profession but in the form of anecdotes and
spontaneous witticisms rather than stock jokes. In addition, it appears
that part of the professional socialization process is the internalization
by mortuary science students of the idea that humor is a devalued part
of their professional role. Thus we find social structural constraints on
the emergence and nature of humor in a professional subculture, and
these constraints seem to operate regardless of individual variations in
cognitive processing, motivation, or personality.

Being ill is serious and thus arouses anxiety and tension. If Robinson (1977) is correct in the conclusions drawn from her study of humor
in health care settings, humor helps reduce that tension and anxiety.
Also, Coser (1965) found that in the hospital, with its distinct status
hierarchy and often anxiety-filled interactions, humor as a communication medium can function to decrease social distance and encourage
less formal, friendlier relations between, say, patient and staff.

But as Robinson (1977) perceived, "When anxiety or tension is too
high, humor may fall flat" (p. 51). If we assume that dying and death

are more serious than illness, then it follows that while humor could relieve anxiety and tension in such a setting, the potential for it "falling flat" looms large. This would explain why, more than the nurse or physician, the funeral director is reluctant to incorporate humor into his professional role performance.

Martineau's (1972) model, which uses the group as the unit of analysis, points out the importance of structural characteristics in determining the (social) functions of humor. The social status of a group or the relative status of interacting groups, their history of past interaction, and the norms of interaction all influence which party is entitled to initiate humor, what form the humor can take, and which topics are acceptable as content.

The humor of funeral directors can be trichotomized into in-house jokes (formal structure; incongruity and its resolution), anecdotes (first-, second-, or thirdhand real incidents that were not funny at the time they happened but, in retrospect, are), and spontaneous humor (puns, one-liners, and witticisms most likely encountered in the context of one's work). In-house jokes and anecdotes tend to reflect the nature of humor in the professional role, while spontaneous humor is more a measure of the individual's sense of the comic.

If we treasure life, then death—which gives limit, meaning, and perhaps even desperation to life—can be perceived as the greatest incongruity of all. Thus, we joke greatly about it. We are also powerless to defeat death; we are inferior to it. Thus, we joke often about it, for humor is both a denial shield and a mechanism through which we can make light of our powerlessness. Because a dead body, which looks human but does not behave that way, is incongruous in itself, we joke about corpses. Because funeral directors are so intimately involved with death and corpses, we joke about them.

In late 1983, the nationally syndicated "Dear Abby" (1983) featured a series of columns on funeral director jokes. After one funeral director complained of the inappropriateness of such humor, Abby glibly responded, "All men are cremated equal." This generated additional protest letters (and not only from funeral directors), but one New York mortician wrote, "Don't let it bother you, Abby, most people in this business have a good sense of humor."

Do they? Most funeral directors do not joke much about death. Perhaps because they have had training experiences that we have not, death is not incongruous to them. If that is the case, death is part of their daily existence, part of their normal reality. Death is what pays the mortgage and puts bread on the table.

Mindness (1971) noted that "a special affinity to certain types of humor (e.g., sexual, hostile, death-related) indicates an unusual need to work off anxiety related to its content" (p. 179). If this is true, then it is not surprising that much of the public jokes about death, funerals, and funeral directors and that funeral directors tend not to joke about themselves or their business. They have relatively low anxiety levels regarding death and thus, according to Mindess' notion, little need to joke about it.

But Mindess also claims that "a strong dislike (of a humor type or topic) suggests an inability to tolerate irreverence about its content" (p. 179). This explains the funeral director's general dislike for public jokes about death and his profession. Defensive and hypersensitive to criticism, the funeral director is adept at finding the injurious needle in any haystack of humor.

Funeral directors are justified in this defensiveness that borders on paranoia. Since 1963, when Mitford's muckraking "The American Way of Death" was published, the profession has been the target of criticism and scrutiny ranging from local to federal levels. Over the past two decades, according to one mortician, funeral directors have lost whatever professional sense of humor they may have had. Twenty years after publication, said another, you still hear a lot of "Well, Jessica said . . . ." In the last 10 years, he claimed, the Federal Trade Commission has spent $14 million investigating the funeral industry. A Federal Trade Commission directive, which went into full effect April 30, 1984, requires funeral directors to itemize all goods and services available to consumers.

In addition to itemized pricing, funeral directors—especially the more traditional ones—are uncertain how to respond to such recent innovations as cut-rate, franchised funeral homes and cremation services that undercut funeral home cremation costs by up to 88% ("Franchised funeral homes to open," 1983; McCarthy, 1983). Their professional integrity is offended by what one funeral director referred to as "the McFuneral," yet a strenuous protest by the profession could effect another public salvo of Mitfordian accusations.

It is suggested by McGhee (1979) and others that a playful frame of mind is a prerequisite for humor. Perhaps this is another reason why funeral directors see little humor in their profession. It is work, not play, and there is nothing playful about it or about the appropriate professional frame of mind.

There is, however, a belief in an association between good mental health and having a good sense of humor. Remarked Mindess (in Blakeslee, 1983), "A person with a lively sense of humor is more flexible, insightful and healthier in a lot of respects. Humor is breaking free from inhibitions" (p. 9). Extant research, while inconclusive, indicates that both incessant humor and a total lack of humor are indicators of abnormal mental health. For the great middle mass of us, however, the jury is still out. While we would probably worry more about a funeral director who was always joking than about one who never smiled, we might think carefully before engaging the services of either type.

The role of funeral director in the death system and of the death system in society is, for the purpose at hand, perhaps best interpreted macrosociologically from a structural–functional perspective. The profession exists because of a socially expressed need. It is in the profession's interest to recruit new members who will not push for major reform and to train those recruits so that they can carry out their role with minimal friction. The funeral director's relationship with the public is symbiotic. If the public demands he carry out his work while maintaining low visibility, so be it. And with a public still uncomfortable with confronting death, with public interactions coming at a time of maximum grief and emotional upheaval, the funeral director is wise in eschewing borscht belt patter.

An occupational analysis of funeral directors on a microsociological level would do well to employ a dramaturgical perspective. The funeral director's role, with its blocking, lines, props, front- and back-stage personae, and audience seems custom-made for such an approach.

While funeral directors seem generally reticent to endorse a sense of humor as beneficial to their professional role, others argue in favor of such behavior. Peter and Dana (1982) write that although one might think the shock of loss and such reactions as denial, grief, anger, and depression would banish humor from the scene, "humor can play a valuable role in the process of accepting loss" (p. 88). While not recommending humor as a substitute for grieving, Peter and Dana feel that "humor is an ally in helping us accept our own mortality and can be a comfort when we are bereaved" (p. 89).

There are two avenues of investigation that would shed more light on the topic of humor in the death-related professions. The first, obviously, is to add to our knowledge by studying other professions, such as obituary writers, casket manufacturers, or emergency room staff, where we would expect to find death-oriented humor used for defense, coping, or superiority. The second is to alter the method of investigation. Mindess (1971) wrote that "much more significant than our humorous reactions . . . are our humorous creations. The spontaneous witticisms we come up with ourselves grow directly out of our personal predicaments" (p. 180). While the loosely structured interviews of this exploratory research are preferable to surveys, participant or nonparticipant observation of the profession would be better still. Only in this way can the researcher truly be exposed to the spontaneous humor that emerges from the work setting, humor that is qualitatively different from the anecdotes recounted here. Through more and varied research we will gain a better understanding of the social and psychological functions of humor for those who deal with it—and us—at the very end of the life cycle.

REFERENCES

Abrahams, R. D. (1978). Towards a sociological theory of folklore: Performance services. In R. H. Byington (Ed.), *Working Americans: Contemporary approaches to occupational folklife* (pp. 19–42). Washington, DC: Smithsonian Folklore Studies (No. 3).

Blakeslee, S. (1983, Aug. 30). Tests show you are what you laugh at. *New York Times*, Sec. C, pp. 1, 8.

Blau, P. (1955). *The dynamics of bureaucracy*. Chicago: University of Chicago Press.

Bowman, L. (1959). *The American funeral*. Washington, DC: Public Affairs Press.

Bradney, P. (1957). The joking relationship in industry. *Human Relations, 10*, 179–187.

Coser, R. L. (1965). Some social functions of laughter: A study of humor in a hospital setting. In J. K. Skipper and R. C. Leonard (Eds.), *Social interaction and patient care* (pp. 292–306). Philadelphia: Lippincott.

Dear Abby. (1983, October 24). *Era*, Bradford, PA.

Dylan, Bob. (1965). *Bob Dylan's 115th dream*. Warner Bros. Music.

Emerson, J. P. (1963). *Humor in hospital setting*. Unpublished Ph.D. dissertation, University of California, Berkeley. (University Microfilms No. 64–5218).

Fine, G. A. (1983). Sociological approaches to the study of humor. In P. McGhee and J. Goldstein (Eds.), *Handbook of humor research: Vol. 1. Basic issues*. New York: Springer-Verlag.

Fox, R. C. (1959). *Experiment perilous: Physicians and patients facing the unknown*. Glencoe, IL: Free Press.

Franchised funeral homes to open (1983, November 7). *Bradford Era*, p. 11.

Holland, N. (1982). *Laughing: A psychology of humor*. Ithaca, NY: Cornell University Press.

Kane, T. R., Suls, J. & Tedeschi, J. T. (1977). Humor as a tool of social interaction. In A. J. Chapman and H. C. Foote (Eds.), *It's a funny thing humour* (pp. 13–16). New York: Permagon.

Klapp, O. (1950). The fool as a social type. *American Journal of Sociology, 55*, 157–162.

Koestler, A. (1964). *The act of creation*. New York: Dell.

La Fave, L. (1972). Humor judgments as a function of reference group and identification classes. In P. E. McGhee & J. H. Goldstein (Eds.), *The psychology of humor* (pp. 195–210). New York: Academic Press.

Martineau, W. H. (1972). A model of the social functions of humor. In P. E. McGhee & J. H. Goldstein (Eds.), *The psychology of humor* (pp. 101–125). New York: Academic Press.

McCarthy, P. (1983, November 27). New cremation service roils state's funeral directors. *New York Times*, Sec. 11, pp. 1, 4.

McGhee, P. (1979). *Humor: Its origin and development*. San Francisco: Freeman.

Mindess, H. (1971). *Laughter and liberation*. Los Angeles: Nash.

Mitford, J. (1963). *The American way of death*. Greenwich, CT: Fawcett.

Munroe, John (Ed.) (1957). *The London Shakespeare*. Vol. 1. New York, Simon & Schuster.

Myrdal, G. (1944). *An American dilemma*. New York: Harper.

Obrdlik, A. J. (1942). Gallows humor: A sociological phenomenon. *American Journal of Sociology, 47*, 709–716.

Peter, L. J., & Dana B. (1982). *The Laughter prescription*. New York: Ballantine.

Radcliffe-Brown, A. R. (1940). On joking relationships. *Africa, 13*, 195–210.

Robinson, V. M. (1977). *Humor and the health professions*. Thorofare, NJ: Slack.

Stephenson, R. M. (1951). Conflict and control functions of humor. *American Journal of Sociology, 56*, 569–574.

Thomas, W. I., & Dorothy S. Thomas (1928). *The child in America*. New York: Knopf.

Vernon, G. (1970). *Sociology of death: An analysis of death-related behavior*. New York: Ronald.

Hopi Ritual Clowns and Values in the Hopi Life Span

CAROL ANN LORENZ
CHRISTOPHER VECSEY

INTRODUCTION

For those interested in studying humor cross-culturally, the North American Indians offer rich and diverse testimony. The three primary areas in tribal life in which regularized humor is prominent are (1) joking relationships, in which persons in particular positions vis-à-vis one another (such as aunt–nephew) enjoy the license of repartee; (2) trickster stories, in which the protagonist displays the range of comic proportions; and (3) ritual clowning, in which ceremonial performers elicit the laughter of their audience. This chapter examines a specific manifestation of ritual clowning among the Hopi Indians of Arizona and aims to demonstrate the importance of this type of humor in defining the Hopi community and its periphery.

THE HOPI PEOPLE

The Hopi Indians are of significance to us because their social organization and subsistence activity are in continuity with the wellsprings of human life. These people have lived in the same villages—

Copyright © 1986 by Academic Press, Inc.
All rights of reproduction in any form reserved.

the western mesa pueblos of Arizona—for over 800 years, and despite centuries of contact with Spanish and "Anglo" invaders, they have persisted with remarkable tenacity.

Their way of life has been termed "primitive," "tribal," or "primal"; but however it is characterized, it possesses the following qualities, many of which form sharp contrasts to the way of modern, "civilized" life. First, the Hopis live in a face-to-face social world. Their society consists of people whose faces are seen regularly, perhaps even daily. Second, virtually all the people whom they see and whom they will continue to see until death separates them, are related either by blood or by ceremonial bonds. Their social world is one in which individuals can claim a kinship obligation from almost anyone they meet. Third, these various relatives possess a remarkable degree of social homogeneity. Although there are classes of Hopis—commoners and chiefs—there is little difference in the subsistence activities or economic life of the two classes; indeed, it is the duty of the chiefs to be servants of the rest of the population. Although some Hopis are better off economically than others, this does not coincide with class differentiation, and there is no spirit of class competition. Fourth, the subsistence activities of the Hopis are primary in the sense that, at least traditionally, each Hopi village produces locally and directly its own means of sustenance. Trade has existed for centuries, but it has been for nonessential items. For their food, housing, and clothing, Hopis have relied on the immediate environment: growing corn, cotton, and other crops; gathering firewood and lumber; mixing their own local clay; and quarrying local stone. Fifth, this homogeneous community of relatives emphasizes the well-being of the group over individual ambitions, with harmony being valued far more than personal success. And finally, the Hopis value tradition over change, affirmation of the community way of life over criticism of Hopi ways. In short, the Hopis are conservatives who uphold their ancient ways and who have a relatively clear idea of who they are and how they should live their social lives (Brandt, 1954; Thompson, 1950).

HOPI RITUAL CLOWNS AND CLOWNING

In their most sacred rituals and in their determination to persist as a people, the Hopis send in their clowns. As among other Pueblo groups, and indeed among American Indian tribes in general, clowning is an integrating element in Hopi ceremonialism. Clowns are part of the bulwark of Hopi society, promoting the Hopis' very existence (see Hieb, 1972a, for an excellent analysis).

The generic Hopi term for clown is *chukuwimkiya*, which may derive from a word meaning "to spring up from a concealed place" (Fewkes, 1892, p.156; see also Harvey, 1970; Hieb, 1972a; Parsons, 1939). There are various types of Hopi clowns, identifiable by their costumes and body paintings.

Types of Clowns

Chuku clowns (Figure 10.1) have two distinct appearances. The *Sikya Chuku* paint their body yellow, with red stripes across their eyes and mouth; they wear sheepskin wigs and red-dyed rabbit fur ear pendants. *Nasomta Chuku* are smeared with whitish clay and blackened around the eyes and mouth. Their hair is dressed up into bunches on either side of the head and may also be covered with mud.

Paiyakyamu (Figure 10.2), a second type of clown, have black and white horizontal stripes painted the length of their body, with blackened eyes and mouth. They wear tight-fitted headdresses with tall, similarly banded horns. Like the *Chuku*, they perform naked, except for a breechcloth or blanket.

Tachuktu, or Mudhead clowns (Figure 10.3), are painted all over with pinkish clay and wear a sacklike cloth mask with knobs containing seeds and cotton. They wear a black cloth from a woman's discarded dress as a kilt or over one shoulder, woman-style. They also

Figure 10.1 *Nasomta Chuku* clown with hair tied up into bunches.

Figure 10.2 *Paiyakyamu* clown with alternating black and white stripes and banded horns (adapted from Roediger, 1941, plate 39).

wear a black cloth around their neck, containing additional packets of seeds.

Finally, the *Piptuku* (Figure 10.4) usually wear white face masks and sheepskin wigs, but their costumes include various forms of motley, ragged, and ephemeral *bricolages*. They burlesque foreigners, wearing Navajo dress, nuns' habits, garish bermuda shorts, or whatever they can lay their hands on (Colton, 1959; Harvey, 1970).

Some of these clowns wear or carry sexual insignia. Some carry food, such as melons, corn, *piki* bread and gourds. Most of the clowns are men, although clowning is not restricted to males. Indeed, it is not even restricted to the clowns themselves. In addition to the *chuku-wimkiya*, there are kachinas and sodalities who perform clowning acts (Fewkes & Stephen, 1892; Fewkes, 1900a, Parsons, 1923). During the New-Fire ceremonial, members of the men's society interrupt a solemn procession to joke and laugh hysterically before continuing their procession in silence (Fewkes, 1900a). In another important processional at the end of the Bean ceremonial, certain kachinas—masked

Figure 10.3 *Tachuktu* or Mudhead clown with cloth mask and black kilt (adapted from Roediger, 1941, plate 40).

Figure 10.4 *Piptuku* clown with white face mask, dressed to parody a Mexican.

impersonators of the gods—pretend that their lightweight baskets of young bean plants are heavy, as a form of prayer for a successful harvest (Earle & Kennard, 1938). Their staggering under the "weight" of the baskets causes much amusement among the Hopi spectators. Other kachinas are known to jitterbug or to play madcap hopscotch and basketball as a respite from their more serious duties. Clowning pervades Hopi ritual (see Earle & Kennard, 1938; Parsons, 1936; Steward, 1931b; Titiev, 1944).

Although there is debate about whether the clowns are truly kachinas (see Bunzel, 1932; Parsons, 1936, 1939), the *chukuwimkiya* appear when the kachinas are in force, approximately from the winter to summer solstices, which divide the Hopi year (Fewkes, 1897b; Hodge, 1896; Titiev, 1944). They no longer possess the formal organization that they had a century ago. Over the past decades the clowns have lost many of their official functions, and some types are defunct at certain villages. Under white intrusions the clowns have subdued some of their scatalogical, sexual, and violent antics, but the clowns persist in the face of attempts by whites to intimidate them (see Frost, 1982).

Clowning Behavior

Hopi clown performances are deservedly celebrated. The clowns arrive at the plaza via rooftops rather than by taking normal paths. After jumping up and down on the roofs, they descend the ladders head first, amusing the crowds with their contrary behavior. They frequently do the opposite of whatever the kachinas are doing: While the kachinas dance, the clowns may stand motionless or sit on the ground; if the kachinas dance slowly in single file, the clowns race around them in a wide circle (e.g., Baxter, 1882; Roediger, 1941; Scully, 1975). The clowns often dance backward, stand on their head, and use inverted speech, saying the opposite of what they mean (Parsons, 1936; see also Fewkes & Stephen, 1892). They also build a "house" in the plaza, using ashes, which they refer to as logs and clay (Simmons, 1971).

The clowns act incompetent, frequently trying in vain to imitate the dance steps of the kachinas (Baxter, 1882). They fall down, eat the wrong things, walk the wrong way; they limp, stagger, and beg for food. Hopi clowns sometimes ridicule deformed, decrepit, or crippled persons in the audience, as well as widows and orphans (Thompson & Joseph, 1965), and they are not above stealing the crutches from a paralyzed spectator (Parsons, 1936).

The clowns also satirize personal and group foibles and eccentricities, such as tippling, philandering, and arguing (Koenig, 1976; Parsons, 1936). It is interesting that today the Hopi newspaper at New Oraibi, *Qua'toqti*, uses images of *Paiyakyamu* clowns to deliver social commentary in their editorial page cartoons. Both in print and in the plaza, the clowns jibe their fellow Hopis (Beck & Walters, 1977).

Foreigners are special targets for the clowns' pranks. The *chuku-wimkiya* mimic foreign speech and wear foreign clothing in their skits. Curly hair is exotic to the Hopis and therefore something to satirize. Often the clowns wear woolly wigs, including some black ones to imitate black Americans (Voth, 1912). The clowns impersonate white traders and shopkeepers (Parsons, 1936), soldiers, and a variety of government attachés, including teachers, social workers, and administrators of the Bureau of Indian Affairs (Earle & Kennard, 1938; Scully, 1975). The clowns comically mime anthropologists (Fewkes, 1892, 1910), priests, and hippies, and they actively taunt student groups, forcing white youths to race them in rigged contests and even humping them (Coze, 1957; B. Williams, personal communication May 10, 1982). Hopi clowns mock not only "Anglos," but also Mexicans, other Pueblo Indians, Navajos, Utes and Apaches (Fewkes, 1892; Parsons, 1936), and even Hopis from other mesas (Parsons, 1936).

The Hopis' own religious leaders, sacred ceremonials, and the kachinas themselves also fall prey to the clowns' jokes. At Shipaulovi, clowns mocked an old priest who officiated at kachina dances the year before (Scully, 1975). Clowns with large gourd penises simulate copulation with impersonators of old women on a sacred altar (Parsons, 1936). Clowns also perform comic dramatizations of Hopi myths and will even grab a kachina and imitate copulation with him (Earle & Kennard, 1938; Parsons, 1917, 1936).

The clowns are excessive in many ways. Some wear outlandish false penises and vulvas (Parsons, 1936). They may display their natural genitals in public, snatching one another's loincloths, pulling one another around the plaza by the penis, plastering their genitals with food and medicine. The clowns copulate after mock weddings, often with inappropriate partners, for example, old women with young boys or humans with animals. Sex reversals are common; and transvestism, as well as bawdy songs, indecent suggestions, and other pornographic excesses occur regularly. The clowns' sexual displays are as often anal and oral as it is genital (Frost, 1982; Parsons, 1936).

Furthermore, the clowns have been known to drink urine and eat excrement and other filth (Bourke, 1920, 1934; Parsons, 1936). They douse each other and fellow Hopis with feces and urine, and at one ceremonial, seven clowns drank 2–3 gallons of urine. This scatology has long disgusted and intrigued prudish whites and has been moderated lately in public performances.

The clowns' eating habits are also excessive as well as scatalogical. Gluttony is a universal trait among Pueblo clowns, and the Hopi *chukuwimkiya* in particular. The clowns are supplied with huge quantities of food, which they stash at their plaza "house" and consume ravenously during the ceremonials (Bourke, 1934; Coze, 1957; Parsons, 1936). They are orally excessive, too, in their loud, babbling talk and puns.

The clowns' violence is equally excessive, reminding us of their historical relationship to Hopi military orders of the past (Parsons, 1923; Titiev, 1972). They are rowdy among themselves, and they rough up spectators and kachinas and sometimes cut white youths' hair or try to strip them. In former days, the clowns would stun and devour a live dog during a plaza ceremonial; this dog represented an enemy, for example, a Navajo (Fewkes, 1897a, 1897b; Parsons, 1936). Today the clowns may attack a watermelon, reveling like warriors in its red pulp as they once did the red blood and entrails of dogs (Tyler, 1972).

But the clowns receive their share of abuse in return. Sometimes they beat each other with yucca whips or sticks (Fewkes, 1891; Parsons, 1936). At other times the impersonators of their Indian enemies thrash the clowns. Even more commonly, the Hopi kachinas administer brutal beatings to the clowns, flogging them unmercifully with whips, sticks, and wooden saws (Fewkes, 1897b; Fewkes & Stephen, 1892; Parsons, 1936). At the end of each ceremonial, however, there is reconciliation among all parties (Parsons, 1936).

Sacrality of Clowns

In light of all the excesses of the Hopi clown performance, it is important to note that the clowns also have nonclowning duties. They serve as organizers of the performances and often play the role of leaders of the kachina dancers; some are known as "fathers of the kachinas." The Mudheads are the first "kachinas" to return to the pueblos at the winter solstice. They likewise precede the kachinas at various ceremonials, and they announce upcoming performances or the arrival of the kachina dancers (e.g., Parsons, 1925; Titiev, 1944). Clowns also arrange for a supply of food to be prepared for a ritual, and they are responsible for keeping spectators in line; in addition, they serve as valets to the dancers, freeing tangled hair or adjusting fallen rattles (Roediger, 1941; Simpson, 1951–53).

They have other solemn and sacred functions. They sprinkle sacred cornmeal on the kachinas and are blessed with meal in return by the chiefs or other leaders (Baxter, 1882; Parsons, 1936). They make prayer sticks and deposit them at shrines (Parsons, 1936; Voth, 1912). They distribute prayer feathers to the kachinas at the close of ceremonials (Parsons, 1936), and they join the elders in thanking the kachinas for their performance and in praying for rains to follow (Parsons, 1936). Often clowns simply sing, dance, and drum in a serious manner (Earle & Kennard, 1938; Steward, 1931b; Titiev, 1944). In this sense the clowns are priests (Fewkes, 1892, 1894), ritually important intermediaries to the gods (Roediger, 1941). Their images on sacred objects such as prayer meal bowls (Frank & Harlow, 1974) fetish vessels (Branson, 1976) and on kiva walls in conjunction with corn, cloud, rain and lightning symbols, bear out this sacrality. Even with declining duties, the clowns have a profound effect on their fellow Hopis.

HOPI RESPONSES TO THE CLOWNS

Appreciation

Hopis respond to the clowns' buffoonery with genuine, profound laughter. It is what the clowns want. As they are heading for the plaza to perform, they say, "May I gain at least one smile" (Sekaquaptewa, 1979, p. 7). The laughs do not signify disrespect for the clowns' roles; indeed, the clowns are highly respected for their powers of fertility, life, and death. The clowns are also loved because they are humorous, they amuse people, and their labors are recognized as a sacrifice for the good of the entire community. They are subject to dietary and sexual restrictions, and their acts are physically taxing. They must endure a variety of indignities, some of them painful. These hardships bring blessings to the community.

In particular, the clowns bring rain. The *Chuku* wear their hair in two bunches representing clouds (Parsons, 1939). The *Tachuktu* knobs are stuffed with cotton, which symbolizes clouds, as well as snow and rain (Roediger, 1941). The corn smut used as a black body pigment is a pictorial prayer for rain, since corn smut thrives on moisture (Parsons, 1939). In general, the clowns are associated with watery places, springs, and wells. They are bringers of rain and fertility (Beck & Walters, 1977). When they jump up and down on the rooftops before entering the plaza, they symbolize rainclouds (Beck & Walters, 1977; Simmons, 1971). All their urine and water play is aimed at providing rain. Their erotic activities also aid fertility of crops, animals, and humans alike (Steward, 1931a), which illustrates the prayer of all Hopi ceremonialism: to promote rain, fertility, and life (see Fewkes, 1896, 1900b, 1903; Haeberlin, 1916; Scully, 1975).

Tension

The Hopis are grateful for the rain and agricultural bounty that the clowns bring. Despite their love and esteem for the clowns, there is nonetheless an element of tension in the Hopi reactions to many of the clown antics. Some of this is generated by the caustic commentary and physical violence employed by the clowns in their social control function. Sometimes this tension derives from the Hopi fear of being singled out as different from other Hopis and being ridiculed in public (Brandt, 1954; Parsons, 1939; see also Thompson & Joseph, 1965). Furthermore, the clowns' mock arguments remind the Hopis of the dangers of rupture in their society, dangers that are as old as the emergence of Hopi society in mythic times. In many ways the clowns are disquieting because they are the antithesis of the ideal Hopi. They are disagreeable, uncooperative, and unpredictable. They are tricksters in the public plaza. They are *kahopi*, or un-Hopi (Brandt, 1954; Hieb, 1972a). The Hopis think of themselves as members of a group—kernels on an ear of corn, they say (Harvey, 1972; Ortiz, 1972)—and the clowns are unbridled individualists and eccentrics, akin to witches (Harvey, 1972; Parsons, 1917, 1939). Even though the clowns are only actors and their eccentricities are laughable, they are also perceived as potential dangers to the established Hopi way.

Another reason for the tension they create is that the clowns are said to be like the dead, and they remind the Hopis of their eventual death. Although some observers have claimed that for the Hopi "there is no real dividing line between life now and life later" (O'Kane, 1953, p.169), it is more accurate to say that "the Hopi betray a great fear of death and the dead" (Eggan, 1943, p.357). In the Hopi myth of emergence, the first death in the world is brought about by the nefarious work of a witch, jealousy, and the most antisocial of folklore characters, the trickster, Coyote (Voth, 1905; Cushing, 1923; Stephen, 1929). In short, death results from antisocial behavior. The Hopis believe that death is really a metamorphosis through which the living become fertilizing coulds and helpful, godly kachinas. There is also a thoroughgoing belief in an afterlife and continued kinship between the living and the dead, and the Hopi religion consists to a large extent of communication with the dead. Yet, "there is the greatest reluctance to speak of the dead, the underworld, or even to identify the katcina[*sic*] with the dead" (Kennard, 1937, p 492).

Hopi burials are quick, tense affairs, in which the face is painted and covered with a cotton mask in order to establish immediately its identity as a dead person, a nonliving person. People hide from the corpse out of fear. Those who dig the grave and bury the body—frightful tasks—must be washed and purified upon completion of the rites (Simmons, 1971).

Thompson (1950) notes that "the spirit of the deceased is propitiated with prayer feathers to forget and not to bother the living and the trail back to the village is ceremonially closed"(p.107). When the burial is done, one Hopi says, "It is best to laugh and joke again as soon as possible [in order to] rid our minds of sorrowful thoughts" (Simmons, 1971, p. 315). The Hopi person expects to return to the mythic underworld from which the Hopis emerged and expects to visit the upperworld as clouds, bringing rain to the living (Thompson, 1950). Nevertheless, the Hopis regard the dead with ambivalence (Parsons, 1939; Titiev, 1971).

As for death itself, the Hopis express distinctive views. Death from old age is a natural event; however, death at an early age is resented intensely. A person who dies early in life is said to show a lack of concern for the living, just as a crippled or sick person is blamed for his or her failing. Sickness, deformity, too early a death—these are antisocial acts in the Hopi world view (Thompson, 1950). Thus, one Hopi woman slapped the face of a corpse, shouting, "You are mean to do this to me" (Kennard, 1937, p.496). A Hopi man said of a woman who died on the day of an important ceremony, thus delaying it: "She could have died yesterday or waited until tomorrow, but she deliberately chose that day to spoil the dance" (Kennard, 1937, p. 496). The Hopis believe that a person who dies too soon has done so because he or she has not concentrated strongly enough on the positive values of this world. A Hopi must focus all will, prayer, and wishes on life, on fertility, on harmony. In contradistinction, "a man who thinks of the dead or of the future life instead of being concerned with worldly activities is thereby bringing about his own death" (Kennard, 1937, p 492).

And yet the *chukuwimkiya* remind the Hopis of death and the dead. It is said that the striped clown bodies represent the bones of the dead (Coze, 1957; Roediger, 1941) and their cloud symbolism refers directly to the ancestors, the fertilizing clouds (Titiev, 1944). In this regard, the following passage from Mischa Titiev is significant:

> Clowns are often equated with the dead; and . . . much of the mockery arousing laughter stems from the notion that since death is the opposite of life, those who represent the dead, as the clowns, should also do and say the *opposite* of what is normally expected. This is a surefire way of arousing laughter; but in such cases the factor of amusement is entirely secondary, whereas the primary purpose is to behave like the dead—that is, to do things *opposite* to the way they are done by the living. (Titiev, 1972, p. 256)

The clowns are also identified with Masau'u, the god of death, metamorphosis, tricks, opposites, war, and blood (Fewkes, 1892, 1897b; Parsons, 1936; Stephen, 1929; Titiev, 1972), the deity who beckoned the Hopi ancestors from the underworld in the emergence myth. Like the dead and like Masau'u, the clowns are fertilizing agents, germinators, sources of existence, yet they are the opposite of living Hopi ways, of normal routine. And so the clowns, like the dead, are both helpful and frightful.

FUNCTIONS OF THE CLOWNS

In a previous attempt to understand these ritual clowns (Vecsey & Lorenz, 1979), we say that their priestly, joking, fertilizing, military, pornographic, scatalogical and excessive connections touch base with all extensions of the Hopi universe, including death and the dead. We emphasize that, in making manifest the fullness of Hopi existence— including representations of the opposites of Hopi norms—they function to integrate Hopi personality, religious life, cognitive categories, and social solidarity.

Psychological Function

The *chukuwimkiya* spring up from the subconscious and integrate Hopi personality by bringing to a conscious level renegade, troublesome, subliminal elements. The Hopis witness these elements, recognize them, and assimilate them into their consciousness (Charles, 1945). Thus the clowns bring about a more complete Hopi self, just as dreams help integrate portions of the subliminal into the whole person (Freud, 1963). In this regard the clowns are not heroes, but underside figures; not egos, but a collective id (Welsford, 1961). Because the clowns reveal subliminal human nature, they are dangerous and worrisome. Their shit and sex, violence and transformations are disturbing. Yet, they offer a release from this ambiguous aspect of human personality by exposing it in a controlled, ritual setting.

The clowns not only manifest the wellsprings of the Hopi self but also put the Hopis in touch with their primordial, earthy origins (Charles, 1945; Disher, 1925). The Hopi clowns represent primeval, unformed matter, a throwback to a time when humans had not fully emerged from nature. Covered from head to toe in clay, Hopi clowns dramatically illustrate the bridging of humans and the earth. They reunite the Hopis with their ground of being, the earth from which they emerged in mythic times (Willeford, 1969) and also with their animal nature (Courlander, 1971; Titiev, 1941).

Religious Function

In addition to integrating Hopi libidinous and archaic impulses, the clowns also serve Hopi religion. First, they make the religion digestible, working like catalysts to break down difficult abstractions and mysteries (Honigmann, 1942). They offer comic relief during awesome rituals, burlesquing the gods and thus bringing the mighty ones down to earthly proportions. Grabbing them down by the throat, they make the kachina-divinities more accessible to their human relatives.

Even though the onlookers know what to expect from the *chuku-wimkiya*, the jokers always surprise them. This element of surprise acts as an intensifier—in this case, to the ceremonial emotion—thus heightening the whole of the religious experience (Desai, 1939). They do not relax their audience; they put the Hopis on alert. They open them up for revelation (Tedlock, 1975). They heighten the sublime by comparison with the ridiculous (Disher, 1925), just as the audience is elevated in status by contrast with the fools before them (Monro, 1951).

Almost by accident, almost by design, the clowns reveal to the Hopis crucial incongruities, which they then integrate (Douglas, 1968). As in William James's (1958) definition of religion, they offer a feeling of disquiet, followed by its resolution. Through the craziness of their performances, they reveal.

Cognitive Function

Their revelations are cognitive, surely. They reveal contradictions between the subliminal and the conscious, between the ideal and the real, between rules and disorder. They bring together within their costumes and actions the contrasting elements of their world. Like jokes, they bind together incongruous elements (Maier, 1932), showing both their similarities and dissimilarities (see Freud, 1963). Through the clowns, oppositions like religion and humor, gods and excrement, are attracted and connected. The clowns marry elements that are normally considered mutually exclusive (Ortiz, 1972). Their motley costumes, their muddy lumpishness, and their stripes highlight the contradictory, ambiguous, polysemous nature of the world from which they spring. They are walking contradictions, living examples of interbanded dualisms, brought together in the plaza for all the Hopis to see. They contradict themselves—by being serious and ridiculous simultaneously—as well as the mundane world around them, and their incongruity serves to integrate Hopi religious elements, Hopi culture, and Hopi personality, as well as Hopi logic.

Clowns will not be tied down to one category any more than will tricksters. They are liminal as well as subliminal (Turner, 1969, 1978). They perform in the plaza crossroads and at the village border, often at the changing of seasons. They move between and around the dancers. Their clowning takes place during intermissions of kachina dancing. One often finds them between buildings, amid the lines of cultural texture and architecture (Titiev, 1944). As liminal figures they join the categories that they cross: nature and culture, fertility and death, funny and frightening, gods and men. They serve to conjoin the many apparent dichotomies of life while establishing dichotomies of their own. The *chukuwimkiya* give formlessness to struture, parody to piety, and thus they rebalance the Hopi humors, as well as the bodies religious and politic, in ritual settings of intense seriousness. Hopi clowns act as physicians—therapists for personality, ritual, and society, integrating diverse elements through their fun (Piddington, 1963; Makarius, 1970).

Societal Function

On an anthropological level, the *chukuwimkiya* attack the restrictions and repressions of ordinary society. They personify vitality attacking rigidity (Sidis, 1913, p. 3, after Bergson). They are the epitome of freedom in a community-minded tribal society, calling into question cultural categories (Charles, 1945; Crumrine, 1969; Douglas, 1968; Parsons, 1939; Zucker, 1967). They are ids in a community of strong superegos. But they are obviously no more destroyers of traditions, leaders of revolt against the order of society and the world, than the tricksters of tribal societies (Vecsey, 1981).

They defy order; but to make the Hopis laugh, the clowns must produce a properly improper inversion (Hieb, 1972b). Their nonsense must make cultural sense to the Hopis (Bouissac, 1976; Stewart, 1979). As performers, clowns are not outside the cultural system, because they are playing a role designated to them (Ortiz, 1972; see also Abrahams & Bauman, 1978). They question; they attack order; they offer freedom, but only within the ritual event. Like folkloric tricksters, they are cultural creations who help regulate symbolic representations of deviancy and make themselves laughable and safe. They offer vicarious revolt, subverting the probability of real revolt (Zucker, 1954; but see Babcock, 1978). They offer catharsis for complaint and actually reinforce Hopi commitment to normal behavior by pointing out deviance. In effect, the *chukuwimkiya* improve the rules of Hopi society (see Vogt, 1976).

The clowns are not only radicals who question the order of things, who cross every conceivable Hopi boundary, but they are also conservatives who question the ability to ask a sensible question of the establishments of tribal life (see Freud, 1963, p. 115; Zucker, 1967). They are cynics and skeptics alike who reduce to an absurd level the claims against society, thus exposing the foolishness of innovation and revolt. They do not offer radical syllogisms, but rather revelatory "sillygisms" that muddy up all logic.

Not only are the clowns ultimately harmless because the threats they pose can be laughed off, but they are also frequently punished for their misdeeds. The audience that laughed uproariously at their misbehavior laughs again at their chastisement. The *chukuwimkiya* are both escape and scapegoat (Zucker, 1967). They offer relief from order, then relief from freedom, thereby integrating the two: order and freedom.

In the process they make the Hopis laugh. At their performances, the Hopi audience—the descendants of the people who once emerged from beneath the ground and wandered over the body of the earth in search of themselves as a people—laugh together like members of a societal chorale. Their harmonic laughter is a praise song to their lifeway in all its contrariness. Their laughter points to and participates in a shared world view, a consensus (Douglas, 1968; Freud, 1963), a mutual acceptance of Hopi life. Their laughter is a socially— as well as psychologically, religiously, and cognitively—integrating phenomenon; it strengthens their bonds on every level of existence (Freud, 1963; Piddington, 1963). They share their laughter and criticism like allies sharing tobacco, like intimate companions sharing a meal (see Burns, 1953).

What is this laughter that they share, which the clowns elicit? It is a physiological and cultural act that helps create, sustain, and express a state of satisfaction. On a biological level, respiration, circulation, and blood pressure increase during laughter, producing a sort of euphoria, an interruption of breathing that confers a soaring sense of breadth, where no reform is necessary (Piddington, 1963). Tribally, the Hopis' clowns produce integrative laughter that symbolizes contentment with their way of life, which they have defended against white encroachments, fostering a tribal state of satisfaction. Even though they are very well aware that total integration and contentment is impossible, their clowning recreation in the plaza helps to recreate and to celebrate the ideal Hopi existence defined in their mythology and experienced in their everyday lives.

CLOWNS AND THE HOPI LIFE SPAN

We notice, however, that the *chukuwimkiya* define the Hopi ideal partially to the exclusion of those Hopis at the extreme ends of the life span: the very young and the very old. The ritual clowns embrace the Hopi middle ground at the expense of its periphery.

The Infantile

The clowns act like unsocialized children. They frisk, cavort, and play. They are socially inept. Their gluttony is like the unchecked appetite of small children at or between meals. Their nakedness also evokes the child in Hopi society. Even their mockery of unfortunates may be likened to the brand of cruelty often practiced by Hopi children. Their sexuality, too, is infantile: uncontrolled, omnidirectional, polymorphously perverse, and simulated (see Parsons, 1917). They are simultaneously anal, oral, and genital. They will hump or suck a burro, an old woman, a little boy, a transvestite, a kachina, an aunt or a spectator, whoever is available for their simulated gratification. Theirs is sexuality without sex, eroticism without adult libido, and it evokes the ready sexual teasing that Hopi boys receive from their aunts.

Hopi society is well known for the license it grants to its young children (Eggan, 1943; Goldfrank, 1966). They receive constant attention; their every cry is appeased with nursings, feedings, and play; their self-willfulness is permitted and even encouraged, in sharp contrast to the self-control of Hopi adults. Not until Hopi children are initiated into the religious orders (accomplished partially by whippings and by the revelation that the dancing kachinas are masked impersonators of the gods, their relatives rather than the gods themselves; see, e.g., Gill, 1977) does the permissiveness toward them cease.

Like infants, the clowns are free from restrictions that adults must honor (Hieb, 1972b; Levine, 1961). Hopi society may share vicariously the freedom from restraint and responsibility that the clowns enjoy. However, clowns suffer punishment for their misbehavior, accepting it without resistance like persons who know the proper authority (Levine, 1961). In short, the clowns set off childish behavior from societal norms. Like foreigners, perverts, and other deviants, the clowns define little children as *kahopi*, virtually foreign beings outside the core of Hopi ideals.

The Aged

Where does this picture of Hopi communalism, as celebrated by the *chukuwimkiya*, leave the Hopi aged? In one sense it embraces them as part of the Hopi whole; in another sense it excludes them from the Hopi community entirely. The key factor is their state of health.

The Hopis do not keep track of age beyond the crucial passage from youth to adulthood. There are no ceremonies marking the transition from adult to old age, and the Hopis make no attempt to guess how old a person is. If a person is active and well, then he or she is not regarded as aged. Old people, unless crippled or blind, work hard and long hours, laboring into their 80s or 90s in the hot cornfields, climbing the steep mesas without deference or sympathy from the young. The Hopis say, "No matter what your age may be, no matter how old you are, you will always continue to do whatever you are able to do" (O'Kane, 1953, p. 26, see also Thompson, 1950). It is not uncommon for blind old men to make their living weaving, and no fuss is made over them; they are merely doing what any Hopi must do to survive and help the community (O'Kane, 1953). The ideal Hopi trail of life, then, is to "live to be an old man . . . and pass away in sleep without pain" (Simmons, 1971, p. 51). Furthermore, one should not dwell upon infirmities either in youth or in old age. Whatever you direct attention to grows stronger; therefore, refuse to give the ailments of old age any attention and they will not disturb you. As a result, the old Hopis will themselves to vigor, with tremendous exercise (O'Kane, 1953). The robust, productive old Hopi shares in the communal affirmation of Hopi life evoked by the clowns.

On the other hand, "it is well known . . . that old people are often neglected by the Hopi" (Brandt, 1954, p. 29). If a Hopi elder is sickly and cannot support his or her existence, there is not a strong Hopi sense that the young and healthy must provide food, shelter, or clothing. A father is especially neglected in this regard since his children are technically more related to the mother in this matrilineal system (Brandt, 1954, see also O'Kane, 1953). One researcher was told that "if a man lets an aged parent starve to death, he does not lose caste. Public opinion, so strong in other matters, is silent here" (Colton, 1934, p. 24). Thus one Hopi describes an old cripple, crawling about and begging from tourists: "Sometimes the [Hopi] children would tease him, take things from him, mock him, and even kick or strike him." Hopi adults teased him kindly, but his relatives "were careless and sometimes mistreated him, even threatening to give him no food" (Simmons, 1971, p. 317).

The explanation for this mistreatment arises from our earlier discussion of death. Just as a person who dies before his or her time is referred to as one who "is mean and wants to hurt other people" (Brandt, 1954, p. 31), the old person who is crippled or useless demonstrates to Hopi neighbors a form of antisocial behavior. The unhealthy old Hopi is regarded as malevolent, *kahopi*. As Brandt (1954) says in his study of Hopi ethics: "when a person becomes so old that he makes no contribution to the family store, resentments tend to develop—or. . . when he ceases to take an active role in Hopi affairs, *he ceases, to some extent, to function as a person in Hopi thinking*" (p. 373, note 4; emphasis added).

The Hopi clowns make clear this exclusion of the unhealthy aged from the Hopi norm. They are grouped with other deviants as objects of derision. Foreigners, perverts, animals, the dead, the deformed, the violent, the crippled, the infantile and the unhealthy aged—these are the characters whom the clowns mock, and as a result of this mocking, a definitional circle is drawn around the standard, ideal Hopi person. If the clowns reaffirm the Hopi way, they also exclude from that way certain *kahopi* deviants. No matter what their age, healthy, productive, old Hopis are included in the reaffirmed Hopi ideal. As for the unhealthy old Hopis, according to the definitions made by the antics of the clowns, they cease to be Hopis, just as young children have yet to become Hopis.

REFERENCES

Abrahams, R. D., & Bauman, R. (1978). Ranges of festival behavior. In B. A. Babcock (Ed.), *The reversible world: Symbolic inversion in art and society* (pp. 193–208). Ithaca, NY: Cornell University Press.

Babcock, B. A. (1978). Introduction. In B. A. Babcock (Ed.), *The reversible world: Symbolic inversion in art and society* (pp. 13–36). Ithaca, NY: Cornell University Press.

Baxter, S. (1882). The father of the Pueblos. *Harper's New Monthly Magazine, 65*, 72–91.

Beck, P. V., & Walters, A. L. (1977). *The sacred: Ways to knowledge, sources of life.* Tsaile, AZ: Navajo Community College.

Bouissac, P. (1976). *Circus and culture: A semiotic approach.* Bloomington, IN: Indiana University Press.

Bourke, J. G. (1920). *The urine dance of the Zuni Indians of New Mexico.*

Bourke, J. G. (1934). *Scatalogic rites of all nations.* New York: American Anthropological Society.

Brandt, R. B. (1954). *Hopi ethics. A theoretical analysis.* Chicago: University of Chicago Press.

Branson, O. T. (1976). *Fetishes and carvings of the southwest.* Santa Fe, NM: Treasure Chest.

Bunzel, R. L. (1932). Zuni katcinas. Washington, DC: *Bureau of American Ethnology, 47th Annual Report,* (pp. 837–1086).

Burns, T. (1953). Friends, enemies, and the polite fiction. *American Sociological Review, 18,* 654–662.

Charles, L. H. (1945). The clown's function. *Journal of American Folklore, 58,* 25–34.

Colton, H. S. (1934). A brief survery of Hopi common law. *Museum Notes, 7,* (21-24). Museum of Northern Arizona.

Colton, H. S. (1959). *Hopi kachina dolls. With a key to their identification.* Albuquerque: University of New Mexico Press.

Courlander, H. (1971). *The fourth world of the Hopis.* New York: Crown.

Coze, P. (1957). Kachinas: Masked dancers of the Southwest. *National Geographic Magazine, 112,* 218-236.

Crumrine, N. R. (1969). Čapakoba, the Mayo Easter ceremonial impersonator: Explanations of ritual clowning. *Journal for the Scientific Study of Religion, 8,* 1–22.

Cushing, F. H. (1923). Origin myth from Oraibi. *Journal of American Folklore, 36,* 163-170.

Desai, M. M. (1939). *Surprise. A historical and experimental study.* London: Cambridge University Press, (*British Journal of Psychology,* Monograph Supplements, No. 22).

Disher, M. W. (1925). *Clowns & pantomimes.* Boston: Houghton Mifflin.

Douglas, M. (1968). The social control of cognition: Some factors in joke perception. *Man, 3,* 361-376.

Earle, E. & Kennard, E. A. (1938). *Hopi kachinas.* New York: Augustin.

Eggan, D. (1943). The general problem of Hopi adjustment. *American Anthropologist, 45,* 357-373.

Fewkes, J. W. (1891). A few summer ceremonials at Zuñi pueblo. *Journal of American Ethnology & Archaeology, 1,* 1-62.

Fewkes, J. W. (1892). A few summer ceremonials at the Tusayan pueblos. *Journal of American Ethnology & Archaeology, 2,* 1-160.

Fewkes, J. W. (1894). Dolls of the Tusayan Indians. *Internationales Archiv für Ethnographie, 7,* 45-73.

Fewkes, J. W. (1896). The Tusayan ritual: A study of the influence of environment on aboriginal cults. Washington DC: *Smithsonian Institution Annual Report.* pp. 683-700.

Fewkes, J. W. (1897a). The sacrificial element in Hopi worship. *Journal of American Folklore, 10*, 187–201.

Fewkes, J. W. (1897b). Tusayan katchinas. Washington DC: *Bureau of American Ethnology, 15th Annual Report,* (pp. 245-313).

Fewkes, J. W. (1900a). The new-fire ceremony at Walpi. *American Anthropologist, 2,* 80-138.

Fewkes, J. W. (1900b). A theatrical performance at Walpi. *Proceedings of the Washington Academy of Sciences, 2,* 605-629.

Fewkes, J. W. (1903). Hopi katcinas drawn by native artists. Washington, DC: *Bureau of American Ethnology. 21st Annual Report,* (pp. 3–126).

Fewkes, J. W. (1910). The butterfly in Hopi myth and ritual. *American Anthropologist, 12,* 576-594.

Fewkes, J. W. & Stephens [sic], A. M. (1892). The Nā-ác-nai-ya: a Tusayan initiation ceremony. *Journal of American Folklore, 5,* 189-217.

Frank, L., & Harlow, F. H. (1974). *Historic pottery of the Pueblo Indians 1600–1880.* Boston: New York Graphic Society.

Freud, S. (1963). *Jokes and their relation to the unconscious.* New York: Norton, (Original work published 1905)

Frost, R. H. (1982). *Pueblo clowns, Anglo responses, and the dance crisis of 1923.* Unpublished manuscript.

Gill, S. D. (1977). Hopi kachina cult initiation: The shocking beginning to the Hopi's religious life. *Journal of the American Academy of Religion, 45,* (suppl.), 447-464.

Goldfrank, E. (1966). Socialization, personality, and the structure of Pueblo society (with particular reference to Hopi and Zuni). In D. G. Haring (Ed.), *Personal character and cultural milieu* (pp. 302-327). Syracuse: Syracuse University Press.

Haeberlin, H. K. (1916). The idea of fertilization in the culture of the Pueblo Indians. In *Memoirs of the American Anthropological Association, 3, 3,* 1-55.

Harvey, B. (1970). *Ritual in Pueblo art. Hopi life in Hopi painting.* New York: Contributions from the Museum of the American Indian, Heye Foundation, p. 24.

Harvey, B. (1972). An overview of Pueblo religion. In A. Ortiz (Ed.), *New perspectives on the Pueblos* (pp. 197-217). Albuquerque: University of New Mexico Press.

Hieb, L. A. (1972a). *The Hopi ritual clown: life as it should not be.* Unpublished doctoral dissertation, Princeton University, Princeton, NJ.

Hieb, L. A. (1972b). Meaning and mismeaning: Toward an understanding of the ritual clown. In A. Ortiz (Ed.), *New perspectives on the Pueblos* (pp. 163-195). Albuquerque: University of New Mexico Press.

Hodge, F. W. (1896). Pueblo snake ceremonials. *American Anthropologist, 9,* 133-136.

Honigmann, J. J. (1942). An interpretation of the social-psychological functions of the ritual clown. *Character and Personality. Journal of Personality, 10,* 220-226.

James, W. (1958). *The varieties of religious experience. A study in human nature.* New York: New American Library.

Kennard, E. A. (1937). Hopi reactions to death. *American Anthropologist, 39,* 491-496.

Koenig, S. H. (1976). *Hopi clay. Hopi ceremony.* Katonah, NY: The Katonah Gallery.

Levine, J. (1961). Regression in primitive clowning. *Psychoanalytic Quarterly, 30,* 72-83.

Maier, N. R. (1932). A gestalt theory of humor. *British Journal of Psychology, 23,* 69-74.

Makarius, L. (1970). Ritual clowns and symbolical behavior. *Diogenes, 69,* 44-73.

Monro, D. H. (1951). *Argument of laughter.* Melbourne, Australia: Melbourne University Press.

O'Kane, W. C. (1953). *The Hopis: Portrait of a desert people.* Norman: University of Oklahoma Press.

Ortiz, A. (1972). Ritual drama and the Pueblo world view. In A. Ortiz (Ed.), *New perspectives on the Pueblos* (pp.135-161). Albuquerque: University of New Mexico Press.

Parsons, E. C. (1917). Notes on Zuni. 2 parts. *Memoirs of the American Anthropological Association, 4,* 149-327.

Parsons, E. C. (1923). The Hopi Wöwöchim ceremony in 1920. *American Anthropologist, 25,* 156-187.

Parsons, E. C. (1925). *A Pueblo Indian journal 1920–1921.* Menasha, WIS: Memoirs of the American Anthropological Association, 32.

Parsons, E. C. (1936). *Hopi journals of Alexander M. Stephen* (Vols. 1-2). New York: Columbia University Contributions to Anthropology, 23.

Parsons, E. C. (1939). *Pueblo Indian religion* (Vols. 1-2). Chicago: University of Chicago Press.

Piddington, R. (1963). *The psychology of laughter. A study in social adaptation.* New York: Gamut.

Roediger, V. M. (1941). *Ceremonial costumes of the Pueblo Indians: Their evolution, fabrication, and significance in the prayer drama.* Berkeley: University of California Press.

Scully, V. (1975). *Pueblo/mountain, village, dance.* New York: Viking.

Sekaquaptewa, E. (1979). One more smile for a Hopi clown. *Parabola, 4,* 6-9.

Sidis, B. (1913). *The psychology of laughter.* New York: Appleton.

Simmons, L. W. (Ed.). (1971). *Sun chief: The autobiography of a Hopi Indian.* New Haven: Yale University Press.

Simpson, R. D. (1951-1953). The Hopi Indians. *The Masterkey, 25,* 109-124, 155-166, 177-185; *26,* 5-12, 87-94, 122-129, 149-160, 179-191; *27,* 11-14.

Stephen, A. M. (1929). Hopi tales. *Journal of American Folklore, 42,* 1-72.

Steward, J. H. (1931a). The ceremonial buffoon of the American Indian. *Papers of the Michigan Academy of Science, Arts, and Letters, 1930, 14,* 187-207.

Steward, J. H. (1931b). Notes on Hopi ceremonies in their initiatory form in 1927–1928. *American Anthropologist, 33,* 56-79.

Stewart, S. (1979). *Nonsense. Aspects of intertextuality in folklore and literature.* Baltimore: Johns Hopkins University.

Tedlock, B. (1975). The clown's way. In D. Tedlock & B. Tedlock (Eds.), *Teachings from the American earth* (pp. 105-118). New York: Liveright.

Thompson, L. (1950). *Culture in crisis: A study of the Hopi Indians.* New York: Harper & Brothers.

Thompson, L. & Joseph, A. (1965). *The Hopi way.* New York: Russell & Russell.

Titiev, M. (1941). A Hopi visit to the afterworld. *Papers of the Michigan Academy of Science, Arts, and Letters, 1940, 26,* 495-504.

Titiev, M. (1944). *Old Oraibi. A study of the Hopi Indians of the third mesa.* Papers of the Peabody Museum of American Archaeology and Ethnology, 22, 1. Cambridge: Harvard University.

Titiev, M. (1971). Some aspects of clowning among the Hopi Indians. In M. D. Zamora, J. M. Mahar, & H. Orenstein (Eds.) *Themes in culture (Essays in honor of Morris E. Opler)* (pp. 326-336). Quezon City, Philippines: Kayumanggi.

Titiev, M. (1972). *The Hopi Indians of old Oraibi: Change and continuity.* Ann Arbor: University of Michigan Press.

Turner, V. W. (1969). *The ritual process: Structure and anti-structure.* Chicago: Aldine.

Turner, V. W. (1978). Comments and conclusions. In B. A. Babcock (Ed.), *The reversible world: Symbolic inversion in art and society* (pp. 276-296). Ithaca, NY: Cornell University Press.

Tyler, H. A. (1972). *Pueblo gods and myths.* Norman: University of Oklahoma Press.

Vecsey, C. (1981). The exception who proves the rules: Ananse the Akan trickster. *Journal of Religion in Africa, 12,* 161-177.

Vecsey, C. & Lorenz, C. A. (1979). *Tricksters in the plaza: Hopi clowns.* Paper presented at the American Academy of Religion Annual Meeting, New York.

Vogt, E. (1976). Rituals of reversal as a means of rewiring social structure. In A. Bharati (Ed.), *The realm of the extra-human: Ideas and actions* (pp. 201-211). The Hague: Mouton.

Voth, H. R. (1905). *The traditions of the Hopi.* Chicago: Field Columbian Museum. (Anthropological Series, Vol. 8, Publication 96).

Voth, H. R. (1912). *The Oraibi Marau ceremony.* Chicago: Field Museum of Natural History, Anthropological Series, Publication 156, 2,(1).

Welsford, E. (1961). *The fool. His social and literary history.* Garden City, NY: Doubleday.

Willeford, W. (1969). *The fool and his scepter. A study in clowns and jesters and their audience.* Evanston: Northwestern University Press.

Zucker, W. (1954). The image of the clown. *Journal of Aesthetics and Art Criticism, 12,* 310-317.

Zucker,W. (1967). The clown as the lord of disorder. *Theology Today, 24,* 306-317.

PART IV

BRIEF EMPIRICAL STUDIES OF HUMOR ACROSS THE LIFE SPAN

When a field is in its infancy, it is often useful to publish pilot studies which acquaint potential researchers with what is possible. By reporting intriguing exploratory work, we offer opportunities for improvement as well as imitation. In this way, we lay the groundwork for the development of fresh hypotheses. In a new field, old methods of inquiry may be inappropriate or too rigid and new procedures should be explored. These studies should not be expected to meet the critieria of generalizability and replicability required by major journals.

There are many, many possibilities for studying humor across the life span. Every chapter in this book has presented the reader with at least a dozen potential research areas. Nevertheless, the fact is that, heretofore, humor has not been studied across the life span. We must aks ourselves, "Why not?" Two possible answers come readily to mind.

First, humor research has not received funding from government agencies because it does not constitute a problem. Public funds are allocated to solve problems and not to pursue ideas. It is unfortunate that we have placed such a heavy emphasis upon funded research areas that other areas with great potential have been overlooked.

 Copyright © 1986 by Academic Press, Inc.
All rights of reproduction in any form reserved.

Second, and even more important, methodological problems abound. Humor is particularly hard to standardize. When standardization and quantification present particular problems, scientists have started their work either with young children, with whom complex issues are more manageable, or with students who are so easy to access that one can easily repeat a technique. Therefore, we feel that, for starters, the publication of preliminary research should be published.

The chapters in this part are all examples of pilot research in humor and aging. Although they are very different from one another, they share the following attributes: (1) the exploration of new domains, (2) the introduction of innovative procedures, (3) findings that are suggestive only (where statistics are applied, they are merely to clarify the exposition by making the presentation of data comparable to other reported studies), and (4) conclusions that are not intended to be conclusive, but rather to develop new hypotheses. These chapters are interesting and provocative, and they are to be questioned. It is our hope that each one will lead to new areas of research.

Ventis, in Chapter 11, looks at the use of humor in the depiction of old people in children's books. Ansello, in Chapter 12, considers long-term relationships between men and women as a source of humor. Tennant, in Chapter 13, considers the role of humor in recovery from minor surgery. McGhee, Bell, and Duffey, in Chapter 14, consider the effect of the use of humor in parenting and other factors that lead to initiation. Nahemow and Raymon, in Chapter 15, tap the knowledge of professional comedians in their appeal to audiences of different ages.

These brief empirical reports are followed by an all-too-brief theoretical effort by Martin Loeb on his deathbed, which begins to delineate an Eriksonian theory of humor. The writing was interrupted by death. It is deeply wished that the theoretical work will be carried on by an inspired reader of this book.

11

Humor and Aging in Children's Picture Books: Is the Joke on Grandpa?

DEBORAH G. VENTIS

INTRODUCTION

Humor has recently been identified as an important source of information about attitudes toward aging. Researchers have found that the elderly and the aging process are usually negatively portrayed in jokes (Davies, 1977; Richman, 1977; Palmore, 1971), magazine cartoons (Sheppard, 1981; Smith, 1979) and humorous birthday cards (Demos & Jache, 1981). Although Weber and Cameron (1978) argue that ambiguity and subjectivity in humor make it difficult to determine what social attitudes about aging are conveyed, Demos and Jache (1981) emphasize the need for examination of the meaning of such humor in everyday life.

Although the elderly are generally portrayed positively in children's literature, there has been increasing concern about stereotyping of aged characters in books (Ansello, 1977; Blue, 1978; Fillmer,

 Copyright © 1986 by Academic Press, Inc.
All rights of reproduction in any form reserved.

1982; Kingston & Drotter, 1981; Robin, 1977; Storey, 1977, 1979). Blue (1978) notes that this concern is based on the assumption that attitudes and stereotypes are formed early, that literature is one important vehicle for their transmission, and that stereotypes will influence one's behavior towards oneself as well as others. Picture books may be particularly problematic because of vocabulary limitations at lower reading levels (Blue, 1978) and the fact that illustrations of the aged in children's books are unrealistic and often portray stereotypes not present in the text (Kingston & Drotter, 1981; Storey, 1977).

Humor and aging in children's literature have not been studied directly, but observations that child characters occasionally make fun of the elderly (Blue, 1978) and that older individuals are often portrayed by cartoonlike drawings (Kingston & Drotter, 1981) suggest that humor may be an important source of negative stereotypes about the aged.

In an increasingly age-segregated society, it is likely that children's attitudes toward aging will be heavily influenced by media presentations of older individuals. Research shows that young children have limited contact with older individuals in or outside of the family (Seefeldt, Jantz, Galper, & Serock, 1977). In discussing the implications of stereotyping of the aged in children's literature, Ansello (1977) observes that there is little likelihood of reducing negative stereotypes through increased contact with the elderly, since there is little motivation for interaction as long as negative attitudes are held. One study (Fillmer, 1982) confirmed that elementary school children are not only more likely to express negative stereotypes about pictures of older adults than those of younger adults, but also express less willingness to associate with the aged.

The purpose of the present study was to investigate the relationship between humor and stereotyping of the elderly in children's picture books. In view of Ansello's (1977) finding that older people comprise only 16.46% of the characters in children's books, books involving the aged as central characters were preselected. It was expected that the elderly would generally be positively portrayed but that older characters might be more likely to be the focus of negative humor than other characters. Gender differences in stereotyping were also explored. No specific hypotheses concerning gender differences were advanced; although Fillmer (1982) found that children stereotyped old men more negatively, some humor researchers (Davies, 1977; Palmore, 1971) have concluded that it is elderly women who are more negatively portrayed.

METHOD

Selection of Books

Subject guides (Dryer, 1977; 1981; Tway, 1981; Yonkers Public Library Children's Services, 1979) and the Library of Congress (1981) *Children's Books* listings were used to identify 37 contemporary children's picture books that deal with aging or have elderly persons as central characters. Twenty-three of these titles were listed as currently in circulation at the Williamsburg Regional Library. Nineteen titles were available for study (see Appendix).

Ratings

Each book was rated by two female senior psychology majors who were unaware of the specific purpose of the study. Raters were first asked to identify each character and indicate gender (male, female, neutral), age (infant, child, adolescent, adult, old person, or other, such as animal, fairy, etc., with age given if possible), and characterization (positive, neutral, or negative). They also summarized the general theme(s) of the story and characterized the general tone of each book (somber–serious, neutral, or carefree–humorous). With respect to humor, they were asked to specify whether any humor was present in text or pictures and the location in the book, the characters involved, whether it was positive, neutral, or negative, and what (if any) theme it conveyed. Humor was defined as ideas or events that are incongruous, absurd, ridiculous, ludicrous, or funny (adapted from McGhee, 1979, pp. 6–8). Finally, they indicated whether any specific attitudes toward aging or the aged were presented and rated these as positive, neutral, or negative.

RESULTS

Characterization

The 77 characters identified were almost equally distributed among three age groups: children (32.47%), adults (31.17%), and old people (33.76%) (there were two nonhuman characters: an infant burro and an adult genie). There were equal numbers of male and female adults and elderly, but 64% of the children were male, and 36% female. Portrayals were overwhelmingly positive or neutral (93.5%) with only

6.5% rated as negative. Those negatively portrayed included a boy, three adults (two male, one female), and one old man. Raters' percentages of agreement for identifying characters, their age, gender, and characterization were .88, .96, .99, and .96, respectively. Virtually all the children were portrayed as grandchildren, the adults as parents, and the elderly as grandparents; only 29% of the characters were presented in nonfamily roles.

General Themes

The grandchild–grandparent relationship was the focus of 12 of the books. Underlying themes included the issues of senility, death of a grandparent or great-grandparent, different views of grandparents, acceptance of grandparents as they are. Four additional books involved grandparents: the focus in two of these was on broader family relationships; in the third, on being appreciative of what one has; and in the fourth, on the value of being unselfish. In another book, a great-grandfather helped a young child deal with sibling relationships. Only two books did not portray families; one dealt with the rejection and loneliness experienced by an elderly man, the other with the value of giving as exemplified by a poor elderly woman.

Humor

The general tone of the books was about evenly distributed between somber–serious (31.6%), neutral (36.8%), and carefree–humorous (31.6%). Although raters percentage agreement was reasonably high with respect to general tone (.74), there was less agreement about whether or not humor was present (.68) and little agreement (.36) about exactly where the humor appeared. Nine of the books were identified as containing some humor. Most of this humor was rated as positive (55%) or neutral (33%) with only one book cited as portraying negative humor. The two raters identified 28 specific examples of humor, most of them involving humorous pictures. Twenty-three characters (12 male, 11 female) were involved in these instances, 43% were elderly, 40% children, and 17% adults. Two adult males involved in these examples had been categorized as negatively portrayed; the remaining characters had been rated as generally neutrally or positively presented. Fifteen of the humorous examples cited involved someone (in nine, an older person; in six, a child) looking or doing something ridiculous (see example in Figure 11.1), eight instances involved grandfathers playing children's games with grand-

Figure 11.1 "Then Kevin tells me about his grandma. When Kevin is sick she brings him things like *Mad* magazine and homemade peanut-butter soup, which she delivers on her Honda 90." From Kevin's Grandma by Barbara Williams, illustrated by Kay Chorao. Illustrations copyright © 1975 by Kay Sproat Chorao. Reproduced by permission of the publisher, E. P. Dutton, a division of New American Library.

children, and the remaining five incidents centered around a grandparent appearing incompetent in some way: a grandmother mistaking a granddaughter for a strange boy, a grandmother screaming at the sight of a frog, two instances of a grandmother getting a grandson's friend's name wrong, and one instance of a grandfather being late although he used to be strict about being on time.

Attitudes about Aging

Attitudes toward the elderly conveyed in the stories were rated as generally positive (58%) with 21% of the books rated as neutral and 21% as negative (percentage agreement: .68). Of the subset of books involving humor, however, only 44% were rated positively, 22% as neutral, and 33% negative. Positive themes centered around the special, caring relationship between grandparent and grandchild, wisdom of grandparents, and the potential for productive, independent living in old age. Negative themes focused on loneliness, rejection, stubbornness, and senility.

DISCUSSION

Both attitudes toward the aged and humor involving elderly characters in this sample of books were rated as generally positive. It seems clear, however, that humor is a source of stereotyping of old people in children's literature. The humorous instances identified almost always involved elderly characters as the focus of the humor. It is interesting to note that, although adults comprised almost a third of the books' characters, the only adults involved in any instance of humor were two men who had been negatively portrayed. Also, as a group, those books containing humor were rated more negatively with respect to the portrayal of attitudes toward the aged than was the sample as a whole. Humor involving elderly characters depicted them as looking or doing something ridiculous, engaged in children's games, or somehow incompetent. Barnum (1977) has observed that "old people in children's literature are almost unfailingly pleasant" (p. 20) and suggests that this "pervasive gaiety" stereotypes the elderly by not portraying a realistic range of emotions. Similarly, the humorous presentation of the aged playing children's games and as being somehow incompetent reinforces the stereotype of inevitable regression or decline in old age.

With respect to gender differences, elderly men and women tended to be the focus of different types of humor. Most of the men looked ridiculous or playing children's games, whereas the women were more likely to be portrayed as inept. This finding seems consistent with Demos and Jache's (1981) observation that older men and women are the focus of different types of stereotypes in humorous birthday cards.

What are the implications of these findings for the development of children's attitudes toward aging? The need to use subject guides to identify this sample of books undoubtedly resulted in a positive bias with respect to portrayals of the aged as well as a disproportionate number of elderly depicted as grandparents, since *aging* and *grandparents* were usually the only relevant subject headings. Presumably books dealing with aging as a central theme present more enlightened views of older people. Given Ansello's (1977) finding that *stranger* was the most frequent relationship category for the aged in children's books, it is clear that this sample overrepresents close relationships with the elderly. Thus, it is likely that these results represent a conservative view of humor as a source of stereotyping in children's picture books. Storey (1977, 1979) has suggested stereotyping can be dealt with by children's use of critical reading techniques in evaluating the images of the elderly that are presented. Ansello (1977) argues that content analysis used in advocacy for portrayal of "the full range of human potential with older characters can serve to narrow the discrepancy between perceptions and reality by socializing a fresh cohort of children to more positive human values" (p. 271). If, as the present study suggests, stereotypes are presented "all in fun," it may be considerably more difficult for children to identify negative portrayals of the elderly or for concerned adults to eradicate them.

A number of issues remain to be addressed by future researchers of humor and aging in media such as children's books. As noted, Weber and Cameron (1978) have expressed concern about ambiguity in the attitudinal content of humor. The results of the present study suggest that the study of humor and aging in some media may also be hampered by disagreement about just what is humorous. Previous researchers escaped this problem by rating discrete examples (of jokes, cartoons, humorous birthday cards) on the nature of the humor portrayed. Isolated pictures, incidents, and so forth from children's picture books could be rated in a similar fashion, but context is clearly important in determining whether or not an instance is humorous as well as in interpreting the nature of the humor present. For example, Williams' (1975) portrayal of Kevin's grandmother (see Figure 11.1) might be viewed as representing a positive view of aging as a time of activity and enjoyment. However, this book is dedicated to a child with a wild imagination and ends with the lines, "I'm not sure I believe everything about Kevin's Grandma. Whoever heard of peanut butter soup?" Thus, the broader implication is that such a grandmother could not possibly exist!

Future researchers should also explore the role of developmental changes in what is viewed as humorous as well as cohort differences in the perception of attitudinal content of humor. As Blue (1978) suggested, children and elderly as well as adult raters could be used to determine how experiences portrayed in children's books are perceived.

Finally, since the present study focused only on picture books with older people as central characters, more information is needed about whether the frequency and nature of humor involving the aged differs from that of humor involving characters of other age groups. Fifth-graders studied by Storey (1979) concluded (among other generalizations about aged book characters) that "there were not many happy books about the elderly" (p. 410). Thus, a paucity of humor about the elderly may be as much of a problem as humor that contains negative stereotypes.

ACKNOWLEDGMENTS

I would like to thank Kathryn Kostel and Wendy Glasser for their assistance as raters.

APPENDIX: BOOKS ANALYZED

Borack, B. (1967). *Grandpa*. New York: Harper & Row.
Brooks, R. (1978). *Timothy and gramps*. Scarsdale, NY: Bradbury.
Buckley, H. E. (1961). *Grandmother and I*. New York: Lothrop, Lee & Shepard.
DePaola, T. (1978). *The clown of God*. New York: Harcourt Brace Jovanovich.
DePaola, T. (1973). *Nana upstairs, nana downstairs*. New York: Putnam.
DePaola, T. (1974). *Watchout for the chicken feet in your soup*. Englewood Cliffs, NJ: Prentice-Hall.
Goldman, S. (1976). *Grandma is somebody special*. Chicago: Whitman.
Jeschke, S. (1978). *Mia, Grandma and the genie*. New York: Holt, Rinehart & Winston.
Knotts, H. (1978). *Great-grandfather, the baby and me*. Brattleboro, VT: Book Press.
Langer, N. (1979). *Freddy my grandfather*. New York: Four Winds.
Lapp, E. J. (1978). *In the morning mist*. Chicago: Whitman.
Lasky, K. (1976). *I have four names for my grandfather*. Boston: Little, Brown.
Lundgren, M. (1972). *Matt's grandfather*. New York: Putnam.
Matsuno, M. (1960). *A pair of red clogs*. New York: World. 1960.
Ness, E. M. (1963). *Josefina February*. New York: Scribner.
Skorpen, L. M. (1975). *Mandy's grandmother*. New York: Dial Press.
Van Woerkom, D. O. (1977). *Tit for tat*. New York: Greenwillow.
Williams, B. (1975). *Kevin's grandma*. New York: Dutton.
Zolotow, C. (1974). *My grandson Lew*. New York: Harper & Row.

REFERENCES

Ansello, E. F. (1977). Age and ageism in children's first literature. *Educational Gerontology, 2*, 255–274.
Barnum, P. W. (1977). The aged in young children's literature. *Language Arts, 54*, 29–32.
Blue, G. F. (1978). The aging as portrayed in realistic fiction for children 1945–1975. *Gerontologist, 2*, 187–192.
Davies, L. J. (1977). Attitudes toward old age and aging as shown by humor. *Gerontologist, 17*, 220–226.
Demos, V., & Jache, A. (1981). When you care enough: An analysis of attitudes toward aging in humorous birthday cards. *Gerontologist, 21*, 209–215.

Dryer, S. S. (1977–1981). *Bookfinder: A guide to children's literature about the needs and problems of youth age 2–15* (Vols 1–2). Circle Pines, MN: American Guidance Service.

Fillmer, H. T. (1982). Sex stereotyping of the elderly by children. *Educational Gerontology, 8,* 77–85.

Kingston, A. J., & Drotter, M. W. (1981). The depiction of old age in six basal readers. *Educational Gerontology, 6,* 29–34.

Library of Congress. (1976–1982). *Children's books* (6 Vols 1–6). Washington, DC: U.S. Government Printing Office.

McGhee, P. E. (1979). *Humor: Its origin and development.* San Francisco: Freeman.

Palmore, E. (1971). Attitudes toward aging as shown by humor. *Gerontologist, 11,* 181–186.

Richman, J. (1977). The foolishness and wisdom of age: Attitudes toward the elderly as reflected in jokes. *Gerontologist, 17,* 210–217.

Robin, E. P. (1977). Old age in elementary school readers. *Educational Gerontology, 2,* 275–292.

Seefeldt, C., Jantz, R. K., Galper, A., & Serock, K. (1977). Children's attitudes toward the elderly. *Educational Gerontology, 2,* 301–310.

Sheppard, A. (1981). Responses to cartoons and attitudes toward aging. *Journal of Gerontology, 36,* 122–126.

Smith, M. D. (1979). The portrayal of elders in magazine cartoons. *Gerontologist, 19,* 409–412.

Storey, D. (1977). Gray power: An endangered species? Ageism as portrayed in children's books. *Social Education, 41,* 529–533.

Storey, D. (1979). Fifth graders meet elderly book characters. *Language Arts, 4,* 408–412.

Tway, E. (Ed.). (1981). *Reading ladders for human relations* (6th ed.). Washington, DC: American Council on Education.

Weber, T., & Cameron, P. (1978). Humor and aging—A reply. *Gerontologist, 18,* 73–76.

Williams, B. (1975). *Kevin's grandma.* New York: Dutton.

Yonkers Public Libarary Children's Services. (1979). *A guide to subjects and concepts in picture book format* (2nd ed.). Dobbs Ferry, NY: Oceana.

12

Male–Female Long-Term Relationships as a Source of Humor

EDWARD F. ANSELLO

INTRODUCTION

Our analysis of humor in long-term relationships begins by considering the cartoon in Figure 12.1[1], which depicts a banged-up hospitalized man and, supposedly, his wife reading to him that his insurance company does not cover acts of stupidity. While the setting is serious, the context is almost immediately transposed: We suspend our perception of realilty while introjecting our selves into this particular scenario; we can almost hear the tone of the wife, matter-of-fact, recounting as she has done so often in the past the litany of his mistakes. We laugh because we identify with one or the other character; we recognize ourselves. We understand the special qualities of his condition and her bedside manner that come from a long-term relationship.

A cartoon (or comic strip) does all of this. It is a disarmingly simple format for, at times, profoundly complex mechanisms. Unlike a joke, where one may be the teller or agent of the message, the cartoon is an outside medium to which the individual responds. While the joke may

---

[1] *Cartoon* and *comic strip* are used to describe the same medium, differing only in format length; hence, the terms are somewhat interchangeable.

Copyright © 1986 by Academic Press, Inc.
All rights of reproduction in any form reserved.

GRIN & BEAR IT   LICHTY & WAGNER

"Your insurance company says they don't cover
acts of stupidity."

Figure 12.1 Cartoon depicting qualities of a long-term relationship. GRIN AND BEAR
IT by Lichty & Wagner. © News Group Chicago, Inc. Courtesy of News America
Syndicate.

require time to set up the necessary ludicrous context through style
and content, the cartoon is nearly immediate. In a single image or
several frames, the cartoon must set up a context, identify its characters, convey values, and tap a sense of commonality in the viewer. At
the same time it must make us laugh or at least smile. Consider how
well political cartoons do this. They depend upon all of these conditions to make a statement in one frame that will produce humorous
responses from laughter to an "ain't it the truth" acknowledgement.

Long-term relationships, then, can enable the humor to take place
and can provide the substance of that humor. Male–female long-term
relationships in mid- and late-life seem to offer a wide range of opportunities for humor. These adult relationships, reflecting years of
male–female interactions, provide a common ground of understanding for gentle assertion of self and "ribbing" of the other gender.

Humor, in general, may be a safety valve, a socially reinforced
mechanism, for the very maintenance of long-term relationships. As
Schaeffer (1981) has observed in his study of a related issue:

> All of our instincts are in the service of survival. But in laughter we experi-
> ence an explosion of pleasure, a vocal and conspicuous display of delight that
> in effect incapacitates us, while it lasts, for any other business. This is an

indulgence apparently granted no other creature. Perhaps we alone have mastered reality just enough so that we feel we have a surplus of physical and mental energy that can be explored for the sake of imaginary pleasure alone. (p. 21)

With regard to cartoon humor specifically, its treatment of long-term relationships may afford us some insights into the issues of sustained relationships, the advantages and disadvantages of knowing another well, as well as the underlying processes of changes in the social ethic of male and female age-appropriate behavior.

Before proceeding we should clarify what aspects of humor and aging we are considering. We are not talking about the humor about aging, as in "You know you are getting older when your back goes out more than you do." We are not examining philosophical, epistemological questions on the theory, nature, or comprehension of humor (e.g., Feinberg, 1978; Fleet, 1890/1970; Froeschels, 1948). Finally, we are not pursuing the etiology or causes of laughter (e.g., Bolinger, 1971; Wilson, 1979). We are considering cartoon humor as reflective of social attitudes and themes and cartoon humor about long-term relationships as potentially instructive regarding values in male—female adult development.

CARTOON HUMOR AND SOCIAL STRUCTURES

Cartoon humor is a mirror, often reflecting marital and social realities. Other communicative media such as literature and television are both mirror and matrix of cultural theory; that is, they serve not only the function of reflecting cultural values but also that of changing them. But cartoon humor tends to be immediate; there is no real opportunity for exposition or sustained involvement as with other media. Hence, it tends to rely upon and to convey commonly accepted cultural values. In this regard, it is not unlike children's literature, which relies upon reductionistic portrayals and simple metaphors (Ansello, 1977, 1978, 1979).

Of course, our social structures are undergoing movement. The deeply set patterns of male—female relationships, including long-term or marital relationships, are undergoing some change. Being a mirror, cartoons can be expected to reflect these changes with varying degrees of insight, precision, and humor. Like a huge underground plate along one of the earth's fault lines that moves slowly but importantly, there is deep shifting in the relationship of one partner to the other in contemporary marriage. Like the plate's movement, sometimes this shifting is barely perceptible, sometimes it causes eruptions and earthquakes. We see this in the cartoon humor of long-term relationships: the struggle for control between partners, the emotional consequences of living closely together, the special appreciation for the other's idiocyncrasies, the adjustments required consciously or unconsciously to the other's shifts away from the traditional status quo.

Today's mid and late-life couples have experienced the earth's movements in their relationships. They have experienced contemporary changes in socially appropriate gender-role behaviors, especially the emergence of the powerful female, in addition to the traditional adjustments and antagonisms presumed to occur normally in a marriage. And so, cartoon and comic strip humor about couples engaged in long-term relationships offers a rich opportunity for insights into cultural themes about marriage, the constant versus the evolving, male and female mid- to late-life transitions, and the consequences of continuous exposure to another. The long-term relationship is an encapsulated microcosm of societal norms undergoing change; and cartoon humor distills the essence of this process.

Unlike McGhee's (1980) research on children's humorous material where some moderate challenge to comprehension seems funnier to the children, cartoon humor about long-term relationships is often baldly straightforward, striking quickly the respondent chord of recognition. Indeed, it may be that the content of long-term relationships humor would be perceived differently by younger persons or by those who have never experienced a longevous relationship. From the perspective of humor across the life span, that which poses a challenge to comprehension may be funnier to the child than to certain adults; that which has little or a certain humorous meaning at one point in the life span may have greater or a different meaning to another whose longer life and longer relationships have forged a different comprehension. Thus, the immediacy of the cartoon humor being discussed offers not a contradiction to McGhee's observation but rather the possibility of a life span continuum on the interactions of comprehension, challenge and humor.

Nahemow (1983) postulates that humor in old age might reaffirm "the integrity of the self despite myriad imperfections and challenges" (p. 10). Indeed, the self does seem to be a factor in many of the cartoons set in long-term relationships: reaffirming the self through the quest for the upper hand over one's mate; reinforcing the sufficiency of the self without need for intrusion or control by the other; conversely, stating the need of one's self to be understood and supported by the other; and so on.

We can relate to this humor because it stimulates what Schaeffer (1981) refers to as the vertical and the horizontal associative dimensions of humor. In the vertical sense, long-term relationship humor has a depth of meaning to our innermost self; the humorous reaffirmations, struggles for control, and foibles strike home. In the horizontal sense, these cartoons apply not just to us but to many others in long-term relationships; our kindredness is reinforced; we are not at all alone.

METHOD

Our research procedure has been casual but educational. From 1979 to 1984 we have examined cartoons published in newspapers and periodicals. The criterion for inclusion in our analysis has been that the average reader could ascertain that the cartoon characters have been in a long-term relationship; famililarity with the comic strip often allowed this, as in the case of "Andy Capp," "Dagwood," "Sally Forth," and "The Lockhorns". Even less objective factors were such things as the cartoonists' drawing of apparent ages of the characters, terms of endearment such as *dear,* and contexts commonly associated with couples, such as sitting near each other in the living room, visiting with another couple, and driving together in an automobile. Validation checks with other adults in their 30s and beyond confirmed that each of the cartoons examined was perceived to represent a couple in a relationship of long-standing.

We analyzed 90 cartoons and comic strips that portrayed adult relationships that reflected years of male–female interactions, providing a common ground of understanding. Just as the comic strip "Cathy" highlights the insecurities of male–female relationships in young adulthood and the need at this time to assert one's independence of potential constraints placed by the other gender, the comics "Andy Capp," "Grin and Bear It," "The Lockhorns," and others add to these dimensions the accommodation to each other and resignation to the status quo that years of marriage or a relationship have created. In addition, the male–female sparring sometimes takes on an extra dimension; for example, the emerging power of the older female, in a fashion quite compatible with Gutmann, Grunes, and Griffin (1980) theory-based observations about the mid- to late-life transitions from expressive to instrumental roles for women. One can also see male responses to this transition in the spouse which are consistent with a psychosexual theory of arrested development.

CONTENT ANALYSIS

Content analysis of 90 cartoons and comic strips published between 1979 and 1984 suggests that they can be seen to reflect at least four interrelated themes relative to long term male–female relationships: (1) the traditional antagonism between the sexes, (2) tension release or catharsis, (3) shared intimacy, and (4) accommodation to gender-role changes.

Antagonism

Antagonism between the genders probably predates history, and so it provides a readily recognizable, if stereotypic, context for cartoon and comic strip humor of long-term relationships. Examples include supposed male superiority, female troublesomeness, the nagging wife, the struggle for the "upper-hand," and other variations. Control may be the underlying dynamic. Representations include the following:

1. The couple sitting in their living room, evening martinis in hand, the man staring determinedly at her and the woman replying resolutely, "You certainly may *not* try to hypnotize me."

2. An apparently late-middle-aged couple, traveling down the highway, she in the frong passenger's seat looking imposing and he behind the driver's wheel commenting, "You must be getting tired, dear. Do you want me to drive on my own for a while?" (Figure 12.2).

Catharsis

Tension release or catharsis may be, paradixocally, one of the healthiest consequences of long-term relationships. While the other person may be the cause of stress, the continued relationship allows a purgation of emotions attendant upon long-term closeness between the couple. Proximity may be the underlying dynamic. Representations include the following:

1. Sally the wife complaining, with an arm full of laundry, that she "just can't do it all." Ted the husband, commiserating, places his hand on her shoulder and replies that he "understands" to which she retorts, "I don't need understanding . . . I *need help!!*"

2. Andy Capp ruminating in his customary position on the couch that "as we get older we tend to get irritated so much more quickly." Out

GRIN AND BEAR IT   by Lichty & Wagner

"You must be getting tired, dear . . . Do you want me to drive on my own for a while?"

Figure 12.2 An example of antagonism. GRIN AND BEAR IT by Lichty & Wagner. © News Group Chicago, Inc. Courtesy of News America Syndicate.

of hearing, she says, "What, Pet?" to which he screams, *"Open your ears, woman!!"* (Figure 12.3).

Shared Intimacy

Lemon, Bengston, and Peterson (1972) maintain that the presence of a confidant(e) for social participation in informal friendship activities is primary for life satisfaction. Primas (1984), examining this position among community-dwelling elderly, found that it is apparently not the informal social activities per se that confidants do together that contributed to high life satisfaction, but the opportunity to share personal beliefs, to confide in one another, to know one another, that matters. People in long-term relationships are likely to develop a special awareness, even appreciation, of the other's idiosyncracies. This theme conforms to what Lopata (1973) had defined as intimacy. It is closely linked to the theme of catharsis and the dynamic of proximity above. Familiarity may be the underlying dynamic here, and, to para-

ANDY CAPP   **by Reggie Smythe**

Figure 12.3 An example of catharsis. ANDY CAPP by Reggie Smythe. © 1980 Daily Mirror Newspapers Ltd. Courtesy of News America Syndicate.

phrase an expression, "Familiarity breeds humor." Like the knowledge that familiarity brings, sometimes this humor can have a biting edge. Consider the following representations:

1. The Lockhorns growling at each other in the marriage counselor's office, the counselor leaning forward in his chair to advise, "You become compatible one step at a time. First, forget about murdering each other."

2. Hagar's wife talking to another woman, apparently in a quiet, reflective manner, "When you've been married as long as I have, intense romantic love diminishes and you begin to feel something else." "What?" the other asks, as the next panel shows Hagar in his customary gear, drinking. "Stuck," she replies (Figure 12.4).

Accommodation

The changes in appropriate psychological structures that follow the parental period have been instructively examined by Gutmann (1969,

Figure 12.4 An example of shared intimacy. Reprinted with special permission of King Features Syndicate, Inc.

1975) and Gutmann, Grunes, and Griffin (1980) Gutmann et al. report a universal "return of the repressed" in both genders, in which men relinquish part of their competitive, production orientation in favor of their more social, nurturant aspects, while women abandon the latter in favor of the more managerial, assertive side of themselves.

Gutmann et al. (1980) state:

> Research suggests that most older individuals, perhaps after some period of mild dislocation, accomodate to their sexual bimodalilty, and begin to live out and even enjoy the hitherto submerged aspects of the self. Accordingly, men can become more openly sensual, more openly dependent, and more openly emotional; whereas women can become happily assertive, less needful of love, more ready to risk the loss of love in trials of strength. (p. 122)

Needless to say, not every accommodation goes smoothly. Add to this the strongly reinforced, traditional roles learned earlier by mid- to late-life husbands, and the stage is set for the cartoonist's pen. Women seek to dominate, while men seek to hold on or get out of the way. Adjustment to new roles may be the underlying dynamic, where the object of some humor may be the dominant or powerful older woman, while the means of the humor may be the man's whining or commiseration. Consistent with Gutmann et al.'s (1980) observations that the older man, faced with the crossover from instrumentalilty to expressiveness and vice versa, may seek to deny and to reexternalize the feminine through drink, the barroom is a common setting in this theme. Humor plays an accommodative role in these late-life transitions. The following are illustrative:

1. Mr. Lockhorn at the bar, hunched over, spies his wife entering the saloon and he comments, "Now I remember what I was drinking to forget" (Figure 12.5).

Figure 12.5 An example of accommodation. Reprinted with special permission of King Features Syndicate, Inc.

2. Older couple in the marriage counselor's office, the man sitting meekly, and the woman barks, "I tell him I want him to stand on his own two feet and do what I tell him to do!"

CONCLUSIONS

Cartoon humor offers untapped opportunities to assess social values. Unlike television, which seeks to be, or has inadvertently become, a socializing medium, cartoon humor is a reflective medium. It is mirror and not matrix. Cartoon and comic strip humor set in long-term relationships can be instructive, especially since mid- to late-life couples have lived through a historical time of substantial alterations of the traditional male–female relationship and are personally at a life span point where psychological structures are being substantially modified. Our preliminary research found these and other issues reflected in the humor. We note four interrelated themes in portrayed long-term relationships: antagonism, catharsis, intimacy, and accommodation. Surely, this area of investigation has only begun to be plumbed.

Further Questions for Study

We have argued that cartoon and comic strip humor is a reflective medium and proves instructive regarding long-term relationships. Consequently, this humor may be educational with respect to values associated with these relationships across historical time. A longitudinal study of "Dagwood and Blondie," for instance, should reveal changes over time in what was considered socially appropriate behavior for each gender, normative marital behavior, and appropriate parent–child interactions in terms of style and content. My daughter's current Archie, Betty, and Veronica, for example, are somehow different from the personae I remember for them. The differences go beyond changes in clothing, speech, and hairstyles, which have all kept pace with the times. To be sure, skirts rose and fell with the fashions and Jughead had long sideburns and shaggy hair during the mid- and late-1970s. Beyond these obvious social "signatures," however, the interactions among the male and female characters are qualitatively different. Betty is more assertive than as I remember her in my youth, and the kinds of activities the boys and girls share with each other seem more varied.

With respect to cartoon and comic strip humor, are there demonstrable changes or differences in perceptions of what is considered humorous across the life span? That is, would longitudinal and cross-sectional study reveal that we differ over time or among cohorts in what we consider humorous? Would there be differences in the triggering mechanism for humor; for example, would the degree of the ludicrous context or the nonsubtlety of the justaposition have to become more pronounced with age in order to stimulate a humorous response? If so, are the changes in what is considered humorous predicted by traits or characteristics of the perceiver? What do changes or differences mean in terms of the perceivers' psychological structures like instrumentality–expressiveness, masculinity–femininity, internality–externality, or sociability, intelligence, or coping skills? Are there changes or differences in degrees of individual senses of humor across the life span?

With regard to the mechanics of cartoon and comic strip humor, there are variations in the use or complexity of metaphors embedded in the humor aimed at readers of different ages. Are the metaphorical nuances consciously or unconsciously created by the cartoonist with a given-aged perceiver in mind? Does the humor of the *New Yorker* or of *Modern Maturity* or of other periodicals targeted for an older readership differ in these dimensions from the humor in publications marketed to younger clientele?

Can cartoon and comic strip humor be an effective therapeutic device for depressed, confused or stressed individuals? That is, is there in fact a verifiable therapeutic value of humor? Can it be used in counseling practice as a coping intervention? Would cartoon humor set in long-term relationships prove especially helpful in counseling with mid- to late-life couples? Does identification with the circumstances of the cartoon's characters, a kind of laughing at oneself, aid not only comprehension of the content, as we have discussed, but also stress reduction?

Cartoon humor is a part of American life. It figuratively wraps our daily lives as it literally wraps our Sunday newspapers. Cartoon humor about male–female long-term relationships seems familiar to us, for it conveys socially recognizable values. We identify and respond; we feel normal or connected to others. Research has begun to assess the mechanisms of this medium, that is, the essential elements or parts of humor and how they interact. To a lesser degree have we examined the functions of humor, that is, humor as a mirror to appraise changing social values and humor as a tool for therapeutic intervention. I believe that cartoon humor with male–female long-term relationships has the potential to instruct us on both the mechanics and the functions of humor.

REFERENCES

Ansello, E. F. (1977). Age and ageism in children's first literature. *Educational Geron-tology: An International Quarterly, 2*(3), 255–274.

Ansello, E. F. (1978). Ageism: The subtle stereotype. *Childhood Education, 54*(3), 118–122.

Ansello, E. F. (1979). Literature, mentality, and aging. In H. L. Sterns, E. F. Ansello, B. M. Sprouse & R. Layfield-Faux (Eds.), *Gerontology in higher education: Develop-ing institutional and community strength*. Belmont, CA: Wadsworth.

Bolinger, Z. B. (1971). *A study of children's responses to cartoons as related to intelli-gence, sex, grade in school, age and father's occupation*. Unpublished doctoral dissertation, The University of Maryland, College Park.

Feinberg, L. (1978). *The secret of humor*. Amsterdam: Rodopi.

Fleet, F. R. (1970). *A theory of wit and humor*. Port Washington, NY: Kennikat Press. (Original work published 1890)

Froeschels, E. (1948). *Philosophy in wit*. New York: Philosophical Library.

Gutmann, D. (1969, April). The country of old men: Cruss-cultural studies in the psy-chology of later life. *Occasional Papers in Gerontology, 1969, 5*, Institute of Geron-tology: University of Michigan–Wayne State University.

Gutmann, D. (1975). Parenthood: A key to the comparative psychology of the life cycle. In N. Datan & L. Ginsberg (Eds.), *Life-span developmental psychology: Normative life crises*. New York: Academic Press.

Gutmann, D., Grunes, J., & Griffin, B. (1980). The clinical psychology of later life: Developmental paradigms. In N. Datan & N. Lohmann (Eds.), *Transitions of ag-ing*. New York: Academic Press.

Lemon, B. W., Bengston, V. L., & Peterson, J. A. (1972). An exploration of the activity theory of aging: Activity types and life satisfaction among inmovers to a retirement community. *Journal of Gerontology, 27*, 511–523.

Lopata, H. A. (1973). *Widowhood in an American city*. Cambridge, MA: Schenkman.

McGhee, P. E. (1980). Development of the sense of humor in childhood: A longitudinal study. In P. E. McGhee & A. J. Chapman (Eds.), *Children's humour*. New York: Wiley.

Nahemow, L. (1983, May 10–13). *Humor as a data base for the study of aging*. Paper presented at the Third Biennial Conference of West Virginia University Gerontol-ogy Center, Berkeley Springs.

Primas, M. E. (1984). *Friendship intimacy, financial security, and morale among el-derly women*. Unpublished doctoral dissertation, The University of Maryland, Col-lege Park.

Schaeffer, N. (1981). *The art of laughter*. New York: Columbia University Press.

Wilson C. P. (1979). *Jokes: Form, content, use, and function*. London: Academic Press.

13

The Effect of Humor on the Recovery Rate of Cataract Patients: A Pilot Study

KATHLEEN FOX TENNANT

> *A merry heart doeth good like a medicine: but a broken spirit drieth the bones.*
>
> Proverbs 17:22

INTRODUCTION

Humor is a funny thing. It is funny that humor is not discussed very much in nursing or medical schools. In nursing books and journals, whole sections are written on the anatomy and physiology of the eye, paragraphs on vitreous and aqueous humor, but not a single sentence on the curative properties of humor. As older adults continue to increase in age and number, nurses will play an increasingly active role in the assessment, care, and promotion of health of elderly clients as they move through the aging process. Every illness of the body, whether it be angina, cancer, or cataracts affects the way in which we think and behave; humor does the same.

There have been few studies attempting to determine the nature of humor used in health care settings (Coser, 1959; Emerson, 1963; Fox, 1959; Robinson, 1970). Humor has been found to be an indirect form of communication that can be used for a variety of purposes: to decrease social distance; to establish relationships; to relieve stress, tension, and anxiety; to avoid or deny feelings; or to facilitate the expression of feelings. Little research, however, has been documented concerning the effects of humor on illness. Medieval physicians told jokes to their patients, but mirth was not widely welcome in the mod-

 Copyright © 1986 by Academic Press, Inc. All rights of reproduction in any form reserved.

ern examining room until 1976, when Cousins (1976) wrote of how he laughed his way to recovery from a degenerative spinal condition. While many doctors discredited Cousins' claim, pointing out that the disease sometimes goes into spontaneous remission, others began taking a serious look at the biology of laughter.

THE FUNCTIONS OF HUMOR

Within this unique world of health and illness, humor serves three major functions: a communication function, a social function, and a psychological function (Robinson, 1977). The emotional messages that need to be communicated within a hospital are usually quite serious: anxiety, fear, anger, frustration, embarrassment, concern, hope, and joy. Patients are frequently uncomfortable expressing these emotions directly, and humor serves to convey these feelings in an indirect manner.

Humor is often a coping mechanism to relieve anxiety in patients; for example, the anxiety about the seriousness of one's illness, the procedures one must undergo, the loss of body parts or changes in body image, permanent disabilities, and threats of impending death are all areas that precipitate the use of humor (Robinson, 1977). In areas where the situation is tense and the anxiety for both patients and staff is high, such as intensive care units, coronary care units, emergency rooms, and operating room, there is often a great deal of joking and humor, which help to alleviate tension and help people to come to terms with the situation in an acceptable way.

Not only does humor allay anxiety, but humor and laughter also produce beneficial physiological results. Laughter exercises the heart and lungs, stimulates the circulatory system, and decreases blood pressure; in addition, it ultimately produces a state of deep relaxation of the muscles and thus promotes physical and emotional well-being (Peter & Dana, 1982).

This pilot study was prompted by the apparent need for many elderly patients in the hospital to tell jokes. The older adults were patients at the Ophthalmology Unit of the West Virginia University Medical Center. The Ophthalmology Unit consists of 11 inpatient beds, five staff physicians, resident physicians, registered nurses, nurse assistants, and other members of the health team including dieticians, social workers, and physical therapists. The purpose of this unit is to treat diseases and disorders of the eye medically and surgically in order to increase or preserve vision and to prevent blindness.

The majority of the patients admitted to this unit are 60 years of age and older and have experienced a visual disturbance with the aging process, namely, cataracts. The role of the professional nurse is to assist the patient in regaining and maintaining independence in daily living activities through the promotion of self-care behaviors, health teaching, counseling, and referral. Thus, the nurse acts as a facilitator of health and well-being by enhancing the quality of life of these elderly patients.

If nurses can establish that humor is essential to health promotion and well-being, humor will become a vital requirement in patient-centered, holistic nursing care.

PURPOSE

The purpose of this pilot study was to determine the effect of humor on the recovery rate of elderly patients after cataract surgery. Specific research questions were:

1. Is there a relationship between patients who score the highest on the Humor Survey and the recovery rate?
2. Is there a relationship between patients who considered themselves an "old joketeller" and the recovery rate?

Definition of Terms

The terms used in this study were defined as follows:

Cataract surgery. Operation under local anesthesia to remove an opacified lens within the eye and replace it with an artificial, intraocular lens implant.

Recovery rate. The length of hospital stay measured by number of days from date of admission to day of discharge.

Humor. The comic or amusing quality of the printed joke as measured by the ratings on the Humor Survey.

Old joketeller. Persons who answered yes, to the question: Do you consider yourself an old joketeller?

METHOD

Sample

The sample consisted of 12 women and eight men ranging in age from 65 to 95 years. The mean age of the women was 73.5 years and the mean age of the men was 78 years. All subjects were patients at the Ophthalmology Unit of the West Viriginia University Medical Center and had undergone cataract surgery 24 hours prior to participating in the survey. All subjects were oriented to person, place, and time as measured by direct question; independent in their activities of daily living; able to speak and understand written English; and able to read the large printed type on the survey. Participation in the study was obtained from each subject on a voluntary, anonymous basis; permission for this study was also obtained from the chairperson of the Ophthalmology Department. Uncontrolled variables in the sample selection that may have had an effect on the outcome of the study included the influence of chronic diseases such as diabetes and hypertension, educational level, culture, religious beliefs, and the degree of social isolation.

Instrument

The Humor Survey was developed by psychologist James Hassett (1977). The 30 jokes were chosen from a list of 75 from jokebooks, from other humor studies, and from personal favorites. The jokes were then pretested on a group of 100 Boston University students and ranked on their average funniness for this group. Five commonsense categories that had been used in previous studies were chosen and five psychologists decided which jokes belong in each group: sexual, wordplay, ethnic, hostile, and silly. The Humor Survey was published in the June 1978 issue of *Psychology Today* with 14,500 readers taking part in the survey.

For the present study, 3 jokes from each category were chosen for a total of 15 jokes. Questions regarding demographics, background, and social data were included on the first page of the survey.

Procedure

The study was thoroughly explained to each subject 24 hours after their cataract surgery. Since delivery, timing, and social setting affect whether or not one laughs, the survey was administered in the private, quiet atmosphere of each patient's hospital room. Each subject was instructed to answer the background data questions and then proceed to the jokes on the next page. The subjects were to read each joke and rate its funniness by circling one number on a scale from 1 to 4. Below each joke was the question:

> How funny is this?
> 1—Not at all funny
> 2—Slightly funny
> 3—Somewhat funny
> 4—Very funny

This was a self-paced study.

PRESENTATION OF FINDINGS

The men rated the jokes as funnier than did the women and therefore scored higher on the Humor Survey (see Table 13.1). This is statistically significant at the .05 level. This finding is consistent with studies of everyday humor that men prefer jokes and are more often than not the joketeller, whereas women are typically in the position of reacting to humor (McGhee, 1979). Studies of American children have found that boys repeat more jokes and riddles than do girls as early as age 6, when formal joking first appears. Pollio and Edgerly found that men in mixed group-therapy sessions were nearly five times as likely as women to try to be funny (see Hassett & Houlihan, 1979). This also holds true for men and women in other cultures. Goldstein and McGhee (1972) surveyed college students in Belgium, Hong Kong, and Philadelphia and found that men were more likely to tell jokes than women.

TABLE 13.1

Scores on Humor Survey and Rate of Recovery from Cataract Surgery

	N	$\overline{X}$	SD	
Humor survey scores				
Males	8	44.13	7.51	$t = 2.36$
Females	12	33.92	10.53	$p < .05$
All subjects	20	38.00	10.55	
Recovery rate				
Males	8	3.5 days	1.07	$t = 1.02$
Females	12	3.9 days	0.67	p (N.S.)
All subjects	20	3.75 days	0.85	

The average length of hospital stay for all subjects was 3.75 days. Women had a recovery rate of 3.9 days, whereas men recovered at an average of 3.5 days (as shown in Table 13.1). While this is not statistically significant, the tendency was for men to recover more rapidly. This seems noteworthy because the men were an average of 4.5 years older than the women and thus might have been expected to recover more slowly.

Furthermore, there was a positive relationship between the recovery rate and humor scores for males: The males who scored the highest on the Humor Survey—53, 53, and 51—had the fastest rate of recovery of 2, 3, and 2 days, respectively. Two of these three male subjects considered themselves to be old joketellers, and the man who scored the highest on the Humor Survey recovered the fastest, staying only 2 days in the hospital.

The female subjects who scored the highest on the Humor Survey— 49, 48, and 44—had a recovery rate of 4, 4, and 5 days. Only one of these women considered herself to be an old joketeller.

Limitations and Recommendations

Several limitations have been recognized from this study which should be objectively weighed in relation to the findings. The printed joke was less than ideal for the elderly patients in this pilot study. Many patients were unable to understand the directions after repeated explanations or unable to read the large-print type due to decreased visual acuity, which is an uncontrolled variable postoperatively. Furthermore, the jokes for the Humor Survey were chosen by 20-year-old college students, which implies a bias even though the older adult respondents in the original survey liked the jokes better than young adults. Perhaps another survey may indeed find a collection of favorite jokes that the elderly person would particularly appreciate. Suggestions for revisions, therefore, include a tape recording of the jokes that have a special appeal for the 65-years-and-older age group.

This pilot study was conducted on a small sample size due to time constraints and, therefore, needs to be further investigated with a larger sample size for statistical purposes. Social and demographic data were obtained, but comparison of cultural groups, geographic areas, and senior center participants and nonparticipants were not analyzed in this study. In addition, extraneous variables such as chronic diseases may have a significant psychological and emotional effect and need to be controlled in future studies.

Implications

Although the findings in this study were quite insignificant; they do point out the need for more definitive and rigorous investigation of the effects of humor on illness. First, more reliable methods and tools for studying humor and for the collection of humorous data in health care settings is needed. Definitive studies of the use of humor in health and illness related to culture or ethnic groups and to certain age groups is needed.

Furthermore, humor as a therapeutic nursing intervention for older adults has implications for nursing practice. Humor as a holistic nursing strategy can be applied to various health care settings as a means to cope with stress and anxiety imposed by environmental restraints. Examples of such situations include a patient confined to bedrest, a patient in isolation, or a postoperative eye surgery patient with one or both eyes patched. Moreover, nurses can be encouraged to explore the role of humor to help prevent or reduce the "burn out" phenomenon: to cope with the stress, pressure and depression inherent in the nursing profession.

Thus, the findings for this study offer implications for nusing research and practice that suggest that nursing should attach more significance to humor in older adults and consider the potential of humor as an intervention strategy.

REFERENCES

Coser, R. (1959). Some social functions of laughter: A study of humor in hospital setting. *Human Relations, 12*(2), 171–182.

Cousins, N. (1976). *Anatomy of an illness.* New York: Norton.

Emerson, J. P. (1963). *Social functions of humor in a hospital setting.* Unpublished doctoral dissertation, University of California, Berkeley.

Fox, R. (1959). *Experiment perilous.* Illinois: The Free Press.

Goldstein, J., & McGhee, P. (1972). *The psychology of humor.* New York: Academic Press.

Hassett, J., & Houlihan, J. (1979, January). Different jokes for different folks. *Psychology Today,* 64–71.

McGhee, P. E. (1979). *Humor: Its origin and development.* San Francisco: Freeman.

Peter, L., & Dana, B. (1982). *The laughter prescription.* New York: Ballantine Books.

Robinson, V. (1970). Humor in nursing. In C. E. Carlson & B. Blackwell (Eds.), *Behavioral concepts and nursing intervention* (pp. 129–150). Philadelphia: Lippincott.

Robinson, V. M. (1977). *Humor and the health profession.* New Jersey: Slack.

Generational Differences in Humor and Correlates of Humor Development

PAUL E. MCGHEE
NANCY J. BELL
NELDA S. DUFFEY

INTRODUCTION

Alford (1983) reported that joking relationships characterize parent–child interactions in about two-thirds of American families. This suggests that parental attempts at humor should play an important role in the child's humor development. However, studies of the relationship between parents' laughter and humor and children's humor development have been rare. Fisher and Fisher (1981, 1983), Fry and Allen (1975), Janus (1975), and Wilde (1968) all found that clowns, comics, and comedy writers tended to have at least one parent (or another close relative) who did a lot of joking and clowning during their childhood. The two studies reported here were designed to obtain information on nonprofessional samples of adults regarding the relationship between ratings of their own current laughter and humor and of the amount of joking and clowning exhibited by their parents. These relationships were tested for both college students and a sample of elderly women. We predicted, of course, that individuals whose parents did

Copyright © 1986 by Academic Press, Inc.
All rights of reproduction in any form reserved.

more joking during their (the subjects') childhood should currently report more frequent laughter and humor initiation.

The same set of studies described above also points to the importance of other aspects of early maternal behavior for humor development. Both for a sample of children (McGhee, 1976, 1980) and professional humorists (Bales, 1970; Block, 1971; Fisher & Fisher, 1981, 1983), mothers of individuals who eventually showed heightened humor development showed a general early tendency toward being nonnurturant and nonmaternal. These mothers made strong demands on their children for early responsible behavior and exposed them to challenging situations more suitable for someone considerably older. These early demands for responsible behavior seemed to predispose these children to greater early interest in humor. Accordingly, the present study also examined the relationship between reports of present humor and laughter and the degree of early maternal babying and protectiveness.

McGhee (1976, 1980) also found that humor initiators showed evidence of high verbal and physical aggression, dominance, and talkativeness throughout the period up to their present age. Similar findings were obtained by Damico and Purkey (1978) with children, by Fisher and Fisher (1981) for amateur comedians, and by Janus (1975, 1981) for professional comedians. The present studies obtained self-reports of current levels of social assertiveness in order to determine whether this relationship continues to hold among college students and the elderly.

Finally, if joking and clowning are relatively stable forms of behavior, amount of current initiation of and responsiveness to humor should show a significant positive relationship with early interest in and enjoyment of humor during elementary and high school. This relationship was also tested in the studies reported here.

The findings reported here should be viewed as exploratory, since both studies relied upon self-report of both present and past behaviors or characteristics of subjects and their parents. In the case of the elderly sample, this recall extended over a period of 50 years or more, leaving subjects open to several sources of bias in reporting information. The validity of the self-report measures used here has not been detemined, but the consistency of information obtained across a wide range of the life span lends strength to the data obtained. The data are viewed as preliminary but are reported here in order to stimulate additional research using stronger behavioral measures of the behaviors described.

STUDY 1: UNDERGRADUATE STUDENTS

Subjects and Method

The subjects were 205 male and 241 female undergraduate students. The humor scale and the background predictor items used in this study are listed in Table 14.1. All of these items were part of a larger questionnaire completed by all subjects (see Bell, McGhee, & Duffey, in press). The six items dealing with different aspects of humor initiation were combined to form a total humor initiation score (alpha = .84 for the six items). Only this total score is used in all analyses reported here. A seventh humor item was used alone as the measure of humor responsiveness. The predictor variables (shown in Table 14.2) were derived from factor analyses (principal components, varimax rotation) of 17 background items relevant to this study. All of the predictor variables were based on a combined score for two items, with the exception of the "assertiveness score," which was based on four items. All subjects completed a questionnaire that included the items listed in both Table 14.1 and Table 14.2 in groups of 50–200 persons in a regular classroom context.

TABLE 14.1
Items Composing the Humor Initiation and Responsiveness Measures

---

Humor initiation
  1. How often do you try to be funny by clowning around or "acting funny" in some way?[a]
  2. How often do you try to be funny by telling jokes or stories that you remember?[a]
  3. How often do you use puns in an attempt to create your own humor?[a]
  4. How often do you come up with witty remarks other than puns in an attempt to create your own humor?[a]
  5. I am usually the one who puns and tells jokes or funny anecdotes in a social situation.[b]
  6. I am usually the one who clowns around (acting silly or funny) in a social situation.[b]
Humor responsiveness
  1. How often do you have a strong "belly laugh" of the type that lasts 5 seconds or more?[a]

---

  [a] Response scale: (1) rarely, (2) two or three times a week, (3) once or twice a day, (4) three or four times a day, (5) more than four times a day.
  [b] Response scale: (1) strongly disagree, (2) disagree, (3) neither agree nor disagree, (4) agree, (5) strongly agree. Direction of scoring was such that a higher score indicates greater agreement with the item.

TABLE 14.2
Items Used as Predictors of Current Humor[a]

Father's early humor
  1. My father did a lot of joking and clowning when I was growing up.
  2. My father did a lot of playful teasing when I was growing up.
Mother's early humor
  1. My mother did a lot of joking and clowning when I was growing up.
  2. My mother did a lot of playful teasing when I was growing up.
Maternal babying and protectiveness
  1. As I recall my childhood, my mother tended to baby me quite a bit.
  2. As I recall my childhood, my mother tended to overprotect me and not allow
     me to have many of the experiences other children had.
Maternal affection/happy childhood
  1. As I recall my childhood, my mother was very affectionate toward me.
  2. My childhood was basically very happy.
Current assertiveness
  1. Generally speaking, I am a socially assertive person.
  2. I am a very talkative person.
  3. I am prone to being verbally aggressive at times.
  4. I am prone to being physically aggressive at times.
Early enjoyment and humor
  1. As I recall, I was especially interested in and enjoyed jokes and other kinds of
     humor during elementary school.
  2. As I recall, I was especially interested in and enjoyed jokes and other kinds of
     humor during high school.

---

[a] Response scale: (1) strongly disagree, (2) disagree, (3) neither agree or disagree, (4) agree, (5) strongly agree. Direction of scoring was such that a higher score indicates greater agreement with the item.

Results

Humor initiation and responsiveness scores were regressed on the full set of predictor variables for each gender in order to determine the most important precursors of subjects' current humor. Table 14.3 shows that, in general, individuals' own early and current behaviors were the best (positive) predictors of their current humor—especially of humor initiation. For both males and females, the greatest amounts of variance in humor initiation scores were accounted for by their present social assertiveness and the amount of enjoyment of humor during childhood and adolescence. Assertiveness was also positively predictive of males' humor responsiveness, while early enjoyment of humor was positively predictive of females' humor responsiveness. The only aspect of early parental behavior that accounted for significant amounts of variance in humor scores was the amount of early humor exhibited by the same gender parent. Thus, fathers' early humor was positively associated with sons' present humor, while mothers' early humor was positively associated with daughters' present humor. It is especially interesting to note that fathers' early modeling of humor predicted the amount of humor initiated by their sons, while mothers' early modeling of humor predicted the degree of responsiveness shown by their daughters. A discussion of these findings will be combined with that for Study 2.

STUDY 2: ELDERLY WOMEN

Study 2 was designed to replicate the procedures used in Study 1 but with an older adult sample. Our original intent was to include both males and females; but since we were only able to test three males in

TABLE 14.3
Regression Analyses of Humor Initiation and Laughter Scores

Predictor variables	Males		Females	
	Standardized coefficient	t	Standardized coefficient	t
Humor initiation[a]				
Father's humor	.17	2.46*	.11	1.88
Mother's humor	−.01	−.10	.01	.17
Maternal prot./babying	.02	.35	−.05	−.83
Maternal affection/happy childhood	−.03	−.48	−.04	−.74
Assertiveness	.27	4.11***	.30	4.96***
Early humor enjoyment	.18	2.52*	.26	4.07***
Laughter[b]				
Father's humor	.01	.20	.07	1.18
Mother's humor	.14	1.87	.21	3.27**
Maternal prot./babying	.10	1.42	.08	1.39
Maternal affection/happy childhood	−.01	−.12	.04	.67
Assertiveness	.18	2.58*	.09	1.42
Early humor enjoyment	.13	1.80	.16	2.39*

[a] Males: $F(6,198) = 7.66$, $p < .001$; $R^2 = .19$. Females: $F(6,234) = 11.72$, $p < .001$; $R^2 = .23$.
[b] Males: $F(6,198) = 3.77$, $p < .01$; $R^2 = .10$. Females: $F(6,234) = 7.02$, $p < .001$; $R^2 = .15$.
* $p < .05$. ** $p < .01$. *** $p < .001$.

the retirement centers visited, only the data for females are reported here. The measures were identical to those reported for Study 1. The subjects were 27 women in their 60s, 70s, or 80s. All of the women tested were recruited as volunteers from two different retirement centers. In contrast to Study 1, these subjects were tested either individually or in very small groups.

The analyses reported for the older adult sample differ from those reported for Study 1, due to the small sample size of the elderly women. Since it was not possible to do a factor analysis on individual items in Study 2, correlations are reported separately for each of the items composing the behavior categories. A global humor initiation score was computed using the first four items listed in Table 14.1.

Results

Table 14.4 lists the Pearson correlation coefficients obtained between both humor measures and all of the individual predictor items. Comparison of this table with Table 14.3 reveals that the pattern of

TABLE 14.4
Correlations between Older Women's Self-Ratings of Humor and Ratings of Early Parental Behavior and Subjects' Own Early and Current Behavior

Predictor	Humor initiation	Laughter	Predictor	Humor initiation	Laughter
Father's joking/clowning	.12	.14	Social assertiveness	.40*	.48**
Father's playful teasing	−.07	.27	Talkativeness	.32	.46**
Mother's joking/clowning	.43**	.39*	Verbal aggression	.38*	.21
Mother's playful teasing	.27	.46**	Physical aggression	−.15	.05
Maternal babying	−.26	.18	Enjoyment of humor, elementary school	.10	.40**
Maternal protectiveness	.29	.19			
Maternal affection	−.19	.05	Enjoyment of humor, high school	.41	.39*
Happy childhood	−.16	−.03			

* $p < .05.$ ** $p < .01.$

significant predictions for this group of older women was very similar to that obtained for college students. With the exception of physical aggressiveness, all three of the assertiveness items were positively predictive of at least one of the humor measures. Also, self-ratings of both humor initiation and responsiveness were positively related to extent of recalled interest in and enjoyment of humor in high school. Only the responsive aspects of humor, however, were predicted by this measure during the elementary school years.

The findings for parental humor are also similar to those obtained for college students in that it was the same gender parent whose early humor was predictive of subjects' own current humor. Thus, recall of amount of early maternal joking and clowning was positively predictive of ratings of both current humor initiation and responsiveness. Positive relationships were also obtained for amount of recalled maternal playful teasing, but this only reached significance for frequency of heavy laughter.

GENERATION DIFFERENCES IN HUMOR

Since the two subject samples completed similar questionnaires regarding their own behavior and early parent behavior, it was possible to compare their responses in order to determine the presence of generation differences in perceptions of both subjects' own humor and the amount of humor exhibited by their parents. Given the considerable differences in the number of women sampled in the two studies, a group of 86 college females was randomly selected from the total of 241 and was compared here with the 27 elderly women. T tests were computed on all of the individual items directly pertaining to humor. The results of these analyses are listed in Table 14.5.

Significant generation differences were obtained for nearly all of the humor items. The younger women reported significantly more clowning, joking, and witty remarks other than puns than did the older women, and they reported more frequent strong laughter as well. Younger women also reported greater enjoyment of and interest in humor during both elementary school and high school, although this difference was only marginally significant ($p < .06$) for the high school period. The younger women also appeared to have grown up in households with more frequent modeling of different kinds of humor than was the case for older women. The younger sample's mothers and fathers were both recalled as having done more joking, clowning,

TABLE 14.5

T tests Computed on All Humor-Related Measures for Younger (Study 1) and Older (Study 2) Female Subjects[a]

Variable	Study	Mean	t
Clowning around	1	3.03	5.10***
	2	1.75	
Joking	1	2.19	2.05*
	2	1.71	
Puns	1	2.01	0.82
	2	1.79	
Other wit	1	2.62	3.48***
	2	1.79	
Laughter	1	2.41	1.83
	2	1.96	
Humor enjoyment in elementary school	1	3.78	2.28*
	2	3.33	
Humor enjoyment in high school	1	4.05	1.89
	2	3.68	
Father's joking and clowning	1	3.41	4.35***
	2	2.22	
Father's playful teasing	1	3.58	5.66***
	2	2.15	
Mother's joking and clowning	1	2.76	3.17**
	2	1.96	
Mother's playful teasing	1	2.94	3.88***
	2	1.93	

[a] For all analyses, $N = 86$ for the younger sample and $N = 27$ for the older sample.
* $p < .05$. ** $p < .01$. *** $p < .001$.

and playful teasing when they were growing up than was the case for parents of the older sample.

GENERAL DISCUSSION

The data obtained here showed surprising consistency across the two samples. In general, ratings of one's own humor initiation and responsiveness in both age groups were predicted by perceptions of current social assertiveness, amount of interest in and enjoyment of humor when growing up, and amount of humor remembered to have been displayed by the same gender parent while growing up. The association of frequent humor initiation with high levels of assertiveness is especially noteworthy, since strong predictions of humor by verbal and physical assertiveness were also obtained by McGhee (1976, 1980) for elementary school children of both genders. This relationship has also been demonstrated for amateur (Fisher & Fisher, 1981) and professional comedians (Janus, 1975, 1981). Thus, it is the socially assertive individual who is most likely to tell jokes, be witty, clown around, or otherwise try to be funny. This appears to hold true at all ages and for professional humorists, as well as for people generally. With the exception of college females, the present findings suggest that this connection with social assertiveness also holds for the amount of laughter shown.

The close association between humor and assertiveness across the life span is consistent with the notion that humor initiation and responsiveness are quite stable across the life span. This view is supported by the fact that the amount of early interest in and enjoyment of humor was significantly predictive of ratings of current humor initiation and responsiveness in both the younger and older women tested here. Among college males, early enjoyment of humor was predictive of reports of current humor initiation but not of humor responsiveness. Thus, once children become interested in humor at some point prior to college—usually during elementary school—they appear to maintain this interest and enjoyment throughout their lives. This conclusion can only be offered for women at this point since no data were obtained for a sample of elderly men. However, the fact that this society generally is more accepting of humor initiation from men than from women suggests that comparable findings will be obtained for men.

The second major finding obtained in these studies is that if parents' own humor and laughter do make a significant contribution to children's humor development, it is most likely to occur with a child of the same gender. It remains to be seen whether this simply reflects relative strengths in identification with the two parents or whether parents do more joking and clowning around with same-gender children. It should be noted that in the college sample, reports of fathers' early humor predicted sons' ratings of their own humor initiation, whereas reports of mothers' early humor only predicted ratings of laughter shown by their daughters. Since recalled early maternal humor was predictive of ratings of both humor initiation and responsiveness among the older women, it may be premature to speculate about the significance of this differential prediction for college students.

The reader is again reminded that these findings should be accepted with caution since they are based on self-report and recall data. However, the consistency of findings reported for widely differing subject samples, age levels, and measures supports the expectation that future objective observational studies will confirm the relationships described here.

The findings of these studies are discussed as if there is a clear basis for arguing that early parent humor somehow helps promote the development of humor skills (or at least interest in humor) in their children. This conclusion should be treated cautiously, however, since it is equally possible that the reverse order of influence was operating. That is, children who became interested in humor for reasons of their own may have triggered increased joking and clowning in their same-gender parent. The fact that amount of parental support (reinforcement) for children's early attempts at humor was not predictive of subsequent humor initiation for either males or females is consistent with this possible reverse order of influence. Unfortunately, these different causal effects cannot be disentagled in this study.

The results of the comparisons between the humor measures of the older and younger sample are especially intriguing. These data consistently indicate a stronger orientation toward humor among the younger than among the older respondents. Thus, the younger sample reported more frequent present initiation of humor and hearty laughter, as well as greater interest in and enjoyment of humor as children. Consistent with this early interest, younger subjects reported that both their mothers and their fathers did more joking, clowning, and playful teasing than was the case for parents of older subjects. This suggests that humor and playfulness may be more generally characteristic of parent–child interactions now than was the case 50 or 60 years ago. The high percentage of joking relationships found by Alford (1983) among American families is consistent with this view. Again, however, it must be remembered that these are recall data, and the older sample may have simply forgotten how much joking their parents did. Finally, this generational comparison is also restricted by the fact that only women were used in the older sample. It may be that humor is simply becoming more acceptable for women.

In addition to underscoring the importance of studying humor development across the life span, the findings reported here also point to the need for studies of humor initiation and responsiveness in the context of ongoing family interaction. Given the apparent continuity of individual differences in humor across the life span, these studies should initially focus on the preschool and early elementary school years. If playful and humor-oriented interaction patterns are characteristic of parents, they should be relatively stable and be manifest in interactions with their children at least by the time they enter school.

REFERENCES

Alford, K. F. (1983). Privileged play: Joking relationships between parents and children. In F. Manning (Ed.), *The world of play* (pp. 170–187). West Point, NY: Leisure Press.

Bales, R. F. (1970). *Personality and interpersonal behavior.* New York: Holt, Rinehart & Winston.

Bell, N. J., McGhee, P. E., & Duffey, N. S. (in press) Interpersonal competence, social assertiveness and humor. *British Journal of Developmental Psychology.*

Block, J. (1971). *Lives through time.* Berkeley, CA: Bancroft Books.

Damico, S. B., & Purkey, W. W. (1978). Class clowns: A study of middle school students. *American Educational Research Journal, 15,* 391–398.

Fisher, S., & Fisher, R. L. (1981). *Pretend the world is funny and forever: A psychological analysis of comedians, clowns and actors.* Hillsdale, NJ: Erlbaum.

Fisher, S., & Fisher, R. L. (1983). Personality and psychopathology in the comic. In P. E. McGhee & J. H. Goldstein (Eds.), *Handbook of Humor Research: Vol. 2. Applied Studies* (pp. 41–59). New York: Springer-Verlag.

Fry, W. F., Jr., & Allen, M. (1975). *Make 'em laugh.* Palo Alto, CA: Science & Behavior Books.

Janus, S. S. (1975). The great comedians: Personality and other factors. *American Journal of Psychoanalysis, 35,* 169–174.

Janus, S. S. (1981). Humor, sex and power in American society. *American Journal of Psychoanalysis, 41,* 161–167.

McGhee, P. E. (1976). Sex differences in children's humor. *Journal of Communication, 26,* 176–189.

McGhee, P. E. (1980). Development of the sense of humour in childhood: A longitudinal study. In P. E. McGhee & A. J. Chapman (Eds.), *Children's humour* (pp. 213–231). Chichester, England: Wiley.

Wilde, L. (1968). *The great comedian.* Secaucus, NJ: Citadel Press.

15

Performers' Views of Humor and Aging

LUCILLE NAHEMOW
ALLEN RAYMON

INTRODUCTION

Comedians who perform regularly before audiences were questioned about how they tailor their material for those of different ages. On the theory that individuals who make a living by making people laugh will have a special awareness of what works with different audiences, performers were interviewed. The process began by developing a common language. Comedians and academics do not usually travel in the same circles; we could not assume that they would refer to comic material in the same way. In order to engender cooperation, or even comprehension, we had to determine that words had the same meaning. In the early stage of the research, some performers were asked to consider the probable reactions of other performers to each question. What categories do performers use to describe their material? Do they use words such as *tendentious* or *mirthful*, for example. Unlike college students who constitute a captive audience, such individuals will not answer questions that they regard as silly or trivial. Therefore, this research was begun as a collaborative process with selected performers. In this way, communication was enhanced.

265 Copyright © 1986 by Academic Press, Inc.
All rights of reproduction in any form reserved.

METHOD

Raymon, the second author of this chapter, is a member of Actor's Equity and a former actor, director, and producer of off-Broadway theater. His personal contacts were invaluable in obtaining the active cooperation of the performers; his communication with them as one performer to another was essential. Data was collected on the performers' professional turf and they assisted in developing an instrument that used concepts and categories that had credence within the profession. Thus, a common language was developed. Comic material was classified according to its form and its content, and questions were asked about the pacing of material.

The questionnaire was in the form of a letter to performers that described the plans for a forthcoming conference on humor and aging and added, "Since you use humor in relationship to different audiences, you know what appeals to people of different ages." They were asked what kind of comedy they used and how long they had been performing. Because some of the performers preferred not to state their age, they were asked to locate themselves within a broad age category. In addition, they were asked whether they thought of themselves as young, middle-aged, or old.

Regarding the audience, we asked whether age was considered an important category. This was followed by a series of questions concerning material used for people of different ages, and a grid was provided for answering detailed questions about form, content, and pacing of humorous material. Performers checked the category they relied upon for young, middle-aged, and older people; multiple checks were possible. Respondents were encouraged to qualify or explain their answers. Then, each performer was asked whether he or she had a personal philosophy of humor and whether it "tells us anything about growing older." Finally, they were asked if they would prefer their answers to be kept confidential or if we should feel free to quote them by name.

Subjects were all volunteers obtained before or after their act at nightclubs in New York City or through Actor's Equity. A range of clubs was sampled from the prestigious Improvisation Club in midtown Manhattan, where performers get a minimum of $25, to the Storefront Blitz, an off-Broadway training club in which performers are unpaid. Questionnaires were also obtained from the Comic Strip and the Don't Tell Mama Club, which are also located in the midtown area. Raymon administered all the questionnaires. When an individual did not understand the questions, he explained them; when someone had difficulty writing down a thought, he assisted. However, the wording of the questions was carefully maintained.

SUBJECTS

Forty performers were interviewed: 30 men, 7 women, and 3 who did not indicate gender. The gender distribution appears representative of professional commedians. It is also characteristic of a differential in the use of humor in the general population. At every age thus far studied, men far outnumber women in the production of comedy. McGhee (1972) has suggested that this is probably related to status in a group and socially defined means of achieving active mastery. Thus, it is interesting that women are now beginning to move into the field in greater numbers. In this sample, more than 50% of the men had been performing more than 5 years, while only 28% of the women had been performing as long.

Respondents ranged in age from under 25 to over 50, with the majority ($N = 24$) being 26–35 years of age. Some had been performing over 20 years, others less than a year. The median was 5 years in comedy. The majority thought of themselves as young, as opposed to middle-aged or old. One performer checked all the categories: young, middle-aged, and old, adding parenthetically, "at different moments of the day."

The type of comedy used by the performers varied widely. The most frequent categories selected were one-line stand-up and character comedy. However, monologue, stories, impressions, clowning and miming, singing, and observational humor were also mentioned. Many of the performers engaged in more than one type of comedy.

RESULTS

The performers differed on the question of whether age is an important category in their conception of an audience; the majority (58%) felt that it was. Arthur Jay, who worked as a comedian for 12 years, primarily as a storyteller, was one who felt it was not an important category. He explained as follows: "I never start out to do anything different from my normal act—I feel if they have come to a club to hear me, they want what I do regardless of their sex, age, etc. I will adjust depending upon reception, but I still think of the audience as simply an audience."

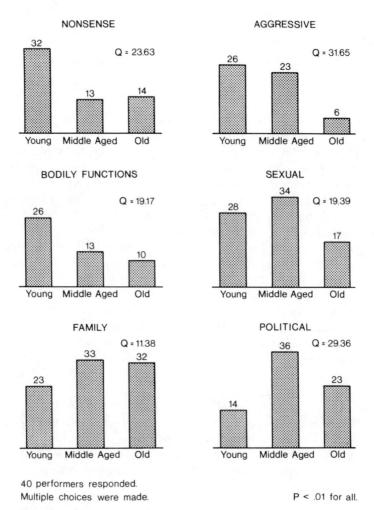

40 performers responded.
Multiple choices were made.   P < .01 for all.

Figure 15.1 Frequency of performers' choice of humorous content for audiences of different ages.

Performers were all asked about the type of material they use for audiences of different ages. They could indicate that they favor one type of humor for one group or check two or even all three categories. Figure 15.1 shows the content of humorous material that performers use with different age groups. Nonsense humor is relied upon most often for young audiences. Although some performers use nonsense humor with both middle-aged and older audiences as well, twice as many indicated that they used this kind of material with the young.[1] Humor based upon bodily functions is also heavily associated with young audiences. Aggressive humor is used most frequently with young audiences, but most of the performers would use it with middle-aged audiences as well. The use of aggressive humor decreases abruptly when the audience becomes old. Nonsense humor, on the other hand, is used as much with old as with middle-aged audiences. Sexual humor and humor based upon family interactions appear to be mainstays across all ages. Although the use of sexual humor peaks in middle age, most performers rely heavily upon sexual humor for all three age categories. Humor based upon family interactions is used most heavily with middle-aged and older audiences. Political humor also peaks in middle-age but continues to be heavily utilized with older audiences.

An interesting picture begins to emerge of the performers' conception of audience interests across the life span. First, by their comments and by the frequency with which performers checked each category straight across the life span, it is clear that there is an underlying sentiment that can be summed up as "a person's a person for all that." At the same time, the consistent statistical significances—all of which were below the 1% level—indicate that different material is used with audiences of different ages. Nonsense humor, jokes that deal with body functions, and aggressive humor are all seen as youthful. With middle age, the more cerebral political humor emerges, along with sexual humor, family humor, and aggressive humor. For older people, family-oriented humor predominates; political humor is heavily utilized, as is sexual humor; but aggressive humor falls off. The suggestion that nonsense humor may begin to reemerge creates an overall picture of a gentler, less barbed humor for the old.

Figure 15.2 shows the frequency with which performers use particular forms of humor with audiences of different ages. As was the case with humorous content, marked differences in frequency of usage emerges with different age categories. Performers expect puns and stories to be most appreciated by older people, next by the middle-aged, and least by the young. One-liners, wit, and satire, however, all show curvilinear relationships. They are utilized most by performers facing middle-aged audiences and, next, with older people. Satire, a very sophisticated form of humor, is considered particularly appropri-

---

[1] The Cochran Q test of statistical significance was used. This nonparametric test measures whether one category is selected more often than would be predicted on the basis of chance. In every case discussed here the chi-square exceeded the .01 level.

ate for the middle-aged. In contrast, put-down jokes are evidently seen by performers as the province of the young; frequencies of use decline sharply with middle-aged and older audiences. This linear decline in the use of put-down jokes with age corresponds with and appears to corroborate the finding from Figure 15.1 that aggressive humor is used much less with older audiences.

It appears that with the single exception of put-down jokes, a wider

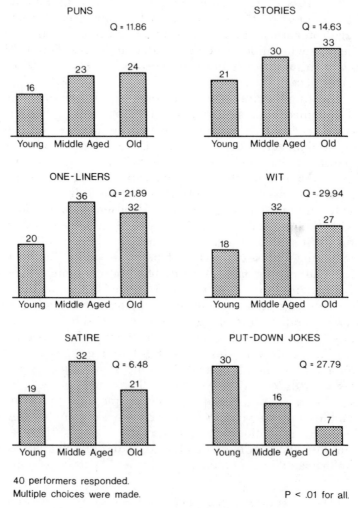

40 performers responded.
Multiple choices were made.   P < .01 for all.

Figure 15.2 Frequency of performers' choice of humorous form for audiences of different ages.

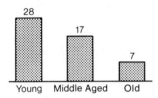

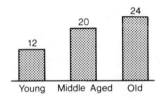

Two performers used a curvilinear model: fast pacing for the middle aged, slow pacing for both the young and the old.

$$\chi^2 = 15.8 \qquad\qquad P < .01$$

Figure 15.3 Frequency of performers' choice of timing for audiences of different ages.

range of humor is used with middle-aged and older audiences. Jon Hayman, a stand-up comedian, 26–35 years of age, who thinks of himself as middle-aged, provides a rationale for this. He states:

Young people are more insecure and thus tend to be more aggressive. They are not as apt to pick up subtleties, nuances, etc. They have less life experience and so cannot relate to as broad spectrum of material as can older audiences.

Figure 15.3 shows that most performers slow down their rhythm of delivery with older audiences. Twenty-eight of the performers would use rapid timing with the young and only 7 would use it with the old. Conversely, only 12 would use slow pacing with young audiences, while 24 would for the old. Clearly, the tendency of performers is to slow down delivery for older audiences; however, this is not universal. Two performers use the most rapid pacing with middle-aged people and slower pacing for both young and old audiences.

PERFORMERS' VIEWS OF HUMOR AND AGING

Probably the most informative material to come out of this research comes from the performers' responses to the question about their philosophy of humor. We quote some of these verbatim and discuss them in the following section. We urge the reader to attend to the following statements, for they attest to the thoughtfulness and insight of our institutionalized comics.

Leonard Drum, character comedian for 30 years, who stated, "quote me, but not my age," says:

No age should ever be underestimated or condescended to. The very young are wonderfully honest in their responses; the elderly are often remarkably indulgent. All ages are grateful for humor that is affirmative, that celebrates life, whether it is silly or profound. We like to see foolishness exposed and happiness triumphant. We know happy endings are not inevitable but we long for and applaud them.

Dennis Wolfbey, a storyteller, says:

Age is a real factor to be considered in humor. Success in humor heavily depends on your ability to communicate that which your audience can relate to. For example, an elderly couple is not likely to enjoy a routine based on cocaine-taking inasmuch as it is highly unlikely that they have much experience with, knowledge of, or concern for cocaine use. Comedic effectiveness requires recognition on the part of the listener. Similarly, an audience of 18- to 19-year-olds is not likely to react enthusiastically to a routine laced with mother-in-law jokes, inasmuch as in-laws are not a pressing priority in their day-to-day existence.

Helen Baldannore, a character actress who has been engaged in comedy for 6 years, states:

I'm 33 years old and a cynic. I think a sense of humor is a person's most valuable asset in life. Our life in this world is not logical—no matter how much we try, we can't make sense out of the things that happen. We all try to make some kind of sense out of the illogical occurances—some use religion, others drugs . . . . I think the healthiest way of dealing is to be able to laugh at and poke fun at yourself and the world around you. If you take this life too seriously, you'll go mad. So it follows, I guess, the longer you maintain your sense of humor, the healthier you are and the easier it makes your life.

Terence Quinn, who explores different kinds of comedy in his work, states:

Only that it is a sharing with others, i.e., fellow humans, of the foibles, bungling, stumbling mistakes and inadequacies that are our lot in life—a sharing summed up by saying let's laugh at ourselves to ease the pain and hurt a little—life is a serious business, but the journey can be eased by humor.

Keith Harrison, character actor–standup comedian who has been performing for 4 years, says:

My own life is constantly salvaged or renewed by using humor. As the daily routine winds up, your stress level comedy becomes more than just a few laughs, it becomes a way of life. As far as age is concerned humor is really not affected, but humor does allow the aging process to become less awesome or feared. Also, laughter is extremely healthy for anyone.

Michael Dacunto, specializing in character comedy, explains:

Laughing at ourselves and our own shortcomings is the best and most healthy humor of all. As we grow older, I think it is much easier to laugh about our problems and that in turn makes them a little easier to deal with.

Ron Darian, standup comic, somewhere between 26 and 35 years of age, who thinks of himself as young, says:

I have worked occasionally in front of "older" audiences and one thing I am conscious of is my tendency to smile and appear to be friendly more. I find that if the older audience cannot relate to my more "youthful" material (horror movies, sex, high school, etc.) then at least they will see a person enjoying himself on stage! Also, since death is common to all humans, you would think much humor would be done about it. (Because it is such a universal experience, it theoretically is one of the best "set-ups" around!) However, I have found in my experience that no other subject comes close to being as taboo. And wouldn't it be somewhat haughty for the young to mock death before those who are older, and thus "closer" to the reality of their fears?

DISCUSSION

A psychologist cannot help but be struck by the insight and understanding of the comics. By and large, their variations across ages are in the directions of which our research and our theories point. However, these are well tempered with repeated statements of commonality across age groups. This, too, is something that covers many pages of any textbook on life span development.

First, the comedians seem to agree that there is a tendency for more overtly aggressive humor to appeal to the younger audiences. In both form and content, the put-down was used more with younger groups. This is very much in line with the theoretical position of Freud, who presented a modified drive-reduction view of humor resulting in the reduction of surplus energy (Godkewitsch, 1976). Freud postulates the psychogenesis of humor as having three stages: *play,* involving pure incongruity without the need for resolution; *jesting,* superimposing joke techniques in which the need for logic emerges; and *joking,* which is tendentious, serving sexual and aggressive moods (Zillmann & Cantor, 1976).

The last is the "mature" stage, and typically, Freud ends there. However, the final stage of maturity is reached by 20 years of age. For our purposes it is very important to note that this is young for an audience. Performers felt that this is the time when hostile humor is most appealing.

Secondly, the performers do not rely upon humor that is based upon bodily functions when addressing audiences of predominantly older people. This is in contrast to the common stereotype of aging that suggests that older people are obsessed by bodily functions. The first author has never found any evidence for this in personal contacts with the elderly. It has always seemed a mere artifact of the considerable amount of research conducted in health care facilities. Though Shakespeare said that the final stage of life was second childhood, research has not corroborated that observation. Even the sick and frail older people do not identify with babies; they are simply treated as such by their younger caretakers. Consequently, it is gratifying to find that performers do not make this unwarranted assumption. (Interestingly, greeting card manufacturers do. For example, there is the singularly offensive card that says, "I only write when I have something important to say. I had a BM today." One wonders who will purchase it; our guess is that it will *not* be an old person.)

It is clear that performers react to the slowdown of older people without knowing about the research findings that demonstrate that reaction time declines significantly with age. It is worth noting that two of the performers indicated that they would use the most rapid pacing with the middle-aged and would slow their presentation for both the young and the old. I get the impression from these protocols that a slightly gentler humor is typically used for the older audiences and that the category *young* in this questionnaire was too broad to pick up differentiation between the very young, for whom a gentler humor might be used, and young adults, who comedians think thrive on putdown and aggressive humor.

The concepts that were developed with performers specifically for the purposes of this study worked well. The categories of form and content of humor and the subdivisions within them were understood by all and seemingly used in approximately the same way by everyone. With hindsight, it is clear that the one concept that we thought we understood best, namely *age*, was ill-defined so as to limit the usefulness of the findings. In preliminary discussions, it had been decided that chronological age might be too rigid a characterization, so the commonly accepted broad categories of young, middle-aged and old were adopted. In retrospect, it appears that when talking about young audiences, some performers were thinking of children and some of adults. Similarly, for the category *middle-aged,* some performers (probably those who associated youth with childhood) included young adults and others did not. This error should be corrected in subsequent research.

This research is obviously preliminary. One of the greatest limitations is in the size and the selection of the sample of performers. It would also be very helpful if subsequent researchers obtained estimates of length of time devoted to comedy and success with audiences. Clearly not all performers are equal, since some handle audiences better than others. It would be helpful to be able to see if differences in philosophy characterizes the relatively successful performers.

We should not forget that thus far we have relied upon the report of performers regarding what makes people laugh; no objective criteria have been applied to tell us whether their assumptions are correct.

Therefore, we urge subsequent researchers to attempt more direct measurement of this phenomenon. It would be necessary to observe audience reactions directly. One could use a laugh meter or independent ratings of audience reaction with built-in reliability checks. In any case, we should determine how audiences of different ages react to each one of the dimensions identified.

The personal philosophies of humor that guided the performers in their work was particularly enlightening. A larger sample of such philosophies should be relatively easy to obtain and extremely useful. In the present study, philosophies were not classified, because there were only 30 responses and those were very varied. Fully 75% of the performers responded in writing to the open-ended question concerning their philosophy of humor and aging; this is an unusually high proportion. (Usually when write-in answers are solicited in a questionnaire that is otherwise limited to check-off answers or one-word fill-ins, it is the exceptional respondent who answers at all.) The number of responses obtained suggests that the question was considered an important one; the thoughtfulness of the responses further supports this conclusion. It is our impression that performers' comments demonstrate considerable psychological sophistication. The words may not be the same as ours, but the concepts are familiar. Several performers reflect themes that are discussed at length elsewhere in this book. Wolfbey and Darian both allude to the issue of cohort-relevant humor, which is discussed by Seltzer, (in Chapter 6, this volume). Three performers, all of whom describe themselves as specializing in character comedy, focus upon the healing nature of laughter, an issue that is pursued by Tennant in Chapter 13. Another three performers discuss the importance of humor as a coping mechanism (see Loeb, Chapter 16, this volume). The performers' responses to this question were quite articulate and deserve careful scrutiny. Clearly, these performers take their humor seriously—analyzing, reflecting, and attempting to see the audience perspective. In general, they show an awareness of their social function in contemporary society.

Vescey and Lorenz argue that in Hopi culture the clown serves a critical social function. They state, "In their most sacred rituals, and in their determination to persist as a people, the Hopis send in their clowns" (Chapter 10, this volume). For the Hopi Indians, the dual themes of clowns as agents who relieve tensions and as individuals who signal social change are developed. Our findings from this small sample of professional comedians suggest that our "clowns" also perceive themselves as having a serious purpose. Humor is a powerful money-making industry in our country. In our society, comedy is used to express common concerns, to defuse troublesome issues, and to form public opinion. The professional comedians evidently understand that this is a serious subject and were very helpful—even conscientious—in this study of humor and aging.

REFERENCES

Godkewitsch, M. (1976). Physiological and verbal indices of arousal in rated humor. In N. J. Chapman & H. C. Foote (Eds.), *Humor and laughter: Theory, research and applications* (pp. 117–138). New York: Wiley.

McGhee, P. E. (1972). On the cognitive origins of incongruity humor: Fantasy assimilation versus reality assimilation. In J. H. Goldstein & P. E. McGhee (Eds.), *The psychology of humor* (pp. 61–80). New York: Academic Press.

Zillmann, D., & Cantor, J. R. (1976). A disposition theory of humor and mirth. In A. J. Chapman & H. C. Foote (Eds.), *Humor and laughter: Theory, research and applications* (pp. 93–116). New York: Wiley.

16

Epilogue: A Nascent Idea for an Eriksonian Model of Humor

MARTIN LOEB
VIVIAN WOOD

INTRODUCTION BY VIVIAN WOOD

Martin Loeb did not forget his commitment to prepare a chapter for this volume. In early April, he asked me to work with him on his paper. We had only a couple of hours, as Martin was very weak and was soon exhausted. From the notes I took and my remembrance of our conversation, I have tried to set down in broad form Martin's ideas for an Eriksonian model of humor in the hope that someone may be interested in developing a full-fledged model. I have taken the liberty of "fleshing out" some of the ideas along lines that I think Martin intended; in some cases, I have undoubtedly done Martin's ideas an injustice.

AN ERIKSONIAN MODEL OF HUMOR

Humor—or what is funny—has been around for a long time, but we have no real definition of humor. Erikson (1963) in his discussion of anxiety in *Childhood and Society* refers to humor as a redeeming human specialty, "the ability at rare moments to play with and to

Copyright © 1986 by Academic Press, Inc.
All rights of reproduction in any form reserved.

reflect fearlessly on the strange customs and institutions by which man must find self-realization" (p. 406)

Erikson continues:

> But the fact remains that the human being in early childhood learns to consider one or the other aspect of bodily function as evil, shameful, or unsafe. There is no culture which does not use a combination of these devils to develop, by way of counterpoint, its own style of faith, pride, certainty, and initiative. (p. 406)

There is the suggestion in the above passage that humor may be a useful mechanism for dealing with the crises posed in each of Erikson's eight stages of human development. Through humor we can sometimes consider things that are too frightening or too embarrassing to consider openly and directly. It has been said that we laugh at that which makes us anxious; joking about it is an attempt to master our fears.

In Erikson's dialectic approach, the individual experiences both trust and mistrust, both integrity and despair, in the process of coming to a resolution, more or less, of each normative crisis. One can adapt to the negative side of Erikson's dialectic if one is secure enough in the positive side; that is, if one has enough trust then one can accept some mistrust. Humor helps us deal with negatives—with the unthinkable—in a light, tentative way.

The writer Leo Rosten (1970), who has defined humor as "the affectionate communication of insight," says that humor "also serves the afflicted as compensation for suffering, a token victory of brain over fear" (p. xxiii). The ability to risk shame or embarrassment requires a certain amount of security. But humor is a mechanism for reducing the risk. By acting in a light-hearted, playful way, one can pretend it was not a serious attempt—that one was just joking, just playing around—if the effort does not turn out well. To be adventurous, to risk oneself, one has to have practice. To dare to take those early risks when one has very little confidence in success requires protective strategies such as humor. Furthermore, the more secure we become, the more able we are to use humor. Once one's sense of identity is secure, for example, the easier it is to use humor to handle aging.

Humor is a very complex concept, and there are many aspects to it. Humor is not necessarily funny, although humor and being funny usually coincide. This Eriksonian approach is merely an experiment in considering humor with a model that is well known. It is not well known as a model of humor, of course, but we are going to see whether Erikson's approach can be applied to a model of humor through consideration of how humor is used at each of Erikson's eight stages of human development.

Basic Trust versus Basic Mistrust

Just as the infant's sense of trust and security is tested by a willing-ness to let the mother out of sight, so, too, is the little joke parents play in which the infant is tossed up in the air and caught by the parent. Sometimes the parent may pretend not to be able to catch the child until the last minute. The child who has been cuddled and held and loved is apt to giggle happily and want the game to go on and on, long after the parent's energy has run out. If, however, the child is inse-cure, she or he is apt to scream with fright. While a certain amount of security is necessary before such games are enjoyable for the child, it is likely that the fun the secure child has enlarges his or her trust in the parent and gives confidence to try other "scary" things.

Autonomy versus Shame

In attempting to stand on his or her own feet, the young child risks shame, which Erikson (1963) describes as "a situation in which we are stared at in a condition of incomplete dress, in night attire, 'with one's pants down'." (p. 252). Almost all young children take glee in shed-ding their clothes and running naked through the house, in showing off their behinds by leaving their "barn doors" open. Little children will stick their fingers in the statue's "crack" and giggle mische-viously. They are able to threaten themselves with shameful acts without losing their sense of autonomy—of self-control. Indeed, per-haps it is only by risking shame that one develops autonomy.

Initiative versus Guilt

In Erikson's view, initiative adds to autonomy the quality of under-taking, planning, and attacking a task for the sake of being active and on the move. In this stage, children are ready for positive, constructive activities under their own initiative. The risk at this stage is guilt. Children may feel that their intrusiveness and activity may have evil consequences, especially if there are harsh parental responses to the child's initiatives.

A major form of self-discipline comes out of guilt. There comes a point when guilt is not a terrifying experience but can be funny largely because guilt is acted out and expressed so that it becomes defused. Jews in particular are noted for using humor as a way of avoiding feelings of guilt. The joke for any particular guilt situation may be referred to merely by number (Joke No. 145, for example).

Industry versus Inferiority

In this stage, children learn that they will gain recognition by producing things—by industry, to use Erikson's term. The potential danger is a feeling of inadequacy and inferiority as illustrated in this joke:

A small boy was sitting at a curb, crying. An old man passed by and kindly asked, "Why are you crying, Sonny?" "Because I can't do what the big boys do." So the old man sat down and cried, too.

Identity versus Role Diffusion

In their struggle for a sense of identity, adolescents are seen by Erikson as having to refight the battles of earlier years, usually casting their parents in the role of adversaries. Humor at this stage is often directed at the bravado of the adolescent (itself a coping mechanism), as in the following Mark Twain story:

When I was a boy of 14, my father was so ignorant I could hardly stand to have the old man around. But when I got to be 21, I was astonished at how much the old man had learned in those seven years.

In today's world with its prolonged adolescence, a certain license is given to a delayed development of a sense of identity. One can joke about role diffusion, of not knowing who one is or what one will become, as is the case of the 25-year-old student who says, "When I grow up, I'm going to be a . . . ."

Intimacy versus Isolation

When one moves from role identity to intimacy, one moves from the larger world into a more intimate world. It is the stage when the young person ordinarily develops an intimate relationship with someone of the opposite sex and marriage is contemplated. The jokes about the bachelor's last gasp of freedom are numerous. There are also marriage jokes about lost freedom—nostalgia about the "good ol' days," when boys could be boys and not have all this responsibility; for example, this statement about marriage:

Marriage is like a violin. After the beautiful music is over, the strings are still attached.

Jokes about old maids and old bachelors who do not make the commitment to marriage imply that they are lonely and isolated: "A lemon that has never been squeezed."

Generativity versus Stagnation

The normative crisis of the seventh stage refers to the middle-aged adult's concern with establishing and guiding the next generation. The danger is that the individual may fall into self-absorption and a sense of stagnation, a sense of going nowhere, doing nothing important. People joke about "going to pot." going downhill. Adolescence is when you think you will live forever, but middle age is when you wonder how you have lasted so long.

A cartoon in the *New Yorker* a few years ago depicts this going nowhere idea. It shows this older couple in their living room and he reaches into the liquor cabinet saying, "Well, shall we get on with our golden years?"

Integrity versus Despair

Fear of dying without believing you have accomplished anything may result in despair. The anxiety concerning death has evidently spawned much humor. In fact, this normative crisis probably has more humor surrounding it than any other, probably indicating how very anxiety-producing the prospect of death is.

An example of a joke in this area is the story about the funeral in London of a comedian that was attended by many old-time comedians who had gathered to say a last farewell. During the ceremony, one man looked up at his neighbor and asked, " 'Ow old are you, Charlie?" "Ninety," replied the old-timer. " 'Ardly worth going 'ome, eh?"

There are numerous jokes about older men and sex that indicate anxiety about waning sexual powers: the one about the frisky, flirtatious 80-year-old man whose ambition was to be shot by a jealous husband or about the man who said his doctor had forbidden him to chase women unless they were going downhill.

Agnes deMille was told shortly after a visit to White House during Gerald Ford's Administration that she had suffered a massive heart attack. "Dammit," she said, "that's what comes from having dinner with a Republican!"

One of the strongest proponents of laughter as medicine and as a coping strategy is Norman Cousins, who is convinced that laughter and ascorbic acid saved his life. In *Anatomy of an Illness* (1981) he describes how he watched old "Candid Camera" and Marx Brothers films; 10 minutes of genuine belly laughter had an anesthetic effect, he said, and would give him at least 2 hours of pain-free sleep. He gives credit to the laughter and ascorbic acid for fighting the inflammation that came with his disease and for his recovery. "Hearty laughter," he says, "is a good way to jog internally without having to go outdoors" (p. 84).

POSTSCRIPT BY VIVIAN WOOD

This chapter has no real ending. I am not sure Martin had come to any conclusions about this topic. However, as you may know, Martin used humor liberally to deal with aging. Through the years, he usually had some kind of funny sign in his office, which students and colleagues appreciated. His last one was "Old age and trickery will overcome youth and ambition."

When Erik Erikson received the chapter for comment as planned, it was after Martin Loeb's death. The editors received the following replay:

Joan and I have read carefully [the paper, "A Nascent Idea for an Eriksonian Model of Humor"], only to come to the definite conclusion that your version of Martin's intended paper is perfect as it is (and that we are pleased that our "model" was of help.) It obviously reflects Martin's way of musing about such a subject and gives your own good form to his intentions. Any attempt to improve on it by arguing about points and terms could only interfere with the statment's freshness, its form and its humor.

REFERENCES

Cousins, N. (1981). *Anatomy of an illness as perceived by the patient*. New York: Bantam.
Erikson, E. H. (1963). *Childhood and society* (2nd ed.). New York: Norton.
Rosten, L. (1970). *The joys of Yiddish*, New York: Washington Square Press.

Author Index

Numbers in italics refer to the pages on which the complete references are cited.

Subject Index